WEBSTER!

An Autobiography by Jack Webster

Douglas & McIntyre
Vancouver/Toronto

Douglas & McIntyre, 1615 Venables Street, Vancouver, BC V5L 2H1

Canadian Cataloguing in Publication Data
Webster, Jack, 1918–
    Webster!
    ISBN 0-88894-706-2
    1. Webster, Jack, 1918–   2. Journalists — Canada —
Biography.   3. Broadcasters — Canada — Biography.   I. Title
PN4913.W42A3   1990   070'.92   C90-091405-X

Editing by Brian Scrivener
Design by Alexandra Hass
Cover design by Arifin Graham
Front cover photograph by Doane Gregory
Typeset by The Typeworks
Printed and bound in Canada by D. W. Friesen & Sons Ltd.
Printed on acid-free paper ∞

To my wife,
the late Margaret Thomson Macdonald Webster

PREFACE

• Some days I get up and feel like a cartoon character with a perpetual dark cloud over his head, a caricature of a real person.
That's what half a century of performing in a single role does to
you. Sometimes you forget: all the world *isn't* a talk show. Jack
Webster doesn't have to growl at the world all the time!

In the course of more than seventy years, I have become a
much more complicated human being than was represented by
the sharp-tongued curmudgeon who appeared on radio and
television broadcasts calling himself, *Webster!*

Think about it. Forty years of print and electronic reporting
in Canada, including twenty-seven years of open-line broadcasting on radio and TV for hours a day—brainwashing yourself
into a special space. I caught myself sitting at the supper table
one night, lifting my cutlery and saying to it automatically: "Are
you on the topic?" Or answering the door at home and asking
the visitor "What do *you* want to talk about?"

Still, I consider myself a broadcast journalist, not a performer. My professional life has been devoted to making people
talk, often about a personal tragedy, sometimes about an
achievement, ideally about a controversy. Not for me the long-
winded quote or the abstract debate. One of my detractors once

said Webster made his living by finding a molehill at 9 A.M. precisely, and building it into a mountain by noon. There's some truth to that, but I always tried to find a molehill that mattered to a lot of people.

Someone said an unexamined life isn't worth living. Well, I was too busy living it to be bothered. Now that I've got the time, I'm surprised at how fast it all seems to have gone by and what a lot I crammed into it. And it's a long way from finished yet!

I wanted this book to reflect Jack Webster the man, not Jack Webster the media figure. I hope readers will see me for what I am, as I do every morning when I shave.

There are things in my life of which I'm proud, others I regret. I've had my ups and downs, highs and lows, good times and bad. But overall I have had remarkably good luck over the years. I was often in the right place at the right time. Mind you, in the news business that usually meant standing at the lip of a precipice and finding yourself staring down into some dark tragedy, like the day the Second Narrows Bridge collapsed sending workmen to their death. I stood at the scene reporting via the radio transmitter in my car. So it goes.

For as long as it took to get the story, I could look at that sort of horror with casual indifference. I was imbued with a hard streak of that fatalism which seems to run through the Scots, a revelation that there but for the grace of God, go I.

Maybe that's why my favourite writer is Kurt Vonnegut. His work seems to revolve around the one question to which I've never heard an acceptable answer—what are people for?

There is an underlying sadness in my personal life that cannot be denied or dismissed. I do not like to dwell on my wife's emotional disturbance. Mental illness remains even today such a dark spectre that it is difficult to dispel the gloom cast by the merest hint of that affliction. Suffice it to say, I am not looking for pity. Margaret and I had our trials and tribulations—her illness was the major one—but we also shared myriad happy moments together. I relish those.

Throughout my career, I was helped beyond measure by colleagues who were tolerant and patient when I was irascible, enthusiastic when I was flagging, and creative when I went blank. I could not have done it without them and I wanted to say thanks to hundreds, but I must restrict the list to those with whom I worked closely: Linda Dutka, Helen Patterson, Gladys Johnsen, Suzanne Boyce, Pat Ellingson, Ann Davidson, Maureen Richardson, Michelle Hull, Heather Doyle, Brian Coxford, Steve Wyatt, Mark Schneider, Ted Routledge, Pam Mason and Janet (Jinty) Wagner.

Thanks, too, to Jean Cormier, Gerald Haslam and Kyle Mitchell who created the Jack Webster Foundation.

And I must mention those who over the years helped me maintain my enthusiasm and drive, sometimes with kindnesses, sometimes with emotional support, and sometimes with a kick in the pants: Marjorie Nichols, Allan Fotheringham, Patricia Carney, Jack and Connie Munro, Pierre Berton, Ron Haggart, and countless colleagues and contacts, political and professional.

I would also like to recognize and thank Ian Mulgrew, who gave me my literary voice and style, and without whose help this book could not have been completed.

And, of course, to Websters everywhere, especially mine!

Jack Webster
Vancouver
July 1990

C H A P T E R 1

• My world fell apart on February 22, 1985. Margaret, my wife, died. I found her just before one o'clock in the morning. She'd fallen out of bed and hadn't the strength to get back up. Margaret had been ill for a long time and her death wasn't unexpected. I called 911 and waited for the ambulance. It was a cloudy night, dry and cold.

The medical attendants worked on her when they arrived, but there was no heartbeat. I climbed in the back of the ambulance with Margaret and we sped towards Lions Gate Hospital in North Vancouver. I don't remember much about our last ride together, except that I listened to the sirens wail as we sped past West Vancouver High School and onto the Upper Levels Highway.

It's hard to explain what goes through your mind when the person who has shared your life for more than fifty years dies. I don't think Margaret was ever really happy with my success in media. She kept clipping books in the early years, and later, when I moved to television, she watched me faithfully every day. She was quite a good critic. But she liked happy programs, the show-biz stuff. She didn't like the serious programs, and most of my work was about sober subjects—politics, labour, social conditions.

I was only inside the hospital for about an hour that night. There wasn't anything anyone could do. I knew that the moment I found her. I stood lost in the lobby of Lions Gate. One of the ambulance drivers offered me a ride home. I was about to accept when, thank God, Jack Munro walked into the hospital.

Munro, perhaps the single most powerful union leader in British Columbia, has been a great buddy of mine since he arrived in Vancouver from the Interior in the early 1970s.

"How did you know?" I asked him. We embraced.

"Val Chapman called us," Munro said. "Her son Stephen was on dispatch at the fire hall and heard the inhalator call. He phoned her."

"Margaret's dead," I told him.

"I'm sorry," he said.

We stood for a moment in the foyer of the hospital. "Come back to my place, Jack, and have a drink," Munro said.

I was glad of the offer.

We arrived at his house in West Vancouver where his wife Connie was waiting with Val. They both offered condolences as Munro fetched me a large Scotch. I drained it, and we moved into the living room.

I sat looking at the lights of the city spread below as Munro got me another Scotch. After he sat down, Connie brought him a coffee—he'd been off the booze for nearly a year, then. I hadn't touched much either over the past year because of Margaret's illness. But right now I needed a few.

The first thing I wanted to do was call our kids and let them know. I didn't want them hearing the news on the radio. I phoned Jenny in Kamloops, Linda in Victoria, and then I tracked down Jack in Seattle where he and his wife Georgie had gone for the weekend. I couldn't reach my other daughter, Joan, in London, despite several tries.

Like a good Scotchman, Munro kept reminding me: "I hope

you're going to remember the bill." It was a joke, of course, but I don't think I ever did pay him for the long-distance charges.

Mainly I sipped whisky, and talked. Probably babbled if the truth be known. I felt an overwhelming urge to explain and justify myself, as if Margaret's death had somehow called into question my entire life. And I couldn't help feeling that I had made the mistake of making my job more important than my family. Munro just sat, listened and, at appropriate moments, got me another drink.

I never actually made a conscious choice of career over family. It was just the way things developed. When Margaret was very sick I'd leave the house at six in the morning and say to myself: "Well, whatever it is, I'll worry about it tonight. Clear your mind and worry about it when you get home at six o'clock."

That was always my attitude. It was the only way I figured I could survive. Now when I think about my life, my career and my relationship with Margaret, I'm not so sure. Looking back, I am overwhelmed—countless television programs, thousands of radio interviews, numerous news stories, columns and editorials. And what is any of it worth? What have I learned? What truths can I impart after five decades of fulminating, muckraking, gossiping, hanging out and carrying on? I'm not sure any of it means anything. I do know Margaret was disappointed that the nice young man she met in Glasgow grew into such a hustler.

Margaret was from a middle-class Scotch family and never really understood my ambition. She told me to get out God knows how many times. Mostly for not being home enough. I was out too often in those days. I mixed a lot. You had to to get ahead.

I'm not sure how the metamorphosis happened. I just got hooked on the excitement of being important, of being involved. I became a news junkie as surely as others become dependent on heroin. I couldn't stop. I loved the adrenaline rush that accompanied every big story. And I couldn't stand the feeling that something, somewhere was happening and Webster wasn't involved.

I remember one of the first telephone tips vividly, even now, half a century later and half a world away. "Be at the Cross at midnight," a husky voice said. I knew who it was, and I followed his instructions.

At midnight, I arrived at Gorbals Cross, the centrepiece of Scotland's most notorious industrial slum, and found a crumpled mass in the gutter. A moment or two passed before I realized that I was staring at a man's body. I could see that his throat had been slashed; the light from the street-lamp glinted off a steel-headed axe that lay several feet from the crumpled figure. Another Saturday night gangland slaying in Glasgow.

The killings seemed to happen every week that year—1936. I was a junior reporter in a city that was an industrial sore on the face of Europe. Its squalor was unequaled and the violence it bred savage. The open-faced razor was the thug's favourite weapon.

Sometimes the dispute was about religion, sometimes football, occasionally love, or the welshing of a bookmaker. Often there wasn't a reason for the bloody assaults that made the city one of the most dangerous in Europe. The Beehive Boys, the toughest gang, even sold protection to the Irish Republican Army when it held its local fund-raising events. The city hospitals were world-famous for developing emergency treatments for glass cuts. Aside from the bodies, every weekend saw countless faces slashed or ripped open in bar brawls and gang fights.

As I knelt that night to see if the man in the gutter was still alive, I wondered what his transgression had been. A hand clasped onto my shoulder like a vice. "Whit are ye doin' here?"

I was startled and glanced over my shoulder and found myself face to face with a police inspector. Relieved, I stammered: "I'm Jackie Webster with *The Sunday Mail* and I was only passing by and saw the body."

That was a lie.

He snorted his disgust and looked past me at the grey, rain-washed face of the murdered man. "Are you going to give him first aid?" I asked.

"No," the policeman said coldly. "If we help him and he dies, everyone'll blame us. Better he die on his own."

It was too late anyway. I stood up as the inspector made sure the man was dead. Then, he opened the victim's wallet and gave me his name. It would make his job easier if I broke the news to the widow, and it would make my job easier back at the newspaper if I had a picture of the dead man.

Learning my trade covering Glasgow's weekend carnage, I had become inured to death. I had tricks for dealing with it even at 17. The man lived in a four-storey tenement in Bridgeton, in the top flat. There were five flats on the landing and I knocked on the neighbours' doors first. One by one, I told them that I had bad news for the family and would they come with me to the door. Only then did I approach the victim's flat. The results were always the same on such missions: Knock, knock.

"Yes."

"Hello, Missus. I'm Jackie Webster from the *Sunday Mail*." Pause. Take a breath. Continue: "I'm afraid I've got some bad news."

"What is it?" She'd look past me over my shoulder at the neighbours.

"It's about your husband. He's been injured in a gang fight." Long pause . . . "As a matter of fact, he's dead."

She'd usually swoon with shock and in would rush the neighbours. While they made her a cup of tea, I would swipe the wedding picture off the mantelpiece so the newspaper had a photograph to accompany my story about the murder. I was the best-damn picture snatcher in town, a bright, brash, nosey parker who was going places.

I had the world by the tail, then. Out of school for only three years, I already had a white-collar job, not a shipyard job. I was on the ladder to success and I was in love.

Margaret was the pretty, proverbial girl next door. I remember the first time I saw her—she was wearing a mustard-coloured coat and a beautiful smile. She'd meet me after work and I'd regale her with the night's adventures. We'd ride the streetcar home, two teenagers in love. That year held the brightest promise for me, the future unsullied by a single regret.

Then, one night, Margaret didn't laugh as usual. The sound of her voice wasn't quite so light, and her eyes didn't sparkle as usual. That night the conversation wasn't about the dream we hoped to share. It was about the child we had conceived.

The news of Margaret's pregnancy shocked both our families. My mother wouldn't hear of a marriage, and my mother was a strong-willed woman. To this day I don't know why I didn't stand up to her. For all my later bluster, I didn't have the force of will to oppose her. I acted like the boy I was, not the man I would become. Margaret was sent into seclusion until the baby was born and a family found to adopt the child.

The baby, Joan, was born, on December 14, 1936. Margaret embraced her for a few minutes before she was taken away. Margaret always said her baby had been "stolen." It was. She didn't sign the adoption papers. I did it all. If the procedure had been challenged, I'm not sure the courts would have approved. But the wishes of a 17-year-old girl did not count in those days and no one listened to Margaret's pleas.

The loss of her first-born gnawed at Margaret for most of her life. I should have married her when she became pregnant. I don't know why I didn't. It tainted the beginning of our life together. Mostly, when we were alone, we watched television and talked about the missing baby. Later, Margaret blamed her subsequent medical problems on that decision, and at my darkest moments I did, too.

Neurosis ate away at Margaret's mind, crippling her emotionally and physically. Ironically, the discipline her anxiety imposed on my lifestyle made me successful. Without it, I undoubtedly would have succumbed to the twin temptations that have ruined so many journalists of my generation, bitterness and booze. Still, Margaret's distress left me mired in guilt-ridden depression. I couldn't help but feel responsible for making her life a misery.

By the time she found our lost daughter, Joan, thirty-six years later, it was too late. Margaret couldn't really laugh or cry because the surgeons had severed the anxiety nerve in her frontal lobes nearly a decade before. That was their answer to Margaret's agoraphobia, her ever worsening fear of other people and unfamiliar surroundings. The neurosis plagued her, and it became my cross.

Oh, there were good times in the early days at nightclubs and cabarets. Even in later years, there were parties and all the Webster women met annually at The Empress hotel in Victoria to celebrate the International Order of Webster Women. And we had some great holiday times together, camping with the kids. There were trips all over British Columbia, to California, Scotland, Hawaii. But then there were times she'd go to Hawaii and refuse to go to the beach. She'd only sit in front of the unit soaking up the sunshine. Eventually, her fears and mood swings became so unbearable, she wouldn't leave the house without me.

Towards the end, I could see her slipping away every time I looked at her. She had been very ill. There had been all kinds of surgery over the years. And there were the prescriptions. It was awful. Pills, pills, pills. All kinds of pills. You name it, she was taking it. Every kind of pill. Margaret was a walking pharmacy. Most recently, she'd been in intensive care with a very, very fast pulse rate and she had not looked well since her release.

Just a few days before the end, I remarked: "You look bloody awful. I'm going to call an ambulance."

"No, you won't," she snapped. I never knew how she would react, pleasantly or sharply.

"Well," I said, "you've got to go and see a doctor."

I coerced her down to the doctor's office and he told her the same thing I had, that she was physically deteriorating. "I want you to go into hospital for three or four weeks to stabilize you a bit," he said. "See if we can cut down some of your prescriptions."

She wouldn't hear of it. "I'll go into hospital when I feel better," she said. "I might go in, say, a week or two from Monday."

I was livid when we left. We argued all the way home in the car. "The doctor wants you in hospital now for a reason," I emphasized.

"I'll go into the hospital when I feel better," she said.

There was no arguing with Margaret. She died at home that night.

Munro handed me another Scotch. As I took it, I saw Val Chapman and Connie Munro standing by the door. Val had her coat on. "I'm heading home, now, Jack," she said coming into the living room. "Call if you need anything."

"Thanks, love." She gave me a hug and kissed my cheek. "Goodnight."

Connie saw her to the door, and then left Jack and me alone. I took another long pull on the whisky.

Munro and I went back a long way, back to my days with CJOR radio and my studio in Gastown. He had just arrived from the Interior and we hit it off. We had become great friends over the years and I can't think of anyone else I could have unburdened myself too. Especially that night.

"At least, I won't have to go shopping any more," I quipped.

"Don't give me that!" he said. "You loved that part of it, wandering around the store, chatting up the old ladies. It kept you in touch. You just like bitching about it. Things will be fine. Don't worry about it."

"But I do, you know, Jack. I always thought we'd retire and spend our last years on the farm together. I guess I should have made more time for her."

"You can't blame yourself," Munro told me. "You did your best. You don't have to feel guilty. It wasn't your fault."

"It feels like it was. Let me tell you about it. . . ."

CHAPTER 2

"It's no' right for a man to carry a parcel. That's what women are for."

GRANDPA WEBSTER

● I was always an ambitious extrovert. I inherited it from my mother, Margaret Edgar Webster, a handsome, warm-hearted woman. She was the power in our house. We called her "Big Daisy" because she always wore her dress one size too small. It's a family trait. I do the same with my suits. Vanity, vanity, thy name is Webster.

I should have been a shipyard engineer, not a reporter. My father, William (Wullie) Webster, must have fitted the pumps on every destroyer, battle cruiser and merchant ship built in Glasgow between the two world wars. The old man, who took a very small dram of whisky, would occasionally concede that he was the finest iron-turner on the Clyde. His father would insist that he, too, had been the finest in his day. Modesty was not a trait the Websters cultivated.

The male Websters were proud of their skill as craftsmen and sang the praises of men who did an honest day's work. My mother was different. She saw no virtue in trades that left men broken, discarded and destitute as if they were little more than used-up draught horses. During the Depression, she determined that her three boys weren't going to come home in grimy dungarees and suffer the fate of the poor, unemployed workers who surrounded us.

She succeeded. The Webster boys inherited Wullie's sentiments and Big Daisy's ambition. Aside from my trans-Atlantic
success in the media, my older brother, Sandy, took elocution
lessons, played the piano and retired as the editor of Scotland's
biggest Sunday paper, the *Sunday Mail*. My younger brother,
Drew, became chairman of the exclusive journalistic cabal
known as the "lobby correspondents," the Fleet Street word-
smiths who wrote the most-important House of Commons stories. He retired as the London editor of United Newspapers, a
chain of provincial weeklies and dailies.

We lived in a red sandstone tenement, in the apartment on
the bottom right-hand side of the close, number 93 Battlefield
Avenue: two rooms, a separate toilet (no bath!) and a coal bunker in the kitchen. There were tiles and stained-glass windows
on the stairs, and gas lamps. So it wasn't that bad. Of course,
there were a hundred kids on the block. And block after block
after block after that. It was a good working-class district beside
the river Cart on the south side of Glasgow.

My mother and father slept in a recessed bed in the kitchen,
shielded with heavy green drapes, and we three boys slept two
up and one down in a hole-in-the-wall bed in the living room. In
winter, we slept together, covered by blankets and a heavy coat
for warmth. If you were in the middle and the coat-tails were
open, you froze to death. The perpetual cry in winter was, "Father, close the coat-tails!"

He'd come and pin the coat-tails together.

My mother gave birth to five boys, but only three of us survived past childhood. Willie died as a baby in the 'flu epidemic
of 1918. Sandy, Drew and I all made it. But it wasn't easy. Wee
Ronnie died of diphtheria in 1936, at nine, the same year Margaret became pregnant. My mother always maintained that her
child died to make room for Margaret's.

Daisy Edgar grew up in the southside of Glasgow. She was a
seamstress, sewing shirtwaists, but her family had a great deal of

pizazz. We called her father "Grandpa Spot," because of his dog Spot. He always waxed his mustache and wore highly polished, patent-leather shoes that he would order new but have re-cut and patched to accommodate his bunions!

He and his step-brother had once owned a chain of bakery shops. The family had been monied, and even when they lost it, they refused to give up appearances.

I remember Grandpa Spot and his step-brother arriving one summer in a big open Buick touring car, dressed in their finery, with a flask of whisky in the glove compartment. Big Daisy was incensed. "Where are you going, dad?" she demanded.

"We're going to the Ayr races," Grandpa Spot replied jauntily. "Just dropped in to say hello."

She cut him dead with her glare and snapped: "To spend your last ha'penny, I suppose."

They chuckled, waved and drove off.

My mother believed in expressing her opinion, forcefully when necessary. My father, on the other hand, was a very quiet, decent, humorous tradesman. All his life he carried a pair of calipers in his pocket. If he saw anything he had to measure it to see how many thousandths it was out. He was a good engineer.

The G. & J. Weir's Cathcart factory whistle blew every day at twelve o'clock, and my father would come home for his dinner. He finished up as a man in a bowler hat, a gaffer, in charge of production. Occasionally, he made a little dandelion wine that he fermented in a kitchen cupboard. But just a jar full.

The Websters were working-class characters. Alexander Webster, my paternal grandfather, was an absolute dyed-in-the-wool conman who liked a wee dram and a good story. He was an old-fashioned martinet who wore a wig to church. As a young man, he had worked in a South American copper mine in Curacao where men were regularly killed by snakebite. Later, he moved to New York but returned to Glasgow when he was introduced to the North American winter.

That's why I'm Scotch and not American.

My mother never liked him, partly because he probably reminded her of her own father, and partly because like a lot of Glasgow tradesmen he believed that women should walk one pace behind and that men shouldn't carry shopping bags. "It's no' right for a man to carry a parcel," Grandpa said. "That's what women are for."

My father and his brother, Andrew, believed that too. Uncle Andrew had a humped-back and my father used to tell us for years it was because he carried bags of coal on his shoulder as a youngster making deliveries. I thought he was telling the truth until I was about 21 and realized they had been pulling my leg. Andrew had scoliosis.

Uncle Andrew was slightly off. He had four watches, two wrist watches and two pocket watches. You'd say, "What's the time Uncle Andrew?" And he'd tell you, checking each of the four timepieces: "Twenty past. Twenty past. Twenty past. Aye, twenty past."

They were different people. But in spite of their sense of humour, they were also incredibly hard men. I remember my father telling me that that Grandpa Webster once ordered him to get rid of his four pet pigeons, which he kept on a window sill. Grandpa Webster came home and found that my father had disposed of all but one. Grandpa took out his tobacco knife, cut off its head and handed the corpse back to my father. "Now you can keep it!"

We were a fairly religious family. I went to church, plus there was Sunday school and Bible class. I believed you must atone for your sins. Then, there was Boy's Brigade, where you drilled with wooden rifles once a week. I wasn't an athletic kid, but we played soccer on an ash-covered field, or hunch-cuddy-hunch where you jumped on somebody's back while he held onto a spiked railing and tried to throw you off. We had some devilish games. Any new kid in the neighbourhood would be conned into going up to the top flat of the four-storey tenement and then coming down shouting: "It's me, it's me, it's me!"

Meanwhile, the other boys had gone up softly behind him and hammered on the doors of all the flats—so when this poor kid came down, the irate housewives would jump out and accost him.

We went to a very good school, Battlefield Elementary, in proper dress: square-toed shoes, knee stockings and a blue jersey, a jacket and a school cap. I always had a big head, size 7¾, and couldn't get a cap to fit. For cheeking the teacher, we got strapped across the palms; one teacher used to rap us across the knuckles with her wooden pointer and just about break our fingers. Intellectual class distinction was obvious in those days: the top of the class were seated in the first five rows, and those at the back were the dummies. I was always in the front, being a whiz at arithmetic and spelling. It was survival of the literate and the devil take the hindmost!

Ours was a Protestant school that accepted Jews as pupils. We'd all file in at one minute to nine, and the teacher would come in, read the roll and say, "All Jews out in the corridor!"

We had nine or ten Jewish refugees in the class, mostly Russians and eastern Europeans. They'd go out into the corridor and we'd parrot the Shorter Catechism according to King James: "Man's chief end is to glorify God and enjoy him for ever more, Amen."

The teacher would open the door: "You may come back in."

And the Jews would return. But apart from that, there was little overt discrimination. The Protestants and the Jews played together and became friends. Whereas the Catholics were "the enemy."

Roman Catholics were a breed apart from us. The Scottish education system was split along religious lines in 1918. Bigotry was pervasive. People who went to Catholic schools we regarded as different. Catholics were outcasts. They had a hard time getting jobs in newspapers, insurance corporations and other establishment firms. It was damnable. We grew up hating them; they grew up hating us. We didn't call their places of worship churches. They were chapels, a sinister word. We'd dash in and out as kids and splash holy water from the font.

Later, covering a minor disturbance during the Orange walk one July 12 as a young reporter, I was beaten up for wearing a blue tie. I was taking notes and one of them came up to me as I followed the parade through a Catholic neighbourhood. He didn't say a word. Just: Wham! Bam! And down I went. I struggled to my feet and saw a couple of policemen standing at the corner laughing.

"Why didn't you do something?" I asked them.

"If ye'r stupid enough to wear blue aboot here, you deserve to be thumped!" Blue was the colour of the famous Glasgow Rangers football team, the Protestant standard bearers, while green was the colour of the archrival Catholic team, the Glasgow Celtic. Many of Glasgow's Catholics were the descendants of Irish families brought over to supply cheap labour for the shipyards in the eighteenth century. They were at the bottom of the economic pile, even more oppressed than the Protestant poor in the human slagheap.

I grew up a kind of environmental socialist and I'm still left-of-centre. You couldn't help it growing up in Glasgow.

Hundreds of thousands of people lived in poverty. Tuberculosis was endemic. The shipyards that had been the industrial pride of Britain were mostly idle; the Queen Mary, partly built, was rusting on the stocks and it remained unfinished until years later when it was needed as a troopship. The great railway mergers had moved the marshalling yards and the associated locomotive industries south along with their jobs.

Labour unrest had been constant since James Maxton and

John Wheatley organized the great strike of 1915 for a wage increase of two pence an hour. Maxton, Wheatley, George Buchanan and Campbell Stephen organized another mass work stoppage in January 1919 for a forty-hour week. The army and police response to the display of worker solidarity left fifty-three injured and a union militancy unseen anywhere else in the world. Then, of course, came the fabled strike of 1926.

I remember going with my father to hear the great communist and labor demagogues in George Square. I must have picked up some of their oratorical skills by osmosis. In those days, you couldn't help being left wing, unless you were blind and stupid. The ordinary people were being screwed into the ground—right, left and centre.

The city bred brutality. Glasgow had the highest infant death rate of anyplace in the civilized world between the wars. Forty-eight of every thousand children died in infancy. On Paisley Road, there were squatters in the Plantation—four tenement buildings that had been built to form a quadrangle. In the backyard, the landlord had constructed another make-shift tenement. The entrances were blocked and those who lived in the upper levels used buckets to haul up supplies of milk, bread, jam and margarine. On one occasion, a baby died and it took several days before police were allowed access to remove the body. I watched them bring the little corpse out.

It was an incredible warren of poverty and desperation. And it had been condemned. But the people refused to leave because there was nowhere else for them to go. They were that afraid of losing what little shelter they had.

No one did anything to correct such problems back then. Death and squalor were part and parcel of growing up. Horrible. But that was Glasgow in those days. Not that it was a town without wealth. It had its share of fancy big houses, wealthy doctors, affluent politicians and rich businessmen. Yet it had hundreds of thousands of people living in one- and two-room apartments, some of them respectable, some of them terrible. Ours, thankfully, was respectable.

Everybody in those days was unionized: my father had been a shop steward in the Amalgamated Engineering Union. He hated Winston Churchill and would never give him a smidgen of credit as long as he lived. Churchill had said: "What free enterprise needs is twelve men for ten jobs." To my father, that meant Tories were committed to ensuring at least twenty per cent of the workforce was unemployed to keep wages low. He was bitter about the capitalist system because Glasgow at its worst was an expression of the very worst of the Industrial Revolution.

The Websters were never short of food or clothes, but we never had luxuries such as a bicycle—a bicycle was a soft, sissy thing anyway, we told ourselves in self-defence.

Early on, I got the itch to make money. I started delivering milk for the Scottish Cooperative Wholesale Society. You couldn't start until you were 12, but I had a bootleg route at 10.

The funniest thing was delivering milk on the morning after Hogmanay, or New Year's Eve, the biggest Scottish holiday. Normally, I clattered up the stairs with the assorted brass-tipped cans bearing gills of cream, quarts of milk and what not. If I have any muscles in my shoulders, it's because I carried those milk cans as a kid. But on New Year's morning, instead of the usual routine—hammer on the door and hand in the can—I knocked politely on the door, gave the housewife a big smile and said, "Have a good New Year, missus."

It was always good for a tip. One year, I made one pound four shillings in tips—and that was a lot of money in those days. If I ever spilled a bit, or took a wee sip, I'd leave the cans open out in the rain for a minute until they were topped up.

I remember stumbling across a suicide one morning as I made my rounds. I got a glimpse of the body hanging behind the front door of an apartment, and fled. The police were trying to get him off the doorhook when I came along.

I earned three shillings and six pence a week for delivering milk and always gave my mother the three shillings. What she didn't know was that I had my own little private, money-making arrangement on the side.

In the pre-dawn hours before the shopkeepers had arrived, I stole magazines and warm rolls to sell at discount prices. I used to sell the comic books—Dixon Hawke, the Rover, the Wizard, Sexton Blake—at half the retail price. The shop charged tuppence; I charged a penny. The shop charged thruppence for seven rolls; I sold them for tuppence. I never really was a barefoot boy, but in hard times my father inserted cardboard into my shoes to keep my feet dry.

My older brother, Sandy, couldn't get up in the morning to deliver milk like I could, but he was very bright, academic and intellectual. One of his teachers thought he could write and recommended him to Sir James Willock, editor of the Glasgow *Evening Times*. Sandy went to work there as an office boy and soon became a reporter. So when I left school two years later at fourteen, I followed him.

Working as an editorial telephonist at first, I took dictation over the telephone from the reporters. You couldn't be a reporter unless you knew Pitman shorthand. We used a system of typing contractions—"g" for "ing," "sd" for "said," and similar abbreviations—that enabled us to type the story at incredible speed. But to earn a promotion to reporter, you had to learn shorthand.

In those days, you only reported what someone said. Verbatim. Nothing but what they said. Period. So shorthand was essential. I spent three months at night school studying Pitman, travelling on the bus to and from work reading mystery novels printed in shorthand, becoming an absolutely cracker-jack shorthand writer.

I used to go to church on a Sunday night, sit in the balcony and take down the minister's sermon. Then, I'd come back and read it to my mother and father. It was to serve me in good stead in Canada. Not the sermon—the shorthand!

I held down three jobs when I was 16, 17 and 18: at the *Evening Times* from 6 A.M. till 2 P.M., I edited, typed and sent the racing reports to the printers; at the *Glasgow Herald*, from 5 P.M. to midnight, I took dictation over the telephone; and at the *Sunday Mail*, on weekends, I worked a twelve-hour shift, from 6 P.M. Saturday until 6 A.M. on Sunday as a reporter, covering the various rambunctious events for which Glasgow was noted.

The city was quite a primitive place in many ways. There was a dance-hall called the Barrowland ballroom located above an open-air market, not far from the city centre. You weren't allowed in until the doormen had searched your hat brim and lapels for razor blades and your pockets for bicycle chains and knives. The women sat down one side of the hall and the men sat on the other side and you had to be very careful who you asked to dance. If you danced with the wrong girl someone would "do" you. That meant he'd punch the bottom of your beer-glass just as you put it to your lips so that it smashed, sending shards ripping into your face. Or perhaps he'd wait until you were outside and carve you with an open-faced razor. In every way, it was a mean city.

As a reporter, I was responsible for covering local police stations. That's when my real education began. In those days, you went to cover a story wearing a shiny black oilskin so that when you went into slum housing you could sit down without picking up any lice or bugs.

In Glasgow, it seemed that every desk sergeant was a big, dour man from the Highlands. We called them "cheuchters," or "Highland stoats," which were little more than vernacular slurs. If you didn't give them a free copy of the first edition at midnight on weekends, they wouldn't talk to you. No free paper, no news! I learned the tricks quickly.

I also developed very good contacts among the gangs of Glasgow. Principally the Beehive Boys, the Billy Boys and the Cheeky Forty. It helped me quickly earn a reputation as a hot young reporter.

We had a police radio in the office and we used to drive around in Wolsley Fourteens that looked like police cars. If there was too much trouble at the scene, you didn't get out of the car. You sat there and pretended you were a young policeman.

That was an interesting time in Glasgow. The Irish Republican Army were very active during 1938-39. They were buying dynamite from Scotch miners at a shilling a stick. The miners would get six sticks to do a blow and they'd use four sticks and sell two to the IRA. But the slum districts in those days were controlled by the gangs.

The leader of the Beehive Boys, Bobby Metcalfe, would sometimes tip me about a big fight, or a killing like the night he told me about the body at Gorbals Cross.

The connection also paid off the night a bookie welshed, triggering a street brawl as the unhappy punters tried to collect. I did the story and then made extra money by filing it with the wire services—the Press Association, Reuters, Exchange Telegraph and Central News. When I came into the office on Monday morning, Harold Bishop Dickson, who was the chief reporter at the paper, said to me: "That was some riot you imagined!"

"What do you mean?" I asked.

"I heard it on the American short-wave broadcast: 'Unemployed mobs riot in Glasgow.'"

That wasn't quite the way it happened. The story had been blown up and sensationalized by editors in London and New York.

It was in those days that I met Margaret. My family had moved to King's Park when I was 16. As I made the early morning trip to work, I used to see this very attractive girl waiting for the same commuter train. She lived not more than a hundred yards away, but she also lived in a world apart. Her family lived in their own, purchased home, a bought house. We rented. There was a big social gap. But I fell in love with her and soon worked up enough courage to talk to her on the train one morning. We hit it off, and soon we began to go out together whenever I had any time.

It was great.

I was working constantly in those days. Margaret would wait for me at the *Daily Mail* office until I was finished and we'd go for coffee and travel home together on the suburban train. I worked twelve-hour shifts and Saturdays back then. God, I was crazy!

But it was a hell of a lot nicer than working in a shipyard. That's what mattered to my mother: whether your hands were clean when you came home and could wear a suit, collar and tie. She never gave up caring about appearances. I inherited that from her, too.

Margaret's family were Presbyterian like us, and her father was a decent man, Donald Macdonald. He was bit of a drinker, but he was also an accountant at J. & P. Coats in Paisley. That was the epitome of success because the firm was one of the world's biggest conglomerates, owning thread factories on virtually every continent. I remember being very envious of a kid in school who got a job with them. It meant instant status and upward mobility.

My mother never liked Mrs. Macdonald, and that may have been why she was so adamant that Margaret and I not get married when we told her of the pregnancy.

At that time, there was no thought of an abortion. Her mother wanted us to get married and so did we, but my mother wouldn't hear of it. She thought I was much too young and that it would ruin the life she had planned for me. Margaret and her family weren't good enough in my mother's eyes.

Daisy was the driving force behind all the Webster boys: she didn't want any of us spending our lives trapped in the shipyards. It was clear my mother saw the pregnancy as Margaret's problem. I never remember any trouble at home at all until then. Everything changed after that.

My mother blamed me for Ronnie's death the year my baby was born. There's a reason for everything, she would say, and I couldn't dissuade her of the notion. My mother was the strongest character I ever knew, and she didn't want anything to interfere with her son's success—and the responsibilities of fatherhood would certainly interfere!

I should have married Margaret. There's no reason I couldn't have married her. I didn't.

Instead, in the traditional Victorian manner, Margaret was banished to an aunt's house on the other side of town. Her pregnancy was hushed up so well that even my friends didn't know about it. I visited her almost daily until the baby was born. Margaret only saw the child momentarily before she was taken away from her. I did not see the baby myself until thirty-six years later. I had no desire to.

At that time, we had no idea who the adoptive parents were, and immediately afterwards our lives didn't change that much. We continued to see each other, we continued to make plans, and I gave no more thought to the child. It was as if I had erased the baby girl from my life.

There was always something to cover in those days: murders, fights, trials and the squalor. God, if nothing else seared itself into my mind growing up it was the grinding poverty. I travelled the length of Britain writing a series on the thousands of migrant men who wandered the country in search of work. They travelled in the back of trucks and I made the journey with them, spending several nights in the flop-houses they called home.

Before you could book a room, you had to fill in a form stating name, nationality and previous residence—for the benefit of the Metropolitan Police. That done, the man behind the grating took your shilling for the night's lodgings. I remember the scenes precisely.

One "doss house" (as they were called) I stayed in was a five-storey building, and on the ground floor and basement there were two reading rooms, a large canteen, bathrooms and the boiler rooms. The other four floors were occupied solely by bedrooms—out of the 1,000 rooms I was allotted No. 798.

The first thing I wanted after a two-day lorry trip from Scotland was a wash and brush up. Downstairs, a hot bath with the use of two towels was thruppence. A shave cost tuppence—and no tipping expected!—and my boots were cleaned for a penny. Afterwards, the stroll through nearby Hyde Park was free.

Inmates of these houses could come in at any time of night. But when I came back around midnight I had to push my way through the eternal crowd of loungers and moochers at the door.

In a canteen, over a jug of cocoa and a couple of slices of brown bread and marmalade, I had a chat with a young fellow from the Rhondda Valley in Wales who had hitchhiked to London to look for a job. "Keep to yourself," he warned. "It's not worth getting sociable to anyone around here, for you never know who you are talking to."

He put me wise to booking a cubicle for a week instead of by the night because you could save half a crown.

When I wanted to go up to my cubicle, I had to wait—with about forty others—at the staircase gate for the attendant who unlocked it every quarter hour. The cubicle was large enough—just!—for the single bed and a chair, but the bed was fresh enough. On the door of each room there was a Yale lock to provide a measure of safety and privacy.

In the bathrooms, men washed hankies, socks and even shirts in the wash-hand basin, and then hung them over the hot pipes near the ceiling to dry. All bedrooms had to be cleared by 9 A.M., but I was down and washed by 7:30.

It was a motley crew that morning in the canteen. There were fellows who obviously had seen better days, mostly "black-coats" with frayed bowlers and shiny suits; fat, once-prosperous men, with sunken cheeks; hard-faced youngsters from the North and West determined to get work; and regulars with hopeless expressions and their own little teapots.

For breakfast I had a large bowl of porridge, a mug of tea, three slices of bread and butter, and a couple of rolls for six-and-a-half pence.

I was just finishing when I noticed a pathetic old fellow at the end of the form on which I was seated. He was a real down-and-out. His shoes were worn down to the uppers, the felt collar of his heavy coat was torn, his muffler had almost slipped out of sight, and a greyish beard straggled over his face. I saw his eyes, through the thick glasses, fastened on the queue at the canteen, and as I had left a slice and a half of bread and one of the rolls I leaned along the seat.

"Here mate," I said, "you can help yourself to this."

The old man started at the sound of my voice, and then mustering all of his dignity, in a freezing tone, I got the answer to my charity: "Thank you sir, but if I wish food I shall buy it."

By 1939, I was a reporter and making good money. A hell of a lot more than my father after a lifetime as a skilled engineer. Writing five, six, seven stories a day, I met a lot of interesting people, and that helped me get ahead.

Margaret and I were married on July 13, 1939, and honeymooned in Belgium. When we returned we bought a house in Giffnock. Thirty pounds down, three pound, one and four pence a month was the mortgage. It was half of a duplex in a good district. We were thoroughly delighted and we started married life quite reasonably and quite happy. But in October of that year, I was back on the continent. War had broken out.

I was lucky during the war. I spent most of it in transport and at headquarters. I joined up on October 4, and one week later, because I could read, write and type, I was the orderly room army sergeant of a dock labour battalion near St.-Nazaire. I got out of France without any problem and later spent four years and six months in the Middle East, some of it in the Western Desert. I finished the war in the Sudan Defence Force as a lieutenant-colonel based in Khartoum.

I returned home in July 1946 and counted up the wasted years. Margaret and I had been married for seven years, yet we had only been together for a total of nine months.

During my absence Margaret had brooded about the loss of the baby even though our second child, Linda, had been born. I returned from overseas bound and determined not to spend the rest of my life in Glasgow. I also didn't want to hear anything from Margaret about a baby I'd all but forgotten about.

Back in Glasgow, I worked on the *Evening News* for seven pounds a week before joining the new *Scottish Daily Mail*. As before the war, a lot of my reporting was about sensational court cases.

In the first big murder trial I covered, a farmer's wife who had conspired with her 15-year-old lover to kill her husband walked away free because of the Scotch verdict, now removed, of 'not proven.' The husband was an incurable drunk who was disliked locally and on this one occasion when he staggered home on a Saturday night the farmer's wife and the young farm-hand were lying in wait.

As the man staggered towards the farmhouse cursing and swearing the wife put an axe into the boy's hand and said, "Go ahead, Jimmy, do it now!"

The boy hit the man over the head and he fell on the long grass badly wounded. Terrified, the assassins crouched a few yards away watching him until dawn. The man rose and staggered towards them. The woman gave the boy a shotgun and said, "Do it, Jimmy. Remember dead men tell no tales."

She was right. The farmer died and she walked out of court free! And it wasn't a surprise to anyone. The people on the jury liked her. Nobody liked her obnoxious husband. "Not proven" really meant "Guilty, but don't do it again."

One of the biggest pieces I did for the *Mail* was on the first murderer in Scottish history sentenced to be hanged after being convicted on the basis of fingerprint evidence. It was a curious case that gave me my first glimpse of schizophrenia.

On a foggy night in December 1945, a disguised railwayman barged into a station office, spraying lead from a Luger pistol. Annie Withers and Robert McPhie Gough, both railway workers, fell dead in the sudden raid on the Pollokshields East railway station, Glasgow.

A third railwayman collapsed wounded in the hail of bullets. He could see the gunman, dressed in a blue raincoat and brown soft hat pulled down over his eyes, stride across the room to the cash drawer and empty it. He turned and fled.

A few weeks later, and months before he was arrested, 20-year-old Charles Templeman Brown boldly walked up and down the same station platform wearing his gunman's clothes to see if anyone would recognize him. But the one man who could, the sole survivor, was not there. He had been transferred to another station.

I saw in Brown's behaviour the vanity of a schizophrenic—a split personality—and I was fascinated by the way he faced death. It was a rivetting experience for a young man such as I was to sit and watch as another young man faced execution.

When Lord Carmont in Glasgow High Court sentenced Brown to be hanged on January 3, 1947, the spotlight turned for the last time on the outwardly emotionless young man. His young sister, who admitted during the trial that at times she hated her brother and had often called him a "coward," collapsed as Lord Carmont passed sentence. But Brown stood impassively in the dock, unaffected by the finality of the moment.

He had been emotionless, too, during the ten months when hundreds of detectives in all parts of Britain sought him for the crime. By day he was a hard-working young railwayman, but by night he turned to his crazy world of hero worship.

Brown was a young man who lived to be centred in the spotlight; he loved to create heroes for himself and to ape them; he loved to lead a life of fancy, which helped him escape his own humdrum job of railway fireman.

After the murder, but before Brown's arrest, sympathetic railwaymen in Glasgow opened a spontaneous and unofficial fund to help the relatives of Annie Withers and Robert Gough. One of the first subscribers to the fund was Brown, who pulled one shilling from the pockets of his overalls, his lawyer said.

I couldn't help but point out in my report that Brown was more generous to himself later when he went to hear one of his dance-band heroes in a Glasgow theatre. Dressed in a white whipcord Sinatra-like jacket he paid 26s for a box.

Brown would not have made it to the death cell at Barlinnie Prison, Glasgow, if he had worn gloves on the night he murdered Withers and Gough. The vital proof that Brown was at the scene of the crime was contained in the evidence of Detective Lieutenant George Maclean, chief of the fingerprint bureau in Glasgow.

He was emphatic that it was Brown, and only Brown, who left three fingerprints and a right-hand palm print in the stationmaster's office, which was robbed of four pounds, three shillings and eight pence on the night of the murders. It was the only clue to the murderer in the possession of the police.

I wasn't happy in Glasgow after the war. It had fed my appetite for broader horizons. I wanted more out of life. My pre-war chief reporter, Harold Dickson, had become the news editor of the London *Daily Graphic*, Britain's worst morning paper, and I followed him to Fleet Street as its night city editor.

The *Graphic* was the social plaything of Lady Kemsley. She cared little for news. One night she even ordered us to airbrush the pizzle off of a photograph of a prize-winning Angus bull. "That's rude," she told us, gesturing at the bull's pride.

Although dumbfounded, we dutifully complied with her request. Needless to say, the farmer was outraged. In his mind, we'd told the world his bulls were eunuchs and he was not amused. Neither were the lawyers. It cost the paper the equivalent of five thousand pounds to assuage the breeder's wounded pride for his pizzle-less bull!

Despite such high-jinx, the *Graphic* had a circulation of about 600,000. The offices were on Gray's Inn Road, in a cavernous, messy, black building. There were the usual cluttered desks and little compartmentalized offices. The foreign news editor was a quiet man who kept to himself. He was just a perfect English gentleman, a distinguished, pleasant, erudite man in a cravat. I had no idea then that Ian Fleming would become the creator of James Bond.

Fleming and I would sit and decide whether we should send someone to Bulgaria or Italy depending on the news of the day.

At midnight at the *Graphic*, by agreement, you received copies of the first editions of the twelve morning newspapers published on Fleet Street. You had to go through each one to see what you had missed. What a nightmare that was.

One night T. Duncan Webb, a reporter, was on the telephone in the newsroom. He beckoned me over and, because of a crossed wire, we overheard a telephone call involving Scotland Yard and the government's board of trade. It was obvious from the call that an investigation was being conducted into a junior government minister. It had to do with cases of champagne, suits and an arms dealer in Israel called Stanley.

I decided to go with the story we had overheard: "A secret

investigation is being conducted into the conduct of a junior minister in the Labour government involving such and such and such and such. . . . "

We didn't use any names in the story because it was the kind of story you didn't dare double-check. Facts would probably have ruined it! Instead, we went and drank beer in Covent Garden where the pubs were open all night. At two o'clock the next afternoon in the House of Commons, Prime Minister Clement Attlee rose and said his attention had been drawn to a report in the *Graphic*. He announced a public inquiry would be conducted.

It was a great feeling of satisfaction to see a government forced to account publicly for its actions after a three-paragraph, front-page story! It was also a relief that the story was accurate, or Webb and I would still be looking for work.

There was incredible competition among newspapers at the time and Fleet Street was a vibrant place. It was like Glasgow before the war. If you went out to get a picture and you didn't get it, you were liable to get fired. I loved the stress and the excitement.

My decision to move to London also sparked a real battle with Margaret.

To begin with, I moved to the city before her, and that was bad enough. I lived in London during the week and every weekend I commuted to Glasgow, a round-trip of roughly 800 miles. I left London on Friday night at midnight, drove for twelve hours to Glasgow, saw Margaret on Saturday, and left Glasgow on Saturday at midnight to return to London.

Our relationship didn't get any better once she joined me in England. I used to leave the house and get the train to town from New Maldon at 9 A.M. and come back home at 9 or 10 P.M. Then I'd get up and do it all over again. It was dreadful and it drove Margaret up the wall. Especially when Jenny, my third daughter, was born, giving Margaret two little ones to look after.

We used to have screaming matches over it. Margaret wanted to go back to Glasgow, but my pride wouldn't let me return home with my tail between my legs. I was doing well on Fleet Street and I decided I would rather emigrate to Canada than return to Scotland.

I just said, "We're going."

And we went!

My brother Drew was the only one of the family who made it down to see us off. Jennifer was four months old and her sister Linda was six.

"Lucky that baggage form came through in time," Drew said as we stood on the platform waiting for the Southern Railway boat-train to take us from London to Southampton. Our luggage had been misplaced by the railway and we thought we would have to leave without it. "Imagine landing at Halifax with no clothes for baby," he muttered

It was a tearful goodbye. "Well, any minute now," Drew kept repeating, "I think that's the guard. No, not yet. Well, I don't suppose little Jenny will ever remember Scotland at all. Don't let Linda lose her Scottish accent. Yes, that's the guard now. You're off. Hey! No, you're not."

A door had slammed and someone now was clamouring to get out. A sudden change of mind? No, only a non-emigrant who had taken too long over her goodbyes. She was sobbing and Drew asked her if she was all right. "What, you've staved your thumb in the door, dear? Oh, never mind. Somebody always does."

He came back chuckling to where we were standing sipping a last cup of tea. "Well, you're off now, folks," he said. "Here, hand over the cups. The Southern Railway wants them back."

We climbed aboard. "No we won't forget the telegrams," I

assured Drew. "Don't you forget the food parcels. Cheerio. Goodbye."

"Goodbye."

The train moved slowly out, and four more Scots were off on the great adventure to Canada. We had chosen Vancouver solely because we had been told it had a temperate climate. We didn't want to live anywhere cold.

Margaret was not happy.

CHAPTER 3

"No, don't cut him down yet, his heart's still beating."

OAKALLA PRISON DOCTOR

• We came to Canada on the *Aquitania,* a Ministry of War troop-transport ship. We had a first-class cabin, and Margaret and Linda didn't leave it for most of the trip they were so seasick. I would take baby Jenny in a Moses basket, go to the lounge and have a drink. It was there that I bumped into a big blustery Canadian named Bill Mahoney, and we became instant friends. Mahoney was returning to Canada after attending a meeting of the International Confederation of Free Trade Unions in Geneva. Neither of us knew how fateful our meeting would become.

Margaret, the children and I disembarked in St. John, New Brunswick, and began the train journey across the country to Vancouver. We broke the four-day, cross-country trip and spent the night at the Royal York Hotel in Toronto. Then we got back on the train again and came to the coast where we spent the first night in the Hotel Vancouver.

I had a couple of thousand dollars in my pocket and a letter of introduction to Don Cromie, publisher of *The Vancouver Sun.* But I was smart enough to know not to use it unless necessary. No editor was going to like a reporter he thought was forced on him.

The *Sun* was in the old World Tower, once the highest building in the British Empire. The *World* newspaper, the building's initial tenant, folded in 1915 and the *Sun* became the main tenant in 1934. It was a landmark and the *Sun* used it as a billboard. A glowing globe was mounted atop the patina-encrusted copper cupola that crowned the slender building. Great streaks of vivid neon leaked down the edges of the polygonal tower.

Inside, the bottom floors were forests of columns. The tower itself was all elevators and circular stairs. The presses were in the basement; the editorial department was on the fourth floor. I walked into the editor's office on September 4, 1947, and asked Hal Straight for a job.

He glanced up at me. "Another bloody Limey," he sneered.

"I'm not a Limey!" I said. "I'm Scotch. And I'm a bloody good reporter."

"Start tomorrow, forty-five dollars a week," he said, put his head down and continued working on whatever he was doing when I walked in.

Straight was a brilliant newspaper man but I always used to snidely quip that he couldn't write his name unless someone helped him hold the pen. He was a fearsome man. He must have weighed 275 pounds and his main buddy, Harry Filion, the chief photographer, was just about the same size. Straight's normal lunchtime break was to sit under a tree in Stanley Park with Filion, Jack Scott, another *Sun* editorial staffer and a bottle of rye. They'd empty the bottle and come back to work none the worse for wear.

Straight was a mean son-of-a-bitch who infuriated or terrified people into producing for him. He had only one rule: "I won't blame you for missing a story, but I'll cut your throat if you miss the follow."

I lived by that credo. So did everyone else who worked at the *Sun* in that era, a stable of writers and editors who became a who's who of Canadian journalism: Arnie Myers, Hal Dornan, Jack Cahill, Cliff MacKay, Stanley Burke, Doug Collins, Gar

MacPherson, Sandy Ross, Jack Wasserman, Don Obe, Simma Holt, Ray Timson, Tom Gould, Paul St. Pierre, Mac Reynolds, Jack Brooks, Ron Haggart and Ron Ferguson. Pierre Berton had just gone east, and I had his old job.

To mention the successes of a few, Dornan went on to become a speech writer for Prime Minister Lester Pearson; Obe left to edit the *Canadian Magazine* and then *Toronto Life*; Gould went to become the head of the news department of CTV; St. Pierre to write award-winning drama and short stories; Ross to *Canadian Business*; Burke to the CBC; Haggart to be senior producer of CBC-TV's *Fifth Estate*, and Timson to the managing editor's job at *The Toronto Star*.

And there were incredible characters. Hughie Watson was my favourite. In many ways, he was a social disaster. A runaway from a dozen foster homes, he had slept in used car lots as a teenager. On one celebrated occasion shortly after I arrived at the *Sun*, Watson was driving along Main Street with a glass of amber-coloured fluid in his left hand when a police car came up beside him at a traffic light. There was a prisoner in the back, so Hughie rolled down his window and yelled: "Hey Mack! If you want to escape get ready to jump at the next light."

The police weren't amused and promptly arrested him, but he was acquitted.

Hughie was always ready for mischief and practical jokes. He enrolled a blind man in the Book-of-the-Month Club and he wrote fictitious letters to the editor and had his various pseudonyms argue with each other. One night with too much time on his hands, he invented the Howe Sound Basketball League. He telephoned the *Sun* and filed anonymous accounts of make-believe games and the mythical seven-foot-tall centre who dominated the league. All of the stories were published! When the scheme was exposed, Hughie laughed himself silly about duping his sometime boss Erwin Swangard. Hughie was never a great newspaper reporter, but he wasn't a bad guy.

There were all kinds of characters at the *Sun* in those days.

Martin Lynch, who had a photographic memory, later went to the *Globe and Mail* where he became a legend for his eccentricities, which included throwing scissors and spontaneous imitations of Gurkha soldiers assassinating their enemies.

Within a week of arriving in Vancouver, Margaret and I bought a little house in Burnaby, which was miles away from downtown and still without sewers. We had a wood stove and an icebox, which had to be refilled with ice every few days. What a come-down for Margaret. No stores, no sidewalks, no street-lights. Ditches out front. Boy did she hate it. I couldn't blame her. Glasgow had had sewers for over a hundred years— even in the slums!

Margaret phoned me in an absolute panic one day not long after we had moved in. The septic tank had backed up into the basement. We didn't even know what a septic tank was! There I was outside in the middle of November with a shovel digging up the septic tank to get rid of the crap in the basement.

Even good days that winter were trying. The house was heated by a sawdust burner, the first I had ever seen. Once you stoked it and got it going, you couldn't control it. It got so hot in the house we were forced to sit on the doorstep with all the doors and windows open. We were amateur Canadians.

It was dreadful for Margaret. The crises were constant. Talk about culture shock! She was pretty unhappy about emigrating and I didn't help much. But we muddled through. The working pace at the *Sun* was nowhere near as hectic and stress-filled as it was on Fleet Street. My first job was the hotel beat, the most demeaning reportorial job on the paper. I went around to the hotels every morning—the Georgia, the Devonshire and the Vancouver—and looked at the guest slips to see who had arrived the previous night.

As I was going through the slips one day, I spotted: "Bill Mahoney of Sault Ste. Marie." It was an amazing coincidence and I rang Mahoney on the house phone immediately. "What are you doing here?" I asked.

"I'm here to drive the Reds out of the trade unions," he replied.

He'd been appointed by Pat Conroy of the Canadian Congress of Labour, because the trade union movement in British Columbia was dominated by the Communist Party, principally Harold Pritchett of the International Woodworkers of America and Harvey Murphy of the International Mine, Mill and Smelter Workers' Union. The Congress, under the leadership of Conroy and Aaron Mosher, wanted to wrest control of the west coast unions from their radical leadership.

This campaign was going to be big news and if I wanted to get ahead, I had to capitalize on it. I went back to the office and asked the great gnome of B.C. newspapers, Himie Koshevoy, the *Sun's* city editor, for the labour beat. And he gave it to me.

Over the next few months, I worked with Mahoney and by January of 1948 the Congress-backed anti-communists had won all twenty-one seats on the Vancouver Labour Council. From there, Mahoney set his sights on winning control of the B.C. Federation of Labour. I led the witch-hunt in print.

At that time, the press unions at the *Sun's* cross-town rival newspaper, *The Province*, were on strike. If I spotted a *Province* reporter at a Labour Council event, I would send a note up to the chairman who would say: "There's a scab in the hall." The *Province* reporter would get thrown out. It was another Webster trick. I learned a lot of them over the years and I wasn't above using them.

Mahoney, who was later to become the national leader of the United Steelworkers of America in Canada, was tackling a group of people who had control of the province's major unions. They exercised that control through a back-room, if not secret cabal, called the Trades Union Council. Their orders came from the Communist Party.

Mahoney would feed me details about money missing from union treasuries. Being unknown in town, I was able to walk into IWA offices, pretend to be a member of the union and get a copy of the financial statements. These backed up Mahoney's contentions and I wrote the stories.

The *Sun*'s management were happy with my work, partly because McCarthyism was rearing its ugly head and my reporting echoed the tenor of the times. I once described Harvey Murphy as "a communist, real name Chernikovsky, trained in Moscow." It was pretty sleazy character assassination.

I attended a Red bloc dinner one night Murphy was speaking and fed a complete report of his vulgar personal attacks on national union leaders to Mahoney. He fed them back east and Conroy launched disciplinary proceedings that culminated in Murphy's suspension from the Congress.

Occasionally, my double role of reporter and agent-provocateur left egg on my face. Mahoney once warned me on the eve of a morning session of a B.C. Federation of Labour meeting in Victoria that he would manufacture a dispute with Murphy and lead his White bloc out in protest to split the delegation, which was making its annual lobbying visit to the government. I filed the story late that night from Victoria for the Vancouver Island edition of the *Sun*.

Unfortunately, Murphy was hung over the following morning and the meeting started ninety minutes late. I felt sheepish having published a story before it happened!

Coming back to Vancouver that night on the CPR steamer, a big logger from the Red bloc grabbed me by the shoulder as if he were going to throw me over the side and menacingly said to me in a broad Glasgow accent: "You'd better watch out for yourself, Webster, you god-damn, red-baiting bastard!"

"Don't talk to me like that you son-of-a-bitch!" I responded.

"Oh," he said, surprised at my accent. "I didn't know you were a Glasgow man. Pleased to meet you."

But members of the Party were quite capable of fighting fire with fire. They used to refer to me as a Liberal pig with his snout in the trough. At one labour council meeting, a woman delegate who supported the communists belted me in the face with her handbag.

I wasn't easily dissuaded. The way I saw it, I was supported by the facts. They had taken over the labour movement and I believed they had to be evicted. I hounded them.

On one occasion Alex McCauslane, who headed the International Oil and Chemical Workers Union, offered me a job. He wanted me to become an organizer because I had the gift of the gab. I was tempted. It was something like an interest-free loan for a car, about $1,000 a month in salary and expenses. But I thought, "No, I don't want to be a union organizer." Who knows, I might have been another Joe Davidson! But Canada already had its fill of U.K. accents among its union leaders.

I think I got on the anti-Commie bandwagon partly out of principle and partly out of opportunism. It was the sort of reporting that would be condemned today, but back then it helped establish me in Vancouver. We eventually won the battle hands down.

Would I do it again? Probably not. I consider myself a reasonably fair reporter except for the way I treated the communists in the early days. I never turned anybody in. Not that I haven't had a few approaches from the RCMP over the years to act as an informant.

"That was before your time, Jack," I told Munro the night Margaret died.

"Yeah," he nodded, "but there are still a lot of IWA members who watch and listen to you because they remember those days."

He got up to refill my glass.

"You know," I said loudly, so he could hear me in the

kitchen, "when we got the Party leadership out of the iwa, I became the *de facto* editor of the union's newspaper, *The Lumber Worker*, at $55 a week. This was on top of my regular job at the *Sun*. I wasn't writing propaganda, just putting the paper out."

It's funny. Ethics came to journalism with the arrival of middle-class salaries, sweeping benefits packages and job security. I don't remember much talk of scruples back in the days when publishers were parsimonious and you could be fired at will.

Munro came back and handed me the Scotch. His coffee smelled strong and thick from sitting on the stove.

"I don't think you should have any regrets about that stuff, Jack," Munro said sitting down again. "The problem with the left-wing is that if you give them an inch, they're quite prepared to take a mile. There isn't much activity out here anymore, you know. There hasn't been for a number of years. They've all moved to Ontario. They still go after me every once in a while."

"Does anybody still remember those days? Anybody still bitch about me?"

"Sure. But just the hard-core guys. The blind guys, the ones who have blinkers on for everything but what the Party tells them, are still upset, but the middle-of-the-road Commie couldn't care less."

Munro held his cup in both hands and blew the steam across the rim. "You know, Connie's uncle John is a commercial fisherman, and a real left-wing member of the party. He had a new boat awhile back and hadn't named it. He told me he was sitting in the net house and had the radio playing, listening to you give someone shit. You were rattling on about fishermen and Johnnie was working on his nets when someone walked in. He said he looked up, hooked his thumb at the radio and said, 'Listen to what we have to contend with.' Meaning you. Then he had a flash. 'Contend? Contend! That's it. Contender!'

"That's what he called the boat: *The Contender*. It's still fishing."

We laughed.

"The bottom line is that you survived and the Reds didn't. But why did you get off the labour beat?"

"That was Straight. He was always coming up with something for me to do. Once he sent me off to get my hair permed for a full-page spread with pictures of the agony and ecstasy of a woman's beauty treatment. Another time he ordered me to panhandle on Granville Street for a story. Then, he had someone in the office call the cops on me for begging.

"Straight never, ever hesitated to intrude on anybody's private grief. And I didn't mind either. I had developed the brass neck approach to reporting. I'd ask anyone anything for a story and be unmoved by their immediate, personal tragedy. So, I was always doing police stories. That's what I had cut my teeth on in Glasgow. They were my forte. And Straight liked my work.

"While I was covering one sensational murder trial, he complained that I was writing only seven columns a day. Spluttered Himie Koshevoy, 'Even Webster's only got two hands!'

"Without skipping a beat, Straight replied: 'Only two hands? Fire the crippled son-of-a-bitch!'"

Munro nearly choked on his coffee.

The most sensational and strangest murder trial I ever covered began on the night of November 9, 1949. A tenderman on the Kitsilano swingbridge discovered a body floating in False Creek. I was at the scene and saw police recover the corpse. It was Blanche Ferne Fisher, a spinster who fitted corsets at Woodward's.

She was half-dressed and her handbag was slung across her chest. The police said it looked like a suicide and that she probably jumped from one of the city's bridges. I contradicted them, calling it a "mystery" death. My story said, "The body of a 32-

year-old department store worker was dragged today from False Creek. Superintendent of the Criminal Investigation Bureau George Lefler said it was an obvious case of suicide but observers suspect foul play."

By interviewing the woman's relatives, I whipped up a storm of controversy. Fisher came from an eminently respectable and religious home, and her brothers and sister would not accept that she was anything but innocently involved. The coroner who conducted an inquest into the death supported my view and concluded that Fisher was murdered by persons unknown.

A month after the body was found, police arrested a strange character walking along a street in Kitsilano. It was late and the man was dressed only in rubber boots, a fisherman's oilskin, a fisherman's cap and, as the police report noted, "his person tied underneath his chin with two bootlaces joined together around his chest." Those words grew to become a legend on the B.C. coast.

The 28-year-old man stood five foot seven and weighed 175 pounds. Police identified him as Fred Ducharme—a friendly but slightly retarded fellow with a lengthy record of convictions for indecent acts, mainly exposing his abnormally large penis. He lived in a shanty-town on False Creek. Inside Fred Ducharme's shack, police found Fisher's watch.

Covering the trial, I became convinced that the killing was more of an accident. On the night of the slaying, Ducharme had indeed sexually assaulted Fisher and tossed her battered and bleeding, but still breathing body into the ocean. If he'd taken her to hospital, she would probably have lived. Instead, he became the focal point of one of the most sensational cases in B.C. history.

Ducharme became the subject of intense speculation, not because his crime was particularly heinous, but because his member was fourteen inches flaccid. He would tie bootlaces around it and loop them around his neck, wearing it like a pendant. At other times, he held the ends of the laces as if they were a set of reins, and let it "lead" him through the city. He spoke of it in the third person!

During the seventeen-day trial, then the longest continuous murder trial in the province's history, Ducharme wove around himself the coat of a split personality, adorned with a fantastic web of romance and glamour. It was a titillating tale to say the least.

Despite the obvious evidence of Ducharme's mental instability and the contradictions that bedeviled the Crown's case, the jury found him guilty of murder after deliberating for ninety minutes.

When asked if he had anything to say before sentence was passed on him, Ducharme protested his innocence. "I still say that I am not guilty," he said firmly, then continued with a slightly jumbled explanation.

The red-haired ex-airman concluded by saying defiantly: "Death is nothing to me."

Ducharme grabbed the bar of the prisoner's box in Assize Court, white-faced, as he heard Mr. Justice A.M. Manson solemnly pronounce sentence. Manson read his sentence dramatically, at times almost overcome with emotion. He halted half-way through the judgment before concluding that Ducharme should be hanged by the neck in Oakalla Prison Farm on June 30, 1950.

I was on holiday when his execution date arrived, but an editor on the *Sun* city desk called and asked me to cover it. "There's no way I'm going to see that man hanged," I said. "He's off his nut."

I considered his hanging a travesty, and was already opposed to capital punishment in general.

In those days, we got black-bordered invitations from Sheriff Frank Cotton of New Westminster every time there was a hanging: "You are invited to attend the hanging of - - - - at 12:01 A.M., on such-and-such a date." The *Sun* always sent a reporter.

I covered the execution of Sonny Jones, a black boxer who had killed a woman with his fists. The court considered Jones's hands a deadly weapon and he was sentenced to be hanged.

It was with some considerable trepidation that I went. There were to be eight jurymen present plus a couple of reporters at the appointed hour. We were ushered into an area near the top of an old elevator shaft in Oakalla Prison. Promptly at midnight, the whole prison reverberated with the shouting of other inmates. Then the unfortunate man was marched into the death chamber with his hands strapped behind his back.

He was placed on the trap. The executioner whipped leather bands around his legs and around his body. He slapped a mask over the condemned man's face, dropped the noose over his head, stood back, bowed to the witnesses, smiled, and opened the trap.

The horrible thing was having to stand there for several minutes while the rope jiggled backwards and forwards. It jiggled and jiggled and jiggled. Underneath, the warden and a doctor had entered the bottom of the shaft. The doctor climbed a stepladder and listened for a heartbeat. "No, don't cut him down yet," he said, "his heart's still beating."

He had to wait until the heart stopped beating before they could cut him down. Fourteen minutes after Jones fell through the trap, he was pronounced dead. I was sickened.

A colleague, Dougie Glasgow, and I left the prison and headed for a restaurant to have a coffee. I was shaken but Dougie just shrugged it off and ordered a hamburger. I just got up and walked away.

Standing in that room watching the rope quiver with a man gasping his last was the most demeaning experience I ever had. I believe being present at an execution would persuade 99 people out of 100 to abolish capital punishment. It is so cold-blooded.

Death is by no means instantaneous. Seldom, if ever, did the doomed man die of a broken neck. He died of strangulation.

Covering courts shaped my convictions about right and wrong and left me with an unwavering belief that capital punishment should never be reinstated. Watching a clearly insane man being sentenced to death for murder cemented that belief.

I oppose the death penalty even for psychopaths such as child killer Clifford Olson. I would simply lock such people away forever with only the bare minimum of creature comforts. If the government reinstates the death penalty, the executions should be conducted in public with live television coverage so everyone can witness the sickening spectacle. Let's see how many endorse it then!

Straight must have figured that no matter what faults I had, or how many battles we had, I had some moral fibre. I remember him calling me in one day in 1948 and snapping: "It's time you did something useful. Expose all of the bootlegging and the gambling in Vancouver."

I stared at him.

"There's something wrong with the police department here," he said. "Go and see what you can find out. I want to know about the bookies, the gamblers and the cocktail bars. They're all breaking the law."

He told me I'd have $300 for expenses. I wasn't to keep the winnings, but I was responsible for losses! And he threatened to fire me if I sampled any of the illicit booze I bought.

"How do you expect me to do this?" I asked him.

"Go sit outside Mulligan's office for a start and interview everyone who goes in or out." Walter Mulligan was the chief constable and Straight was convinced he was crooked.

I sat outside Mulligan's office every day with an atmosphere of ice around me. When any civilian emerged, I'd say: "What were you complaining about?"

Half the time it was some allegation of police brutality and I'd bash off a story in time for the final street edition. It seemed that every prisoner got out of the jail elevator or the paddy wagon bleeding or hobbled from a "fall" that occurred during the ride. But the real story was on the streets.

Vancouver was a wide-open city in those days. Gambling, prostitution and bootlegging were rampant. Every cigar store was a bookie shop. Every so-called private club was illegally selling drinks to the public. The place was full of blind pigs. If a policeman gave you a ticket for speeding, deliver a couple of bottles the next day and the ticket vanished. The police force was something else again—rotten at the top. This was the frontier and the town was absolutely wide-open and corrupt. It was the Casablanca of the West Coast.

All in all, I spent two weeks living in a downtown hotel, cavorting in clubs spending the *Sun's* money. I remember going to the Dodson Hotel. Two policemen stood guard on Hastings Street. Downstairs in the billiard parlour, the tables were covered with cloth and there were wickets for $2 bets, $5 bets, $10 bets and pay outs. The off-track commentary from Santa Anita was playing through overhead speakers.

All over town it was the same. You could drive up to the bootleggers and get a bottle of rye any time of day or night. There was one on Seymour Street. You drove up behind, honked your horn and bought a mickey of rye for roughly $3. There was a whorehouse on Richards Street.

At The Penthouse night club, on Seymour Street, they sold soft drinks at exorbitant prices, but everyone had bottles under the table. A bell would ring to let patrons know the police were on the way. That meant drink what remained in your bottle and leave it empty; or place it under the table and deny it was yours if the police asked. The dry squad would come in, wander through and they'd done their duty. There wasn't any illegal drinking going on at The Penthouse as far as they could see.

I was absolutely baffled, coming from Britain where things were fairly well ordered. The *Sun* ran my exposé across the top of page one: "Gambling Rife Here, *Sun* Probe Reveals:

"Hundreds of professional gamblers operate in the city, many of them taking part in illegal games—mostly poker—which take place after hours in city clubs, in phony sports clubs and plain illegal joints.

"Bookmakers, their employees, touts and runners, operate in beer parlours, cigar stores, hotel lounges, taxi offices and what amounts to open 'betting halls.'

"Bootleggers, free from competition from any all-night liquor store, supply liquor freely on telephone orders, sell it to personal callers and even dish it out by the glass in private 'lounges.'"

But none of the authorities responded despite the *Sun*'s unrelenting crusade. My front-page reports were backed up by a series of hard-hitting editorials demanding a public inquiry. They were ignored. If there had been hot-line shows, I am convinced the corruption would have been weeded out in a much shorter period of time.

I covered the Legislature in Victoria briefly for the *Sun* in 1952. Margaret and I lived in a motel on The Gorge for awhile. But she was very unhappy and didn't want to move permanently to the Island. It wasn't especially auspicious for me to come back to the *Sun* and say I didn't want the political beat, one of the paper's plum assignments. As a result I began a stint of working on the desk—a brief respite from reporting that lasted barely six months.

I was the assistant city editor for a short while and then I was named city editor. I failed miserably. I wanted to rewrite everything. It had to be my way or no way. I never was capable of being an executive. I didn't like delegating because I always thought I could do it better. And I only wanted to concentrate

on one issue a day. I preferred three or four stories about different aspects of the same subject rather than several stories about
a variety of subjects. In retrospect, I can see that a major blow-
up between Straight and me was inevitable. It wasn't long in
coming, especially when I went back to reporting.

I quit ostensibly because of an overtime dispute.

My problem was triggered by the suicide of Walter Pavlicoff,
the number one wanted criminal in Canada at one time.

Pavlicoff had shot and killed a bank manager. Later he had
escaped and been recaptured. It did not take long for the jury to
bring in a guilty verdict. And as Pavlicoff stood in the box to be
sentenced, Mr. Justice Manson said to him: "Is there anything
you wish to say before I pronounce sentence?"

Pavlicoff leaned forward and shouted—"Yes. You bastard.
You were determined to hang me from the moment I walked
into your courtroom."

The judge, shocked by the attack, turned to me and another
reporter at the press table and told us that he was in command
of the court and we would not report the prisoner's outburst.

He then sentenced Pavlicoff to death.

After the *Sun* wouldn't print the story I had written about
Pavlicoff's behaviour and the judge's order, I sent a copy of it to
an opposition member in the House of Commons, who raised
the matter with the minister of justice. Thereafter, Manson was
known as the "Hanging Judge."

While in the Oakalla prison death cell, Pavlicoff committed
suicide. I got the phone call about midnight from a friend of
mine who ran Royal Oak taxi. "Hey, Jack," he said, "I've got
the guard here who discovered Pavlicoff's body.'

I was on holidays but I got out of bed and raced down to the
taxi office to get the details. Pavlicoff had managed to smuggle a
razor blade into his cell and slit his wrists after the evening bed
check. He bled to death. I got the guard to draw a diagram of
where the body was found and I was in top form when I arrived
at the *Sun* about four in the morning with my scoop.

They held the home edition for me and the story ran under an "exclusive" flag. I went home later as happy as a lark.

Ten days later, when I returned to work, I kept waiting for Straight or someone to say, "Good job, Jack. Well done, thanks." But nothing happened. I was really put out by the indifference and promptly submitted a ten-hour overtime bill at double-time as a means of registering my displeasure.

Well, the bill came back with a message scrawled across it from Straight: "Webster is paid over scale. No overtime."

I went to the union, but they wouldn't support me. So with great ostentatiousness, I went to the secretary-treasurer of the B.C. Federation of Labour and asked him to come and see me in the *Sun* office. I made sure everyone knew I was going to grieve this all the bloody way.

Straight relented, only because fighting the grievance would have cost him even more money. Feelings were so bad that Straight called me in about a week later and said: "You're nothing but bloody trouble."

I wasn't in the mood to put up with that, so I retreated to hyperbole. "The day you die of overweight, Straight," I said, "I'll be one of ten-thousand people who will dance on your coffin for joy."

He exploded. "You're fired!"

"I quit," I sneered, and stomped out.

C H A P T E R 4

"Either you confess and tell the truth, or you take this and blow your head off."

R A Y   M U N R O

● I left the *Sun* full of bravado, but my anger towards Straight cooled quickly with the realization that I wasn't going to have a pay cheque anymore. I wasn't sure how I was going to earn a living and for the first time in my adult life, I was worried about it. Fortunately, radio station CJOR offered me a job. They wanted me to do a daily, ten-minute current affairs program. They also wanted me to read the morning newscast or the sports report whenever anyone was sick.

I didn't know the first thing about radio and I was sure it was a dying medium. The advent of television was upon us and radio, everyone said in 1953, was on the way out. I wasn't enamoured with the idea of going to work every day in the basement of the now-demolished Grosvenor Hotel on Howe Street, adjacent to the old courthouse. But I needed the job and the $125 a week.

"If you're going to succeed on radio," Jack Short, a veteran race-track broadcaster told me when I first arrived at the station, "you need a trademark. A tag for promoting the next broadcast. How about, 'precisely'? 'Listen to Jack Webster at 6:10 P.M. *Precisely!*' What do you think?"

I liked it, used it for thirty-five years, and it caught on. People still call me Mr. Precisely!

My biggest worry was content. I was never a writer of any note. I only turned a phrase by accident. Or theft. The thought of reading on air only self-generated material was daunting.

My greatest strength in the newspaper business had been court reporting. I love covering trials because they reflect what's really going on in a community. Any community. Wander into a courthouse anywhere, and within days, probably hours, you'll know what goes on behind the manicured lawns and sculpted hedges and inside the skid-road hotels. It's also easier journalism. The story is already shaped. The lawyers have synthesized both sides and everything is presented to the court. All you do is record the details. Working the court beat, you always had time for lunch at the West Coast Central Club, or the Hotel Georgia.

That's why I was nervous leaving the warm womb of the Vancouver *Sun*. You couldn't take tape recorders into a courtroom. The skill that had made me an accurate reporter was shorthand. I returned to the office to edit and type my notes, or I edited them as I read them over the telephone to a transcriber. I would learn to do exactly the same thing with a tape recorder.

We had no portable tape recorders in those days so everything pretty well had to be done in a studio. Or you had to transport a huge, two-piece Magnacorder to the scene and set it up. I felt like a hotel porter when I went out to do an interview.

The first ten-minute program took me nearly three weeks to prepare. It was about the Liquor Control Board and its odd licensing procedures. I discussed the origin of the board and Pacific Brewers Agents and tried desperately to explain the esoteric workings of what was little more than a political patronage machine. My second program was an interview with American labour leader Walter Reuther, who had just survived an assassination attempt in Detroit. My third was with Victor Jory, a wonderful, popular actor of the time.

I was never any kind of intellectual but I was a hell of a good brain-picker. I have a knack for asking questions, and I am not reluctant to ask tough ones. Once you've told a woman she's a widow and then asked her for a couple of quotes for the morning edition, you can ask anyone anything.

For each important interview, I composed ten questions on the back of an envelope. I'd plough my way through the list and if there was still tape left, I'd ask any that had occurred to me while I was listening to the answers. I went straight for the jugular. Inflection was paramount. I wanted to sound tough even if I wasn't asking the world's toughest question. I sat leaning forward, giving the impression that I was ready to pounce. Really hard-nosed radio reporters were a scarcity in North America then so my technique stood out.

The skills I'd learned as a print journalist stood me in good stead, and I was incredibly brash. But I was flying by the seat of my pants, figuring out what worked and what didn't work by trying it. There were memorable crashes.

In an interview with U.S. General Lucius D. Clay, who ran the Berlin airlift, I asked: "The *Daily Mirror* said last week that Eisenhower was an amiable bungler. Do you agree?"

He looked at me, grabbed the microphone and said: "If Eisenhower was an amiable bungler, he was an amiable bungler who bungled his way to victory!"

Then, he threw down the microphone and stormed off, leaving me scarcely enough tape for my program. It taught me to save the tough questions until last, until after I had recorded enough for my program.

Jimmy Hoffa, the crooked U.S. labour boss, side-stepped every thrust during an interview about the management of Teamster pension funds, and afterwards said to me with disgust: "Where do you come from?"

"Scotland. Why?"

"Oh," he said, "I thought you had crawled out of the goddamn woodwork."

It must have taken me almost two years to relax and sound

more conversational, less accusatory. I had to learn to conduct a newsy conversation, not an interrogation. I had to learn to interview people who weren't politicians, celebrities, newsmakers or public figures. I had to learn to coax common, everyday people who normally didn't speak in public to talk on radio. And I had to do it live—there was rarely time to edit tapes because I was on every night.

Every day, I broadcast a short show called Spotlight at noon and my main program, City Mike, at 6:10 P.M., precisely. I also recorded ten two-minute opinion pieces on Friday that were aired over the weekend as Capsule Comments. It was quite a grind.

It made me hustle and it paid off. Within months of my departure from the *Sun*, Straight was forced to eat a bit of crow and splash an "exclusive" Webster story on page one again. I alone got the post-race interview with Roger Bannister when he broke the four-minute mile against Australia's John Landy during the 1954 British Empire Games in Vancouver. Straight bought a transcription of the tape for $500, but I insisted on a byline as well.

Quitting the *Sun* had not been my proudest moment and I always had a burning desire to prove Straight wrong.

But by 1955 the drudgery of having so much work to do for what was not a lot of money, forced me to consider eating humble pie myself and return to the *Sun*. Then, the provincial government at last ordered a public inquiry into graft, corruption, mismanagement and laxity in the Vancouver city police department under Chief Constable Walter Mulligan. What became known as the Mulligan Probe rekindled my enthusiasm for broadcasting.

I suspected the inquiry was going to be the most talked-about story in the city. Vancouver was infamous for its sybaritic, laissez-faire lifestyle. Aside from its home-grown characters, the city attracted meandering global miscreants. My own stories about gambling and bootlegging in 1948 indicated the police force was patently corrupt, but no one had done much about it.

Six years later, Mulligan's malfeasance came to the attention of Eddie Moyer, a reporter for *The Province*. He learned of the payoffs through his fishing buddy, Detective Sgt. Len Cuthbert, the cop who collected the graft. *The Province* wouldn't run the story, so Moyer gave it to Ray Munro.

Munro was an ebullient, good-looking reporter who had left Vancouver for Toronto. He was a Damon Runyon character who carried a .45 automatic and drove a car equipped with red flashing lights and a siren. I met him about a week or so after I joined the *Sun*. He was walking about the newsroom with a huge pair of shears, cutting off reporter's ties and giggling insanely. When he got to me, I picked up a pair of giant scissors and said: "Cut off my tie and these will be in your belly!"

He laughed uproariously and we became instant soul-mates.

We covered a train crash in the Fraser Canyon one year and rented a plane to fly to the wreck site. He was a pilot.

"You know I was forced down three times during the war," he told me nonchalantly as we flew towards the derailment. "Last time, my bloody cannon exploded during a run at a sub. Forced me down into the Channel and left me pretty bashed up."

Later, while we were flying below the level of the highway in the Canyon, he leaned out the window and snapped pictures of the wreckage while holding the joy-stick between his knees. On the way back, we ran out of fuel and made an unscheduled landing on the airfield at Flood. We were stopped by some gentle, friendly, welcoming blackberry bushes.

Munro had since left for the East where he worked for a Toronto tabloid called *Flash*, a racy irreverent publication owned by Lou Ruby whose son Clayton would become one of Canada's foremost lawyers. *Flash* trumpeted the corruption story using all the hyperbole its star reporter could muster: "Rape of Vancouver! Munro tears mask from crooked law in gangland Eden."

"A police chief who took a piggy bank—a deputy chief whose secret activities and fits of rage are the talk of a neighbourhood—crooked detectives and enough intrigue to make the fictitious Mike Hammer look like a Lavender Lad— that's the talk of this port city today!

"Ever since 1947 when Walter Mulligan was named Chief of Police over the objections of more than half the force, the general public, caught up by this master spellbinder's oratory and broad beaming smile, have been labouring under the delusion that honesty was the byword of local law.

"Hah!

"Since that date in 1947, immorality among police at even a very high level, bribes taken, fixing and just plain stealing, have been going on in the public's own front yard and they've either been too blind or too scared to blow the whistle.

"*Flash* is blowing the whistle here and now and calling upon the clean people of Vancouver to stand up and be counted— and clean out a City Hall administration heretofore so powerful that not even three daily newspapers could buck it."

Munro even went to Detective Sgt. Cuthbert, handed him his .45 and said: "Either you confess and tell the truth, or you take this and blow your head off."

A few days later, on June 24, 1955, Cuthbert went to the toilet and shot himself in the stomach. He survived.

Munro made it impossible for the establishment to continue to look the other way. He made life in Vancouver sound like a seedy soap opera—corruption in the police department, moral misconduct by police officers, gamblers operating at a furious pace with immunity from police raids. The Mulligan Probe was the result.

The chairman of the commission of inquiry was Reginald H. Tupper, Q.C., a dignified, handsome man who was well entrenched in the local legal establishment. I approached him and asked for permission to install microphones in the hearing room so that I could broadcast the proceedings. Tupper blanched. "No way! Absolutely not."

I was determined to cover the probe, and get the last laugh on Tupper, so I decided to report the proceedings by shorthand, verbatim if possible. I was still a whiz at Pitman: fast and accurate. The great beauty of shorthand is that while you're taking complete notes you can edit as you go. There's enough slow conversation so that you can go back over and finish the sentences for the speaker. No one seems ever actually to finish a sentence when giving evidence in court. I immediately went out and bought a half-dozen shorthand notebooks.

Every day for two months, I attended the hearings. The probe started in the old courtroom downtown and then it moved to City Hall where the council chambers doubled as a make-shift courtroom.

I'd work on my notes during the breaks in a nearby alderman's office and go on the air at one o'clock with a twenty-minute summation of the morning's evidence by simply reading my notes. The nightly broadcast I did from CJOR's studios on Howe Street.

I began each evening with the same introduction: "This is the full story that was not in the *Vancouver Sun* today and won't be in the *Vancouver Sun* tomorrow."

The station cleared the evening schedule and I'd read all of the day's evidence from my notes. Some nights, I'd be live on air for two hours or more continuously. I didn't have to work to make it entertaining, it was detailed and fascinating—the humiliation of a police force. The day's program was re-broadcast entirely at midnight. In effect, we had discovered Talk Radio and didn't know it.

It was wonderful stuff: a police chief who stole a piggy bank containing $22 and split it with his partner; a scarlet woman on whom he lavished presents and cash; a senior detective so racked by conscience he shot himself, and assorted other sordid accusations.

I'd read the day's evidence for an hour, sometimes two. I acted the parts and dramatized questions and answers. People sat in their cars on the Vancouver Island highway to receive the broadcasts. I got mail from Alaska and California where my broadcasts had been heard by people with receivers picking up the skipped radio signal. The hearings exposed a two-bit skein of graft and corruption that hardly rivalled Chicago in the Twenties. It was incredibly entertaining.

Tupper treated Mulligan and his lawyer Tom Norris, Q.C., with contempt. He refused to intervene when Norris's family was attacked by a nasty story in *Flash*. Norris flounced out never to return. Tupper refused to let Mulligan testify before all the evidence against him had been entered. That meant the chief of police had to sit on his hands while his reputation and character were dragged through the mud for months on end.

Mulligan's graft system was exposed when an honest policeman turned down the payoff.

Detective Sgt. Bob Leatherdale was approached by Mulligan in May 1949, upon his appointment to the gambling squad. The police chief indicated to Leatherdale that there was an agreement among police, local bootleggers and gamblers. "Cuthbert knows all the arrangements, he'll see you," Mulligan told him, according to Leatherdale's testimony.

Leatherdale, who said he wasn't quite sure what Mulligan was suggesting, went to see Cuthbert, who made it clear. "There's no use beating about the bush," Cuthbert told him. "We might as well talk straight. The chief wants money . . . he thinks things should open up a little."

Leatherdale thought about it and said: "No thanks."

"I'm sorry you changed your mind," Cuthbert replied, somewhat taken aback. He had assumed that since Leatherdale had talked to the chief, everything was fine. "I've already seen Nick

[Madiuk, an admitted bootlegger] and made arrangements which now have to be changed. But you've got guts, Bob. I wish I had done the same thing."

Indeed, he did. Especially when he learned Leatherdale was testifying against him.

Cuthbert admitted accepting bribes but claimed to have received very little money. He said his own greed and ambition got the better of him and he pointed the finger at Mulligan for enticing him into corruption.

Cuthbert received his promotion because he was a long-time Mulligan crony. He had made detective sergeant even though he had been disciplined and busted in rank for hanging out with criminals. He had also been suspended for "loose conduct" during an investigation in 1945. Mulligan, his superintendent, had given him commendations over the years to help him climb back up in rank.

On the day he was promoted to detective sergeant, Cuthbert testified that he and Mulligan stood at a window looking down on the bustling crowds on Main Street. He said he asked Mulligan: "Well, chief, what are your policies?"

"There are no policies," Mulligan had told him. "That's your beat," he said nodding to the milling people below. "Clean it up."

Cuthbert said he was always confident whenever he accepted packages of money or free bottles of liquor, that if he were caught the chief would protect him. Whenever he called Mulligan and the chief couldn't talk, Mulligan would say, "O.K. Charlie, I'll see you later Charlie." Or, "I'll make a note of it."

But Cuthbert refused to say who else in the department got paid off. When pressed, all he would say was: "Those men who I knew I could trust but whose names I cannot now recall." He claimed the payoffs had only been made in 1949 and were not part of any ongoing or established system of graft.

Eleven detectives subsequently testified. All said the same

thing and in my opinion most of them withheld evidence. I had never seen so many big, burly men, whose memories were as sharp as tacks during any criminal trial, testify one after the other: "I don't remember, I can't recall."

I made up a little jig for the broadcast after hearing several sing the same tune: "I don't remember, I can't recall, I don't remember, I can't recall, I don't remember."

It was a travesty. Huge, seasoned police officers who couldn't remember anything when it came to their colleagues. Supt. Harry Whelan killed himself on July 14 rather than be cross-examined. We never really found out why. Some said he was trying to keep a family skeleton in the closet, others that said he had a guilty conscience. I thought he was an honest cop.

I don't think the inquiry ever got to the bottom of the mess. Tupper gave the detectives the benefit of the doubt in his final report: "There is no firm and sufficient ground for the allegation that any of these men [except Mulligan and Cuthbert] has been corrupt."

Hogwash! More than simply the chief and his bagman were dirty.

The gamblers and the bootleggers weren't any more forthcoming. Some testified they'd been operating for years and had never been busted. But no one would come out and say flatly they'd paid off Mulligan or anyone else. One of them, Bruce Snider, said that he didn't even know Mulligan.

"You do not know Walter Mulligan?" Tupper repeated incredulously. "He was the chief of police."

"No, not to my knowledge," Snider replied.

"To your knowledge you don't know him or haven't met him?"

"That is correct."

"Did you ever pay any money to Walter Mulligan?"

"I did not."

"I mean by that either directly or indirectly?"

"I did not."

"Did anyone on your behalf pay any money to him or any-body on his behalf?"

"They did not."

"Do you know Helen Douglas, the chief's mistress?"

"I do not."

Douglas was the scarlet woman in the whole affair and with-out her, the inquiry would have lost much of its allure. She had been Mulligan's girlfriend and was to be the principal witness against him. Douglas was expected to act like a scorned woman and Tupper allowed her to appear in disguise. She was so cov-ered up she could have been in purdah! She wore a wig and her face was hidden behind a veil. Those features you could discern were obscured under heavy, heavy makeup.

Helen Douglas testified using her maiden name even though she was now married.

"I kept company with him," she said when questioned about her relationship with Mulligan. Kept company! She was his mis-tress from September 1944 until the fall of 1949.

They had talked of marriage shortly after their affair began. Mulligan told her he would get a divorce and leave the police force. Douglas told him that was something he might regret, given his rank of superintendent. "Think it over well, I told him."

He did—for five years. Since he had decided not to marry her, they split. "I don't want revenge," Douglas insisted, refus-ing to play the scorned woman. "Not five and a half years later."

"I was a single woman," she said. "I saw no one else."

She lived on East Georgia Street and Mulligan would visit her a couple of times a week. He'd drop in for the afternoon, some-times for the evening. But always during the week. He paid for trips to the Okanagan, Vancouver Island, Montreal and Seattle.

Mulligan also lavished gifts on her: a diamond ring, two large pieces of unset jade, a zircon ring, a Chinese teak chest, a typewriter and assorted other baubles. There was money, a twenty here, a ten there, and an occasional fifty. Mulligan also gave her $2,200 to buy a small love-nest out in Langley.

But while Douglas could remember the tiny details of her lover's attentions, like the policemen she had trouble recalling any details of his criminal activity. Oh, Mulligan occasionally spoke about gambling and graft, she testified, but she wasn't sure what he meant when he talked about $500 payoffs from gamblers Bruce Snider and Leo Bancroft.

"Did he say anything to you to indicate whether or not he was receiving any of that money?" Tupper asked. "Did he indicate to you whether or not he was receiving any money? Any money at all?"

"My impression was that he might have been," Douglas replied evasively. "There are a lot of gamblers in the city and the way of money coming from them—it was discussed various times. I guess there was some money being paid out," she said in a barely audible voice, "but I don't know to whom. It was his business, not mine."

She had the impression he was on the take, that was all. About all Douglas would concede is that the money Mulligan gave her to buy the Langley hideaway was probably not from his salary. She couldn't explain why she sold it in 1952 for only $500.

She and Mulligan split in 1949, and during the breakup Douglas testified that Mulligan boasted of getting $38,000 from gamblers that year. She testified that the plan Mulligan mentioned involved a divided city: west of Carrall Street would be controlled by two big-time gamblers, while another criminal controlled the eastside. Each would pay Mulligan and the police $5,000 a month. At least that's what Douglas thought was to happen. She wasn't sure.

Upon seeing newspaper stories of the impending inquiry into his conduct, Douglas had burned the diary she kept while having the affair with Mulligan. He had also called her a few times to establish what she would tell investigators. She told him she had burned the diary and also destroyed photographs of them together. She spoke to him again about four weeks before testifying.

There was a litany of minor complaints against Mulligan, including the theft of the piggy bank. Everyone who could throw mud at the man, did. He sat through most of it. But on October 12, he withdrew. Mulligan claimed it was because he was being destroyed by rumour and hearsay evidence, but the truth was writ large on the wall.

Mulligan had tried to forestall the inquiry in April of 1954 by writing a private letter to the chairman and commissioners of the police board. In it, he claimed to be under siege from nefarious forces who wanted to discredit him and the police department.

He wrote that he had the names of two police officers involved in this plot, also the name of a Social Credit member of the Legislature and charged that three employees of a Vancouver newspaper were also involved in the conspiracy. Mulligan concluded: "In respect to any charges that might be levelled against me personally, I can assure the board that I am ready to meet them at any time, and if only they can be brought out in the open where I can come to grips with my opponents, I feel confident that any allegations made will prove to be unfounded."

It was a prescient piece of prose: fortunately, Mulligan's lame attempt to divert attention and blame some yet-unseen conspirators had been ignored. Now, several months later, Mulligan knew it was only a matter of time before he faced criminal charges.

The day after Mulligan announced he would no longer appear at the inquiry, he went to the U.S. consulate and obtained a visa. He fled across the U.S. border and refused to return to Canada.

In the end, Tupper found Mulligan "guilty of corruption in

taking money directly and indirectly from those unlawfully carrying on business as bookmakers." But no charges were ever laid and Mulligan's extradition from California was never sought.

The inquiry was really an exercise in damage control. The legal and political establishment of Vancouver wanted to restrict the effects of the scandal and play down its implications. To be fair, Tupper was overwhelmed by tentative, guarded and qualified answers. But he still fudged it all in a report that was duller than dishwater.

Mulligan's flight was not unexpected. No one really wanted him to testify and reveal how rotten things actually were. Mulligan later got a job as a parking official at the L.A. international airport. He apparently ran into Tupper once, and neither spoke to the other.

Mulligan finally returned to British Columbia twenty years later and retired to Victoria. I went to visit him and he was quite polite to me even though I had mercilessly exposed him.

"It's nice to see you after all these years," he said.

But after we had exchanged pleasantries his wife appeared in the doorway and started screaming: "Jack Webster! You ruined my life! Get out of here! Get the hell out of here!"

It was my turn to flee.

The incident reminded me about the effect of the medium, the power of media exposure to destroy lives. All I did was report what happened. But in massive detail. Forty days the commission sat. I did millions of words on the air. Millions and millions of words on the air.

I won a Beaver award—the highest accolade in Canadian broadcast journalism at the time—for the Mulligan programs. The judges said the award was "for ingenious, accurate and exciting coverage of a sensational police probe hearing; for the indomitable effort of CJOR news director Jack Webster who, denied the entry of a tape recorder, edited and delivered up-to-the-minute reports of pertinent testimony from shorthand notes; for outstanding public service in keeping Vancouver residents abreast of a highly significant event."

Straight had been right all those years before. Some of my friends in the legal profession didn't look so good in light of their lackadaisical treatment of the original complaints. Even now I'm annoyed that I didn't push the issue hard enough in 1948. Probably that realization helped me appreciate Straight more and we became great friends and fishing buddies. I gave the eulogy at his wake.

Although the Mulligan probe had been manna from heaven for my career, my family life had deteriorated.

I was hustling, picking up as many jobs that could be done quickly and without much thought or effort. The ambition that drove me out of bed as a youngster, continued to burn. I worked morning, noon and night. Even on weekends and holidays, if there was a way to make a buck out of it, I found it.

One afternoon I got a call saying Robert Muir, the president of the Royal Bank of Canada, wanted to see me. I went around to his hotel room and he said: "You're that Scotch reporter."

"Yes, what can I do for you?"

"I want you to do a job for me."

"What kind of job?"

"I want a confidential report on how sixteen of my branch managers in British Columbia are doing, their standing in the community, the kind of service they deliver, that sort of thing. Think you could do it?"

"How much are you willing to pay?"

"Fifty dollars a day."

"Sure."

I arranged a vacation and headed off into the Interior with my tape recorder, Margaret and the three kids.

I would arrive in town and ask around about the local bank

manager's character. I gathered whatever gossip was floating about. Then, I'd phone the manager and ask a few questions and see what kind of service I got. Afterwards, I'd go see if he had the Royal Bank newsletter on display, and if not, that was a black mark against him. I'd ask to see the manager, clock the time it took before he saw me and then gauge how I was treated.

It's something I'd never do today, and I feel kind of sleazy admitting to it now. Several of the managers were scolded for their laxity; a few were transferred. But I was doing so many different things in those days I didn't think a great deal about the ethical concerns that seem to preoccupy so many of today's reporters.

When I wasn't out covering something, I gave speeches to service clubs. I conducted current affairs classes for Royal Canadian Mounted Police and army recruits, earning between $40 and $50 a class. I spoke on issues such as press attitudes towards police and gave them tips on handling the media. The army would fly me over to Victoria and back. It was a great way to develop contacts.

Margaret and I saw a lot of the country doing that sort of thing, and it wasn't all work. We did have a lot of good fun. Throughout it all, though, her fear of the outside world worsened. She suffered various neuroses and began to manifest what would later be identified as agoraphobia. The frequency of her withdrawals and her obvious misery led me to move back temporarily to Scotland in 1957. She was so unhappy and alone in Canada that we thought returning to Scotland might help.

I didn't just up and leave. I arranged with CJOR to continue producing five taped programs a week, and the CBC commissioned me to do two radio documentaries, "Footloose in Scotland" and "Footloose in Ireland."

In Glasgow, we bought a large house in a good district and I began writing a column for *The Sunday Dispatch*, and to work for Roy Thomson's new Scottish television station.

I had met the Canadian media tycoon in 1949, before he had finished building his a financial empire. We were together on the inaugural Canadian Pacific Airlines flight to Australia and on the plane he asked me if I would mind writing stories for his newspaper in Timmins, Ontario. "I'll pay you $5 a story," he said.

I just laughed. "Get someone else, you're too cheap for me."

Thomson hired me to be the first newsreader on Scottish Television and to organize the station's newsroom in the old Theatre Royal. He was still cheap and didn't pay me too well—only twenty-one pounds a week. But he was a good chatty guy with a passable collection of off-colour jokes and we got along all right.

The sponsor of the newscast was Ever-rite Samuel Watches and every evening I opened the program by saying: "The time is now six o'clock by my Ever-rite Samuel Watch." Then I'd read the news.

Afterwards, I did a short interview.

But two things quickly caused controversy in Scotland: my accent and my aggressiveness.

People wrote the newspapers saying they strongly objected to my Canadian accent!! I had only been out of the country for ten years but they said I sounded like a foreigner! And, they said, they were sick of my aggressiveness. They really objected to one particular interview I did with a Scottish trade union leader.

There was a dispute in the shipyards about which union was responsible for moving a wheelbarrow from one side of the yard to the other. The jurisdictional squabble ballooned and the unions threatened to close twenty-two miles of shipyards if it wasn't settled. I asked a secretary of the Scottish Trades Union Congress to appear on my program, and he did.

After indicating it was the silliest labour problem I had ever heard of, my first question was: "What machinery do you have to stop this incomprehensible jurisdictional dispute that could possibly close the whole of the Clyde on Monday morning at 6 A.M.?"

He looked me in the eye and said: "If we have any machinery, sir, it's none of your business."

He got up and left the studio. Interview over. That's the attitude that killed the shipyard industry on the Clyde.

My *Sunday Dispatch* columns had also become a local irritant, especially one about aging, leaking gas lines that ruptured under sinking tenement buildings and had caused several homes to explode, leaving a trail of people dead and others poisoned in their sleep.

I got a memo from a managing editor of STV with a note enclosed from the Independent Television Authority saying: "It would seem unwise that your newscaster be expressing his opinions in print in a newspaper column."

The ultimatum was that I could do one or the other: drop the columns if I wanted to appear on television. They didn't want a television presenter expressing his opinions.

I didn't think I had changed, but clearly I had. I didn't fit in any more in Scotland. I'd been out of the country scarcely a decade—I hadn't changed. They had. The aggressiveness and spirit that had characterized the Scotch reporters between the wars and afterwards was gone, it seemed.

Fortunately, the waning of my fortunes coincided with an offer of a job in Vancouver from radio station CKNW. They were offering me double the money I had been getting at CJOR and the use of a company car.

Even Margaret was glad at the prospect of returning to Canada. We had only been in Scotland for six months and the winter hadn't gone well. The family all had been afflicted with the Asian 'flu, and Margaret wasn't as enamoured with life in Scotland as she thought she would be. Her father was dead, as was my mother by this time.

Before we made a final decision, I went to Roy Thomson and asked him for a raise. "Not a chance," he said, "I can get the best newspaperman in Scotland to read the news for twenty guineas a week."

"Get one," I replied.

So, with Margaret's blessing this time, we returned to Canada.

It was a godsend for me professionally. I could ask people straight questions again. They were still touching their forelock in Scotland. It actually felt good to get back to the old daily grind of City Mike, Spotlight and those ten Capsule Comments before leaving for the weekend.

C H A P T E R 5

"Webster! If the bulls come in here, the guard dies, you die and we all die. Go tell the warden!"

G E R A R D   C A I S S Y ,   H O S T A G E   T A K E R

• Crime was long the mainstay of my reporting. The courts and police dockets provided endless grist for the mill. I knew dozens of junkies, pimps, burglars, small-time hoods and other round-ers. Their picaresque exploits made marvelously entertaining material for television and radio. The stories of their lives pro-vide a clearer picture of what is happening in a city than the boosterish twaddle usually provided by local politicians or the chamber of commerce.

One case I championed involved a man who died in solitary confinement after two weeks of being fed only bread and water. John Wasylychen was being punished by the warden for de-stroying government property: to wit one pair of socks worth $1.95!

A classification officer smuggled a page of the punishment book out to me so I could prove what happened. The story forced then-federal Minister of Justice E. Davie Fulton to re-move the warden and order procedural changes to ensure such a tragedy didn't occur again.

But I wasn't always so successful.

One morning a man arrived at my studio with a number of

Indian carvings he had created. He told me his name was Lloyd Bright and he was on a day pass from Mountain Prison. "I want to sell the carvings to get a stake," he told me. "It'll help me get re-established if they ever let me out."

It was a quiet morning and I put him on the air saying anyone who wanted to buy one of the tiny totems at $10 a piece should come to the studio. I bought a big one for $125, and we sold the rest to listeners who poured into the studio. We collected about $300 in cash and cheques and I gave the money to Bright.

"When are you returning to prison?" I asked as he was leaving.

"I'm going back tomorrow morning on the bus."

A week later I got a phone call from the prison asking me what had happened to the man. I told them I had put him on air, gave him some money, and that was the last I saw of him. "You, silly, bloody fool!" the corrections officer said. "You financed his escape. We'll never see him again."

They didn't.

But Bright was not a major criminal. Like others, he was more of a nuisance than a menace, who had been indefinitely imprisoned because police, prosecutors and judges were tired of dealing with his antics. Thank goodness life-time prison sentences for habitual petty criminals have been abolished.

Drugs were always a serious problem in Vancouver and the root of much of the crime. There were about 1,400 addicts in the city, according to the best police estimate at the time. I embraced the drug issue as a cause celebre in 1959.

Covering an inquest into the death of a junkie one day, I heard the coroner ask a policeman where the addicts got the syringes and eyedroppers they needed to inject the heroin. The detective replied matter-of-factly, "Just down the street at the local drugstore."

I found it hard to believe that drugstores were selling hypodermic needles over the counter and went immediately to a store on Main Street. I approached the clerk, a man in his mid-forties who was wearing a fawn-coloured smock, and said, "I want a packet of Export A please and sell me one of those kits, will you?"

"What kit?" the man replied.

"You know," I said casually, "the eye dropper and the fine needle."

The clerk looked at me nonchalantly, reached to his left and opened a drawer revealing a large number of small envelopes. He handed me one. "That will be fifty cents plus three cents tax."

"Tax?"

"The government's got to get its cut. Don't blame me."

I made some light conversation about a parking ticket I had just received and left.

The drugstore promptly sued me for the story I broadcast that night and I responded by laying a complaint against the pharmacist with the provincial governing body. The druggist had his licence suspended but won it back on an appeal. The lawsuit against me was dropped, although the practice itself continued: improper, perhaps, but not illegal. Now we give addicts free needles.

Curly Gregory was the first junkie I ever put on the air. I believed that not many people had ever met a heroin addict or truly understood what many of them did to survive, especially in the late 1950s. I thought, why not give them a first-hand glimpse?

"How do you raise money?" I asked Curly.

"Oh," he said with some verve, "I'm a very experienced shoplifter. For instance, today I got away with a good camera and a good suit."

His habit didn't interfere with his enjoyment of life as far as he was concerned. "Well, thanks very much Curly," I said ending the interview. "And where are you going now?"

With the most delicious chuckle, he said: "I'm going to work."

"What do you mean?"

"I'm off to steal!"

The heroin problem subsided briefly in the early 1960s during a police clampdown on pushers and addicts. On one occasion, the police brought out the dog squad at midnight to herd about two hundred addicts who were hanging out at Pigeon Park, moaning about the lack of supply in town.

One addict I knew by the name of "Ducheyne," decided to commit suicide by giving himself an overdose. He was in his mid-forties and had often visited my Gastown studio. When he decided to end it all, he hung his only suit in his hotel room with a hundred-dollar bill pinned to it along with a note saying he wanted to be buried in the suit and the money was to pay for the service. He shot himself up with a cocktail of heroin and seconal and then jumped out the window. But he was on only the second floor!

The police found him unconscious. When he was finally released from hospital and he returned to his room, the suit and his money were gone. Later I learned one of his suppliers sold him a packet of poison because he owed $3,000. He died after injecting the toxic cap.

Many Vancouver addicts in those days fled to Britain to escape the persecution. Britain was heaven on earth for them. They could obtain all the drugs they need—legally—and virtually for ha'pennies. Canadian authorities were truly delighted to see the problem of caring for these addicts shifted to the backs of the generous British health care system.

The British treated addiction as a physical sickness. In Canada, we considered possession of even the most minute quantity of narcotics a major crime. We forced our addict to support his craving for heroin by wholesale crime, theft, robbery or prostitution to raise the cash. There, a junkie only had to find an understanding doctor.

Armed with a CBC television crew, I tracked one particular Canadian junkie who had fled to the happy hunting ground for heroin and found a growing colony of between forty-five to fifty of them in London. Illicit drugs, which could cost them $10 to $50 a day in the Vancouver underworld, could be bought from chemists' shops for a mere two shillings under the National Health Service, or 10 shillings as a private patient.

Irvin Hess, a 38-year-old addict I'd known well while he lived in Vancouver, agreed to appear on camera for me. He was cleaning taxi cabs at Hackney and was on a maintenance program that provided him with a legal supply of morphine.

The camera followed Hess as he went to Boots the chemist and bought his drugs. Then it followed him into the Regent Palace Hotel in Piccadilly Circus. He was cooking up the drugs in his spoon when the lights went out. I went out into the corridor and found a unionized electrician yelling. He'd interrupted the power supply to the television lights. "Who put that plug in here without my permission?" he hollered.

I explained the situation to him, slipped him a couple of quid and he put the plug back in again.

Hess had a prison record stretching back into his youth and he said he needed four fixes every twenty-four hours. As he hit the vein and pushed the plunger injecting the dope, he looked up and smiled: "In Vancouver, I dared not use my drugs and needle until I had barricaded the door. That way if the Mounties came crashing through I could at least finish my fix and have time to dispose of the evidence."

"If they caught me at it again I'd go to jail for life," he said, explaining his flight from Canada.

To combat the menace of drugs, the RCMP were armed with

all-powerful writs of assistance. These gave them total power at any time to break or enter anywhere in their search for drugs and to use whatever force was necessary.

"Here in Britain everything is different. What I'm doing is legal. I don't care who comes in and sees me. Furthermore," Hess added with a grin, "do you see my new teeth? Before I left Vancouver a year ago, the RCMP knocked them out while searching me for drugs."

I knew of an addict who died when apprehended by two RCMP officers who thought he had heroin hidden in his mouth. He did, but in forcing open his clenched teeth with a set of keys the policeman jammed the bundle of heroin into the man's gullet and he died of suffocation.

"The first thing I did in Britain," Hess said, "was to have new teeth put in by the National Health Service. Cost me a quid. I'll never go back to Canada. Britain is the place for me."

"Britain is wonderful," he repeated as we left. "God bless the National Health Service."

Later, I interviewed a woman doctor on Harley Street who said to me: "We're very happy to be helping these Canadian drug addicts. They all need help. They're all entitled to maintenance doses of morphine. But," she asked, "why is it that everyone of them that comes in here steals something from my desk?"

"Because they are all thieves to begin with," I told her.

Most of those in B.C. who craved heroin had picked up the habit in prison. Every addict I knew had been a delinquent before he got the monkey on his back and just about every one had picked it up in jail. In the B.C. Penitentiary, you could order your drugs and they would be delivered to you over the fence on credit.

Conditions inside most of the institutions were deplorable. I did all kinds of stories on the prisoners' cries for help. I served on a jury that made a series of recommendations aimed at improving prison life after a slew of men in Oakalla slashed themselves with razors so they would be transferred to a hospital.

My empathy with convicts was why three inmates with a guard as hostage demanded that I be the go-between when their escape attempt went awry. It was nearly 10 P.M. on April 19, 1963, when Tom Hall, warden of the B.C. Pen, telephoned me at my West Vancouver home. "Mr. Webster," he said, "we've got some trouble at the Pen. I wonder if you could come out and help us."

"What kind of trouble?" I asked.

"Well, we've got some prisoners who won't go back into their cells. They want to speak to Prime Minister Pearson or Webster. We can't get Lester Pearson so we're calling you."

I picked up my tape recorder and headed for the federal penitentiary at New Westminster. "Don't get taken hostage," my 21-year-old daughter Linda joked.

I drove the sixteen miles to the prison in only twenty minutes. Inside Hall's office, I learned what had happened.

At 7:30 P.M., guard Patrick Dennis called "time" to the eighty convicts using the auditorium-gymnasium. Dennis motioned them up the hundred-foot tunnel to the domed main building of the prison. The men took their last swipes at volleyballs, put away the badminton racquets, and stacked the few folding chairs that had been used. Those who had been lounging on the tumbling mattresses got to their feet and all filed slowly into the tunnel.

Suddenly, three men at the rear of the line seized Dennis and hustled him back to the gymnasium's shower room. They had laid their plans carefully. They trussed Dennis with copper wire, forced a side door and ran for the forty-foot outside wall. Their plan was to try to scale the wall on a length of heavy electric wire weighted at one end. Each man carried a prison-made knife and a Molotov cocktail—an electric light bulb filled with gasoline and fused with a twist of rag.

A guard on patrol spotted the men before they reached the

wall. He fired three shots in the air and loosed his guard dog on them. One of the convicts lit the fuse of his gasoline bomb and hurled it at the dog. The Molotov cocktail exploded prematurely and flaming gasoline seared the man's own face and body.

The three men sprinted back to the washroom where Dennis was struggling to escape from his hastily tied bonds.

Even before the guards in the main building knew what was happening in the washroom, they reacted to the sound of shots by slamming the barred door of the gymnasium tunnel and fleeing. Behind them they left fifteen convicts in the tunnel besides Dennis and his three captors in the washroom beyond. There were also between two hundred and three hundred prisoners, mostly drug addicts, milling about in the main part of the jail refusing to go back to their cells. Everyone feared the worst.

The leader of the three men holding the guard at knife-point was Gérard Caissy, a 28-year-old serving seventeen years for armed robbery in Quebec. He had been transferred from St. Vincent de Paul penitentiary as a troublemaker among his fellow French-Canadian prisoners. With him were Nelson Bernard Wood, 27, serving eight years for holding up a jewelry store and beating up the proprietor, and Wayne Carlson, a 20-year-old Regina man serving four years for burglary.

"I don't know what they want," Hall said, "and I can't authorize you to negotiate with them."

"So, what do you want me to do?" I asked Hall.

"I can only ask you to go down and talk to them."

"OK," I said, and picked up my tape recorder.

"You can't take that down," Hall said.

"Why not?"

"It would be a breach of the penitentiary regulations."

"If I do not take my tape recorder down, I ain't going. That's my insurance policy."

Police Superintendent Woods Johnston, who was also at the briefing, interjected: "Tommy, make up your mind. Let Webster take his recorder or we'll go down and kill the lot."

A guard let me through a locked door into the main dome—into the midst of a milling, yelling mob of prisoners. "They're not causing any real trouble," the guard told me, "but they refuse to go to their cells and because of what might happen down there . . . " he nodded toward the door of the gymnasium tunnel, "we've decided not to take the chance of using force."

Some of the men spotted me and yelled: "Hey, Webster! We want to talk to you too."

The prisoners crowded round, wanting to talk to me. I knew many of them and it took me about twenty minutes to fight my way through the mob.

"You'll have to wait," I told them, "until we see what's happening with the guard downstairs."

One of the fifteen men accidentally isolated in the tunnel stood near the door, closely watching every move of the guard as they unlocked the door for me. The man told me later that he had nothing to do with kidnapping the guard. "If the guards had tried to rush the tunnel when they let you in, I was to shout to Caissy—and that would have been the end of Dennis," he said.

As I walked down the tunnel a man ran up the slope from the washroom and frisked me for weapons. He was Carlson, a thin, pinch-faced youth with bristling hair. During the twelve hours we were to spend together I came to call him, mentally, "the punk."

Carlson led me to the washroom and into a weird and garish scene: a bare unpainted concrete room, windowless and odourless. Around the walls were ranged six shower stalls and six toilets without doors, and four urinals. Two bright bare bulbs hung from the ceiling, illuminating a frightening sight.

Caissy was standing in one of the toilet stalls. In one hand he brandished a knife inches from the throat of Dennis, who was hunched on a straight-backed chair. His wrists were twisted behind his back and bound with copper wire. From his wrists the wire ran in a loop around his neck. Behind him Caissy had the wire in his other hand. He kept jerking the wire as he talked to me, so that it cut into Dennis's neck.

"Mr. Webster, Mr. Webster, you be okay."

His voice was so heavily accented as to be almost unintelligible. He had a habit of repeating every statement. "You be okay. But if we don't get what we want we kill the guard . . . we kill the guard! If they shoot, you die too. We'll die together."

I felt chill. I instantly knew I was locked in with a man who was quite mad. The impression was heightened by his staring eyes, his jerky movements, and by the angry red burns that streaked one side of his face where the bomb he threw at the dog had backfired.

The prisoners explained that they had heard rumours that a fellow inmate who had been moved to Riverview psychiatric hospital had died or been killed. They were breaking out to make sure their friend was all right.

Dennis looked so calm in his dire plight that I thought he must be numb with fear. But on the rare occasions when he spoke his voice was quite normal. He was, I concluded, simply an unusually phlegmatic Englishman. When he was given cigarettes (and once a cup of tea) he'd say casually, "Loosen that wire a bit, chum—I can't swallow."

He argued casually with his captors: "Why are you doing this to me? I haven't been a tough guard, have I?"

Caissy agreed. "Not a bad guard . . . not bad—but a guard all the same!"

Only once did Dennis show emotion. Toward three o'clock in the morning it occurred to me that I had better get a message to my wife that I was all right. "If anybody phones my wife," he said emphatically, "there's going to be hell to pay when this is over. She doesn't know anything about this and it will only scare her to death."

Margaret, my wife, had got the news that I was a hostage from my brother Sandy, at the *Sunday Mail* in Glasgow. He had spotted a wire story about my involvement in the riot and called her to find out what she knew, which was nothing.

Within minutes after I entered the washroom, some of the fifteen prisoners drifted in from the other end of the tunnel. They looked on the scene with strangely apathetic expressions, as if they were watching a not very exciting show but had nothing more interesting to do at the moment. Presently, they drifted away again and I could hear the sound of volleyball in the gymnasium. One of the drifters, though, started to advise me on how to conduct the negotiations with Caissy and his companions. I knew him—Rocky Myers, a disbarred Vancouver lawyer who was serving six years for conspiracy to attempt to bribe an RCMP officer to protect a proposed gambling operation at a place called Wigwam Inn.

"Mind your own business," I told him.

Caissy began jerking the wire again and shouting incoherently. It occurred to me that he was actually in pain, and I asked him. "Hurt like hell," he admitted.

"You've got to have a doctor," I told him. "If I call the prison doctor will you promise not to try to hold him—and not to do anything stupid while I'm gone?"

He agreed.

Back upstairs, I assured the elderly prison doctor he would be in no danger. He refused to descend into the washroom, but said he would have some pills sent down. I returned to the prisoners and a few moments later the tranquilizers arrived.

The pills might have calmed Caissy, but someone had written on the envelope, "Caution—two or three pills will make you sleepy."

"They're trying to drug us," Carlson said, and he and Caissy rejected the pills. Bernie Wood started to eat them like candies.

Then I switched on my tape recorder for the most macabre

interview of my career. Microphone in hand, not twelve inches from the face of guard Dennis, who sat mute and bound with the knife at his throat, I interviewed the men who were threatening to kill him.

For the next fifteen minutes, until the tape ran out, I questioned them and listened to their complaints, or mainly Caissy's, for he did most of the talking. Wood's chief resentment was that after the judge had sentenced him to four years for robbery with violence, the Crown had appealed the sentence and the appeal court doubled it. Moreover, he had not been given credit for the six months he spent in jail awaiting trail.

Caissy's grievances were more complex and varied: He said he was dying of throat cancer and could not get treatment in prison, which explained his cold-blooded attitude toward Dennis—"What does it matter if I die of a Mountie's bullet since I'm dying anyway?"

He insisted I look down his throat to confirm his diagnosis. All I could see was a clean dental plate and a gullet inflamed from too much smoking.

Caissy's demands in exchange for Dennis's life were a medical examination for himself, no reprisals against any of the three, and they wanted John Peters, the inmate they were worried about who had been moved to Riverview, brought to the gymnasium.

Wood wanted to be transferred to Stoney Mountain prison in Manitoba because his wife hated Vancouver and wanted to move to Winnipeg where she would be among relatives and friends.

Caissy and Carlson wanted to be moved to St. Vincent de Paul penitentiary in Quebec. "I don't speak English good," Caissy explained, "so nobody understand me and I don't understand nobody here."

But his most insistent and puzzling demand was that Peters be produced. "Who is this Peters?" I asked.

"You know him!" Caissy snarled. "You broadcast about him when he appeared in court a few months ago."

The name clicked in my memory. Three months before I had reported a habeas corpus application in the Supreme Court at Vancouver. A slim young American-born convict had appeared in person to speak for a writ he had prepared in his cell. He claimed he was being held illegally under a sentence of twenty years for armed robbery in Ontario.

It was true that Peters had a horrendous record of violence in the Kingston, Ontario, penitentiary. Once he had thrown gasoline on a fellow prisoner and set him afire. In 1961, he was a ringleader in Kingston's hostage riot. He and another convict cornered five guards in a kitchen and, brandishing a straight razor and a boning knife, had threatened to cut off their heads one at a time and roll them down the stairs to where the prison officials were assembled.

But it was also true, as I said in my radio report at the time, that if half of what Peters claimed at his habeas corpus hearing was true there should be a full investigation. Peters tried to convince the Supreme Court that the Ontario Provincial Police had made a deal with him. He claimed police told him that if he pleaded guilty to half a dozen unsolved crimes, some of which he did not commit but which police wanted to mark "solved," they would get him off with an eight year sentence. Instead he was sentenced to twenty years.

Transferred to New Westminster, Peters had become friendly with Caissy. Peters's story had apparently aroused a sort of twisted loyalty in Caissy. Then Peters had disappeared. Caissy told me bitterly that the prison rumour was that after a tussle with a guard Peters had been put into solitary confinement, beaten with a baseball bat, and eventually transferred to the criminal wing of Essondale Mental Hospital, four miles from the Pen.

There in the gymnasium washroom, as Caissy brooded on the

fate of his friend, the presence of Peters suddenly became his most urgent demand. He brandished his knife within a fraction of an inch of Dennis's jugular vein and shouted: "You get Peters here right away or the guard die!"

Trussed in his uncomfortable harness, Dennis puffed a cigarette as if he had not heard a word of Caissy's tirade. The angry criminal then turned Dennis over to Wood and beckoned me into a corner of the washroom. (Seldom, and each time only for a few minutes, did Caissy let the others guard Dennis.)

In the corner Caissy's tone changed suddenly from anger to wheedling. "If you can get a bottle of whiskey smuggled down," he whispered, "I'll split it with you."

Next the three men got together and started to voice hysterical fears that no matter what deal they made through me they would be double-crossed. I decided that this wasn't getting us any nearer to saving the life of the guard. I told them I was going upstairs to talk to the warden, after which I would telephone a broadcast over CKNW, giving their demands and the officials' answers. They could listen to it over a radio that would be brought into the washroom.

Warden Hall agreed to relay the prisoners' demands to the commissioner of penitentiaries in Ottawa, and I went on the air via telephone to CKNW: "I am authorized to announce that the commissioner of penitentiaries has been asked to approve the transfer to other penitentiaries of three men who are now holding a guard hostage at knife-point. I have agreed to act as personal escort to the three convicts until they are transferred later today."

When I came through the tunnel this time, Caissy's gang seemed pleased with the broadcast, but then we hit another snag. I told them I was confident permission would be obtained within minutes to transfer them. I wanted to know at what stage the guard would be released. Caissy became hostile. The guard would not be released he said, until he himself was safely in the yard at St. Vincent de Paul.

How could this be done? He had a maniacal answer. He would take the guard with him at knife-point as a hostage on the plane. Both Dennis and I scoffed at this.

"Even to save the life of a guard," I told him, "the authorities will only go so far. Try and be slightly reasonable if you want to get out alive."

"All right," said Caissy, "we'll make them bring carpenters into the gymnasium and build a big wooden box, maybe even a steel box. The four of us will get inside and be bolted in. They can ship the box to St. Vincent de Paul and when they open it in the yard there, I'll release the guard."

I couldn't think of an answer to that proposal except that it was crazy.

Caissy became impatient to hear the result of the warden's call to Ottawa, and I headed upstairs once more. Once again I had to bull my way through the drug addicts who were still milling about.

Outside the dome that formed the central area of the prison, Mounties in full riot gear—at least six of them wearing gas masks and standing with tear gas guns at the ready—stood guarding the main door. Billies and rubber hoses were laid out on the counters outside the yard, and two hundred fully armed RCMP men were lining up in the yard.

The warden told me he had been given a completely free hand by Ottawa to handle the situation as he thought best. It was decided, however, not to give in too quickly to their transfer demands or it might lead to new and more nonsensical demands.

At 2:45 A.M., knowing the trio were tuned to my station, I made another broadcast. I had to fight every news instinct to keep out a dramatic description of the scene in the washroom.

"I am authorized to announce," I said, "that formal permission is expected momentarily to transfer the three men to the penitentiaries of their choice, provided the guard is released unharmed. . . ."

I headed downstairs again, but this time the milling convicts would not be denied their chance for publicity. These convicts, while not yet rioting, were in total but passive control of the dome area.

A delegation of addicts, Jack Dillon, Ed Beaver, Frank Guiney and others, took me to the prison's audio room off the main dome and began to question me. It was a bloody Alice-in-Wonderland nightmare.

What did these addicts want to talk to me about? Brutality? No. Food? No. Conditions in the jail? No. They wanted a public meeting about establishing in Canada the British system of legally supplied heroin for addicts!

Their spokesmen stressed that they had no part in Caissy's gamble. They merely wanted to take advantage of having a reporter in the jail. They complained about the laws that enabled judges to send men away for life or until cured of the habit. They asked that representatives of the RCMP and the B.C. Narcotic Addiction Foundation be brought to the jail to discuss the situation with the addicts.

They were most bitter about the tactics of the Crown in charging addicts as habitual criminals, and cited the case of a sick man, aged 69, who had been sentenced in this way. I told them I didn't believe this could happen, whereupon they produced Frank Wilson, an elf of a man, fifty years on the habit, who told me, "I'm at the end of my life and they throw the book at me. Why? The last judge I was in front of thought a two-year sentence was sufficient. I had a heart attack twenty-two months ago, and the doctor told me it won't be long anyway until I die, so perhaps it doesn't really matter, but why did they have to slap this 'habitual' on me?"

"There's nothing I can do right now," I replied. "And a man's life is still in danger."

I left them and headed down again to Caissy's stronghold. I was confident we were near a solution. I was to tell them that the transfers had been officially approved. I hoped to evade the question of John Peters's presence. Cocky and confident I strolled into the washroom, but before I could speak the phone in the tunnel rang. Carlson answered. He finished the brief conversation, racked the phone and shouted, "The boys are backing us up! They've wrecked dormitory X-1. They've smashed everything. The bulls are using the hoses."

I told him somebody was hoaxing him, that the convicts in the main building had done nothing violent since the incident began at 9:30 and now, past three in the morning, were not likely to start anything. I started to tell them my "good news."

Then all hell broke loose in the main dome. I don't know what started it. Nobody does. We could hear the heavy tin cups rattling tier upon tier of the cell doors, then the shouting and screaming of mob panic as the cons ran riot and smashed everything in sight—toilets, washbasins and television sets. There were sudden, sharp explosions and the shouting and screaming died down.

My stomach sank because I knew this could be the trigger to panic Caissy into slitting the guard's throat. I needed no urging when Caissy ordered me: "Tell, the warden if he attacks us, the guard dies, and you die too, Webster."

Then the cry went up, "It's gas!" And the lights went out.

The tear gas began to seep down the tunnel corridor into the gymnasium. This was the most dangerous moment for Dennis and me. "Webster! If the bulls come in here, the guard dies, you die and we all die. Go tell the warden!"

With Wood at my back with his knife, I moved quickly to carry out Caissy's orders.

I scurried to the tunnel telephone and dialed local 18 in the main building. My language was scarlet. I told Tommy Hall: "For God's sake, what's going on? Don't attack this place or we are all dead, including me! Stop the firing! Stop the gas shells!"

Hall assured me that no attack was being made on the washroom.

When the gas continued to seep in, the fifteen convicts in the gymnasium grabbed every loose object in sight from pop bottles to metal cups and slung them at the fibreglass panels high on the wall to try to smash them and let air in. But the missiles bounced off the tough paneling.

About this time I realized that I, too, was trapped with Pat Dennis. The guards near the tunnel gate had been forced to retreat as the men in the dome rioted, and they took with them the key to my escape. Later, the guards told me they had waited as long as they could, and then had to get out under cover of the tear gas bursts, or be torn to bits by the convicts.

My recollection of the next hour is confused. I remember when the canteen upstairs was ransacked, and the convicts happily running up and down the long corridor with arms full of bread, tea, cigars. I had run out of cigarettes so I gratefully grabbed a share of the stolen cigars.

At the end of that crazy hour some semblance of sanity had returned to the washroom, where Carlson and Caissy had taken the precaution of keeping wet towels round their heads.

I began to negotiate again. My first demand was that I be allowed outside to make the final deal with the warden. But while Caissy was semi-apologetic to my face he would only say: "You can't go now. Not unless they send down the priest, Father Barry, or John Norfield (the assistant deputy warden) in your place."

I was a hostage too, and I was scared witless. It was my turn to shout. "You promised me safe conduct. Now you threaten to double-cross me. But I'm the only man who can talk for you."

I told them too of an "emergency" exit I had found and which I could safely use. In the long tunnel corridor there was another barred gate which led past a projection room to an outside door.

Caissy, Wood and Carlson ordered me out of the washroom so they could discuss the situation among themselves. (I didn't know until days later when I talked to Pat Dennis that the trio discussed letting the guard go and holding me as a more valuable trade.)

While they made up their minds, I moved into a side room which had a barred grating to the outside. Dawn was breaking and outside I could see the feet of RCMP men waiting for their orders.

I shouted for John Norfield and began negotiating for my own release. Caissy wouldn't leave Dennis but Wood and Carlson joined me. Norfield promised all armed men would be cleared from my escape route.

It took a lot of argument, but after about another half hour Caissy agreed to my proposition that I was his only hope, and grudgingly he allowed Wood and Carlson to let me out.

Cautiously they opened the barred gate leading off the tunnel. At the far end I could see the other door open, and tape recorder in hand I scrambled out to safety. I felt a bit of a heel, as if I had left a sinking ship.

Warden Hall was waiting for me outside. The rioters in the main jail had been quelled by the tear gas. Many sections of the jail were a shambles. Miraculously no one had been injured or killed.

The prison yards were now jammed with fully armed RCMP officers. Warden Hall told me that a detachment of soldiers would arrive at any moment from Chilliwack as a double precaution against a mass breakout. The prisoners were being brought out into the open to let the cell blocks clear of tear gas. As they came out they were penned in by solid rings of armed guards and Mounties.

Warden Hall and I were faced with two major problems before we could free Dennis. We still had to produce Peters, and I had to find a formula for the handover of the guard if and when I escorted the convicts to the plane.

First we had to stop for a press conference. The front office of the prison was jammed with radio, television and newspaper reporters, all hungry for information—and some of them pretty annoyed that one of their number had been on the inside. I was pretty annoyed, too. I had made only a few stiffly worded announcements over my radio station, and here I was doling out the news to rivals. Not all of it, of course, but ten times more than I had been able to broadcast myself.

Warden Hall personally booked plane seats for the three convicts; for Caissy and Carlson on the 10:20 TCA plane to Montreal, for Wood to Winnipeg later in the day by CPA.

I returned to the washroom. "We've got to hurry up and close the deal," I urged. "You'll miss your plane. Why not bring the guard out now? I promise to stay with you till you get to the plane."

Wood and Carlson were patently softening, but after conferring with Caissy they hardened. "No deal—not until you bring Peters."

Again this shadowy man locked in an insane asylum was the stumbling block.

The warden and I had another conference. "If you want to get the guard out alive we'll have to produce Peters," I said.

Warden Hall deserves credit for cutting red tape quicker than ever before. Peters had been handed over officially to the provincial authorities as a mental case. The application would normally have gone from New Westminster to Ottawa, to Victoria, to the superintendent of Essondale. Instead, Hall called the doctor in charge of the asylum and explained the urgency of the situation. By 7:20 I was able to again talk to the prisoners.

"Caissy," I said, "Peters is coming. Your planes are fixed. Your transfers are today."

This time Caissy was calmer but still tightly in control of his gang. "I want Peters inside with us," he said.

"You're crazy," I told him. "You've turned the whole prison system on its head. They won't let Peters join you inside."

"Well," he reflected, "bring him down to the window, then

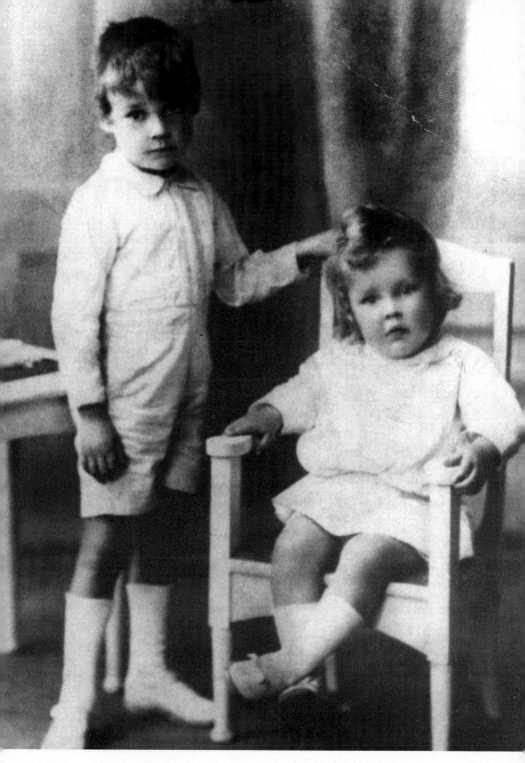

Webster in a dress! That's me sitting with my elder brother Sandy standing beside me in Glasgow, 1920.

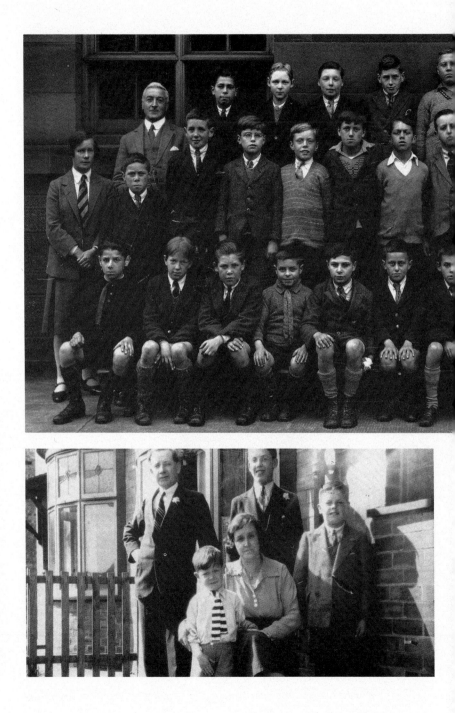

Margaret and I captured during that fateful summer in 1936 when she became pregnant with our first child, Joan.

TOP LEFT: *My class picture from Battlefield Primary School in Glasgow, circa 1926. I'm the earnest-looking boy, third from the left, in the front row.*

BOTTOM LEFT: *The Webster clan at Stockton-on-Tees: dad William, mother Daisy, Sandy, me and wee Ronnie, who died in 1936.*

Margaret and I cut our wedding cake on 13 July 1939 with the help of best man Norman Adams and maid of honour Betty McLellan.

RIGHT: *I spent much of my time during the Second World War in the Middle East, where I learned passable Arabic. Here, in 1944, I'm visiting Haifa, Palestine, in what now is Israel.*

The Webster family in 1953 shortly after I made the switch to radio from the Sun: from left, there's Margaret, Linda, Jenny and Jack's in my arms.

The Canadian Websters at the Saltspring Island farm during the summer of 1982.

RIGHT: *I left school at 14, but in June 1983 Simon Fraser University conferred on me an honorary Doctor of Laws degree.*

FACING PAGE TOP: *Here are my grandchildren visiting the Glen Falls Divide Farm on Saltspring Island in 1980, from left: Angus, Fiona, Jessica, Meghan, Alexis and Duncan.*

Daisy Webster's three sons all became media success stories. Drew, me and our late brother Sandy on Fleet Street in 1984.

Fishing is a passion especially with my grandsons. Here, from left, the guide helps Duncan, me and Angus display our day's haul in 1985 from off Port Alberni.

My son Jack and I after my investiture in the Order of Canada at Ottawa on 7 November 1988.

warn those bulls and guards that I don't want no sniping at me when I'm talking at the window. If they shoot at me, Wood and Carlson will kill Dennis."

At 7:40 Peters drove up in a prison truck, manacled and between two guards. I leaned in the door and said, "Take off his manacles."

Warden Hall nodded.

My luck was still holding because when I mentioned my name Peters's grim face changed to a smile. He leaned out to shake my hand. He, too, had heard my broadcast of his case.

"Will you help me to save the life of the guard?" I asked. This was Peters's moment of glory. "Not the guard," he said, "but I'll help to save Caissy, and if the guard gets out too, I've no objections."

Peters and I walked to the window. Carlson came and asked Peters: "Is it safe for Caissy to come?"

Peters nodded, and moments later Caissy appeared.

"Hi, John," he said.

"Hi, Gerry," said Peters.

"We got a guard in here," gloated Caissy, "and the boys have wrecked the rest of the place." Then he said, inconsequentially, "How are they treating you in Essondale?"

"Wonderful," said Peters, who was smartly dressed in faded blue jeans and a dark cardigan. "Wonderful," he repeated, "but look what I had to do to get out of that hole."

He slipped his jeans down to his ankles and his shirt up to the neck. His body was a mass of thin red scars: self-inflicted razor wounds. It turned out that Peters had been in the hole, as prison gossip had it. He told me his dreadful sentence for his altercation with a guard was fourteen strokes, thirty days on bread and water, and "indefinite disassociation"—the technical term for solitary confinement—for as long as the rest of his sentence. He had slashed his body three hundred times with a razor blade to prove he was insane and get out of the hole.

I let Peters and Caissy chat for few minutes alone. This strange, violent pair seemed genuinely to like each other.

"Come on," I urged after a while. "We've met your every term."

"I don't go from here," said Caissy, "until something is done for my friend John Peters."

I promised I would get a lawyer and see if I could arrange a court hearing on Peters's sanity.

They had one more condition. I must broadcast the terms of the release. I did so. At exactly 8:45 Caissy and Carlson walked out the side door. With Peters, I walked them through the lines of grim-faced, heavily armed RCMP men and soldiers.

Quickly, the two convicts were taken down to a storeroom and dressed, handcuffed and driven to the Vancouver airport. Peters and I traveled with them in the same panel truck. As soon as that plane took off, we raced back with a police escort the fifteen miles to the jail. Once again Peters and I went down the grassy slope to the window. This time Wood appeared with Dennis, still bound with wire. "It's okay," said Peters, "the boys are on the plane."

Wood and guard Dennis emerged, Wood still holding the knife at the guard's back.

"You better give me the knife," I said. Wood gave it to me, then he reached out again.

"Give it back for a minute," he said.

Like an idiot I did. Wood cut Dennis's bonds. He handed the knife back to me. The time was 11:00 A.M., Saturday, April 20, 1963. I was exhausted, but I headed to the station, downed a couple of quick Bloody Mary's and began broadcasting the tapes I had made during the ordeal. I was on air continuously for the next two hours.

I sympathized with the plight of prisoners. I always had a soft spot for people down on their luck, and that's how I viewed criminals: as people who needed a helping hand. Besides, the system was brutal. I thought the corrections system was staffed with too many stupid, unfair and arrogant individuals who acted like little dictators. The inmates had no one else to champion their cause, and I knew they formed a part of my faithful audience. Every week, released prisoners visited me to ask for a handout, for help to find a job, or just to tell me their troubles. They came to view me as their unofficial, two-bit ombudsman. I relished the role.

CHAPTER 6

"Jack Webster, up to his old tricks in B.C., a belligerent and common fellow . . ."

BARBARA FRUM

• The national exposure that followed the prison riot led inevitably to several job offers from large Toronto-based media companies. Several were lucrative and enticing. The southern Ontario–Quebec corridor is the largest media market in Canada. But Eastern Canada in general and Toronto in particular has always left me cold.

I had become well enough known by then that Barbara Frum could take potshots at me in a *Saturday Night* magazine article about national journalists: "And lastly on Sunday there's Jack Webster, up to his old tricks in B.C., a belligerent and common fellow who revels in his man-of-the-people origins and indicates them with a long, back-hand wipe of the nose that starts at the wrist and ends savouringly at the fingertips."

No wonder I didn't get along very well with the Eastern media mafia in the beginning! Honestly, I'm more couth today, and Barbara is a good friend.

I didn't regard myself as a celebrity, but being well known made life a hell of a lot more pleasant. I always got a seat in a busy restaurant.

My fleeting trips across the Rocky Mountains into that land of snow, ice and massive pollution bring out a beast that lurks within my otherwise tolerant soul. I disliked Eastern Canada, partly because I didn't know it very well, and also because there seemed no incentive to get to know it better.

My hate affair with the East began in 1948 when as a reporter, I was trapped in Toronto's Royal York for a week in winter. "The biggest hotel in the British Empire," it boasted. I knew then that the Empire was doomed.

I have never yet been able to locate downtown Toronto. Even the department stores are hidden. And there is no point in asking directions. It's either too hot or too cold for people to be bothered to answer civilly. I suspect they're all taught at school in the East to snarl, "Dunno!" at any stranger.

I am aware of the architectural beauties of Toronto. I always thought Jarvis Street, for instance, should be preserved for all that's ugly and bad. The O'Keefe Centre would look better had it been constructed of weathered beer barrels. It looks like a prison with neon signs. The oyster shell of city hall is impressive, but it can scarcely be functional.

I do have sympathy for the industrial heartland of our divided nation. I shudder when I look out over Toronto in wintertime from the window of my hotel room. The landscape grimaces at you. Occasionally, there is visible a patch of dirty greenery on an otherwise sooty, snowbound horizon.

God help the little serfs in the East, scurrying miles to their brick-built suburbia, their cars coughing and the freezing rain hitting the windshields. My idea of hell (apart from listening to federal election results in B.C. three hours after the polls have closed in the East and the government already decided) is to be condemned forever to drive through an eastern blizzard.

We in the West seldom see the impressive emissaries from the East. All any of them wants to do on the West Coast is talk about the god-damned constitutional crisis—not about anything that really matters to us.

They're out of touch with reality. That's the problem. Westerners still have a hard time comprehending the Easterners' pre-occupation with the constitution or Quebecers' passion about separatism.

But mainly I wouldn't move east because of Margaret. She didn't want to move. Even when one station wined and dined her, promising three free trips to Scotland a year, she said "No!"

Coupled with my own ambivalence towards moving east, Margaret's opposition hardened my resolve. I didn't want to cause her any more anguish than necessary. Over the years, Margaret had been gradually losing her ability to function outside the home because of a morbid fear of impending doom beyond the garden gate. Uprooting my family again, undoubtedly would have aggravated her condition.

Margaret first became ill back in London in 1947, just before we emigrated to Canada. She was anxious and depressed. But the doctor and I both thought it was because she didn't want to move to Canada. For despite her troubles, Margaret was a stubborn, pertinacious woman.

In Canada she became extraordinarily unhappy and emotionally upset at times. She required regular medical attention. The doctors said Margaret had developed an "anxiety neurosis" and they recommended psychiatric therapy. It didn't help.

Over a decade, Margaret's anxieties got worse. Some days she was so afraid of other people and the outside world that she couldn't force herself beyond the front door. She was convinced that if she ventured outside, she would drop dead. She would retreat into the shelter of the house again and remain inside until I returned home. Every trip was for her an ordeal.

I believe her agoraphobia was a subconscious way of controlling me. It was her way of trying to make me slow down. I had to be with her, not off somewhere chasing fame, fortune or another story.

Living with me was anything but easy. I worked both ends of the clock for years. Margaret didn't have my ambition. She always wanted me to quit and take it easier.

Margaret wanted me to go back to Glasgow and work from eight-to-four, five days a week, and eight-till-noon on Saturday, as a regular reporter covering the high court. I couldn't do that. It would have bored me to death. It would have been hell. And I did everything I could to avoid that fate.

All my friends knew about her illness. Fellow reporter Jack Wasserman knew and he was very good with her.

Wass and I had become close during my days at the *Sun*. I liked his style, his chutzpah and his spunk. He was a good friend and before Margaret's illness confined her to the home, we would occasionally frequent downtown clubs such as The Cave, or the Arctic Club, as a foursome—Jack with his wife, me with Margaret.

I can remember the fun we had going to see Lena Horne, Mitzi Gaynor and Sammy Davis, Jr. One night, with Jack Scott, the famous *Sun* columnist of "Our Town," we prevailed on Jack's wife Grace and Margaret to go to a strip club, Isy's, on Georgia Street. Those were the days when bare-breasted beauties were allowed only as decoration to night club acts. That was bad enough, but when Red Foxx, the comedian, used the "F" word, Margaret showed her Presbyterian background. She got up and registered her disgust to the manager in a loud voice, and stormed out. We followed meekly behind.

Over the years, Wass and she grew very close. She could talk to Jack at any time. About the only other one of my friends that Margaret was close with was Marjorie Nichols. But that came much later, in the 1970s. In those days, Wass was it. And during her really troubled periods, I was glad of his emotional support.

Some of the problems our family weathered because of Margaret's violent, uncontrollable mood swings were terrible, a nightmare . . . but you can't dwell on them.

She spent more and more time in hospital receiving every conceivable treatment. She had insulin therapy and electro-shock treatment. I witnessed one of the sessions and was horrified to see her body convulse as the current jolted her.

"Never again," I said afterwards, and she had no more.

One of the toughest aspects of being an immigrant family is that you have no family resources to rely upon. You are on your own.

I remember once in the early days when Margaret was quite sick, I went to a local minister and asked if he could help me. He gave me the back of his hand. It makes you feel humble, to say the least.

And the first time Margaret was treated in a private hospital I had to borrow money to pay the bill before she could get out. I was walking down the corridor in the *Sun* when Sam Cromie, the assistant publisher, spotted my hang-dog look.

"What's wrong with you?" he asked.

My emotions always show in my face. "I've got a problem."

"How much is the problem?" he asked.

"About $500."

"Go down and see Charlie," he said, "he'll give you the money. You can pay it back on payroll deduction."

Sam never did take the money off my pay cheque.

Money was always a problem in the early days. There were dozens of prescriptions for all kinds of drugs. Sometimes, I thought the doctors were turning her into a junkie. I owed drug-stores and taxis a small fortune. It cost a couple of hundred dollars a month to get Margaret back and forth to the doctor in New Westminster. We managed, but it pushed me to work more and more and do everything that came my way.

Whenever Margaret was in hospital, I had babysitters and housekeepers to help with the kids. Neighbours helped in the early days when her bouts of illness weren't so severe. Later, I hired help through the Ministry of Human Resources. I remember having to teach one woman how to scramble eggs and another how to make a decent cup of tea—to heat the teapot first. Then they had to get along with Margaret. She fired one housekeeper because she wouldn't get her cigarettes from the corner store. She was right to axe her.

Still, things got really bad in 1960 and the doctors said her neurosis was so deep-seated it was necessary surgically to sever the "anxiety nerve." They recommended Margaret undergo a pre-frontal leucotomy: a form of lobotomy.

We had all kinds of discussions with psychiatrists, neuro-surgeons and other doctors. Most thought the operation would give Margaret more enjoyment out of life. We both agreed to the surgery; I have regretted it ever since. There was an irrevers-ible change in Margaret's personality.

About six weeks after the operation, the doctor's said it hadn't worked and they wanted to commit her permanently to a psychiatric hospital. I said, "No," and took her home. I brought her mother from Scotland to help nurse her back to health. Six months later, Margaret did make an astonishing temporary re-covery. She got up one morning and said, "I'm going to drive my car again."

And did.

She was better for some considerable time, then suddenly re-lapsed. I don't know what happened. Her personality changed subtly at first and then more so. She couldn't cry and she sel-dom laughed. Margaret began to worry endlessly.

The terrible thing about it was that there was no way to undo what had been done. You could not put back together the pieces of her personality. You could not put back together the pieces of her brain.

The shock treatments had left Margaret with gaping holes in her early memory, but they didn't erase her desire to have her lost child restored to her. I grew totally convinced that Margaret's emotional problems were entirely connected with the "stolen" baby.

She had not approved the adoption. I had registered the birth and signed the adoption papers. She always maintained the baby had been illegally taken from her. She had no say in any way, shape or form as to what happened to the child. Her parents arranged the adoption and I dutifully signed the legal documents as the child's father.

Margaret begged me for years to find her daughter. She talked endlessly about the child and constantly worried about what happened to her. I told her to forget it, but she persisted. It is the only other thing in my life that she repeatedly asked me to do: "Find my daughter."

I made a half-hearted attempt once, in 1957, when I was working at Scottish television. But I really didn't want to find the baby and dredge up the past. I could see no good coming from it.

The only clue I had was the name of the lawyers who had handled the adoption. When I went to the office on St. Vincent Street in Glasgow it had closed down and there was no indication where they had gone. If I had been properly aggressive, I would have found the lawyer through the law society in Scotland and gone to see him.

I didn't. Not then, not ever.

C H A P T E R 7

"We've got to overthrow all these menopausal old men like Jack Webster who don't take dope, and don't know what it's like to be high, and who are filling our airwaves with bull."

J E R R Y   R U B I N

• Against my will in 1963, I was dragged kicking and screaming into the talk-show business. I had the usual journalistic attitude and sneered at the first Talk Radio programs. I didn't want to be someone who chatted up little old ladies in running shoes about the change in life. I was being a snob about this Johnny-come-lately form of communication.

But the incredible Pat Burns, gruff voiced, well-informed, first-class demagogue, had exploded onto the Vancouver radio scene on CJOR. His "Burns Hotline—Go ahead, Doll!" was visibly cutting into the dominant ratings of my station, CKNW, which proudly billed itself as "B.C.'s most listened to station."

They wanted me to compete against him as a hot-line host. They convinced me to give it a try by explaining how much more money I could earn. I was earning good money, and the station provided a car. They doubled it!—to $3,000 a month, and as my audience grew, they promised, so would my salary. And it did.

The late Jim E. Boughton, Q.C., negotiated my first six-figure contract in 1972. He picked up the phone and talked to Bill Hughes, station manager at 'NW. "Hello Bill, it's Jim Boughton. I'm Jack Webster's lawyer, as you know, and it's negotiation time again."

Sitting in his office, I only heard Boughton's side of the conversation. "Oh. . . . Oh. . . . Oh, oh. . . . Is that so? . . . Oh!"

Hughes was obviously screaming at him. "How dare he ask for six figures? Well, let's talk later. Bye."

I left Boughton's office thinking there was little chance of a big raise that year. About twenty past six that night, I was sitting in my little studio, quite uneasy. Hughes always had the capacity to upset me—usually by complaining: "Oh, Jack, did you have to do that program on such and such." He always did it on the day before I went on holidays so I'd have a miserable vacation worrying about his next complaint.

Hughes came into the tiny studio that night five minutes before I was to go on air. He was enraged.

"How dare you have your lawyer phone me and ask for that incredible amount of money!"

I took a deep breath.

"Bill, do you want me to go on the air tonight at half-past six or do you not want me to go on the air?"

"You've got to go on the air," he fumed, and barged away.

I phoned Boughton at home and said, "Boy, have we got trouble!"

Boughton said, "Don't leave the studio!"

At seven-thirty, as I was preparing to go home, he called back. "We're meeting Jimmy Pattison (who owned rival radio station CJOR) in the William Tell Restaurant at eight o'clock."

When we met, Vancouver's most famous used-car dealer came straight to the point. "I'll make a deal with you here and now before we finish dinner. Tell me what you want."

"$110,000," I replied without a blink. "I want to go nine to noon. No night-time program."

Pattison looked at me.

"Half-past eight to noon," he countered.

"I want eight weeks holidays, then, too," I said.

"You got it."

He turned to Boughton. "You write the contract. Anything you put in the contract is O.K. with me."

My contract with CKNW required me to give thirty days' notice. The following day, I went to the Bentall Centre and saw Hughes. He could hear me greeting the secretaries and bellowed from his office: "Oh, oh. Here comes the Oatmeal Savage."

I smiled obsequiously as I entered his office and gently placed my resignation on his desk. He stared at it as I turned and walked out.

My inaugural radio talk show on CKNW was broadcast daily at 6:30 P.M. precisely, from the station's studio in New Westminster. I had two telephone lines and one secretary. I worked out of there until they built me a studio in the Hotel Georgia and I was on air 9 till noon, and 6:30 to 7:15 P.M.

That was a great location because you were in the centre of the action. Things happened around you. Once, just as I broke for the 11 A.M. news one morning, a waitress rushed into the studio in hysterics. "There's been a shooting in the lobby," she stammered.

I grabbed a tape recorder and raced down stairs. There was a body on the floor. "It's Jimmy Hill," I blurted into the recorder. I knew Hill as a colourful Howe Street character. "He's dead," I said bending over the body. "I see one, two, three, four, five bullet holes. He's dead! No! Wait a minute. He's not! His eyes are open! He's alive!"

The gunman was being held by a sous-chef wielding a very large butcher knife. Jimmy, against all odds, recovered.

There was always excitement in the Georgia.

Later, I had my CJOR studio in Gastown, two rooms at the top of Gaoler's Mews. One room was equipped to function as my studio and the other was a little sitting room equipped with a tiny fridge and bar. I decorated them in cedar panelling salvaged from an old barn. Wasserman had suggested the location because he was across the hall. We were so close personally, it seemed a perfect location. Music promoter Bruce Allen was next door. The Irish Rovers and a couple of professional types were also neighbours.

The problem was I only had regular windows on the studio, and whenever city work crews were in the area with their jackhammers, I had to beg the city engineers to postpone the racket until I had finished my show.

My research staff was my secretary and myself. I relied on my contacts and newspapers to identify stories for me to chase. A single news story could spark several programs, especially if you could tap into a vein of community outrage. I never used a script or detailed notes. A few shorthand memory aids were enough. Too much detail bogged me down and made for dull conversation.

I had a formula: Read and mark the newspapers, select a few current events worth chasing, make a few calls and compose the story. I tried to be ubiquitous, querulous, critical and nosey. Those are the qualities I still believe any good hotliner must possess.

The art on air was screening the callers—I learned to identify people by the tone of their voice. I always had an ear for the subtle inflections and cadences of speech that betray class, character and circumstance. Just as I knew who the voice belonged to that night I got the tip about the man murdered at Gorbals Cross. By the end of my twenty-seven years of open-line broadcasting, I swear I could recognize a thousand distinct voices.

Cutting off callers without the audience realizing it was a quick-fingered skill. I'd listen intently for the end of a logical thought and then whip the call out of the circuit. It made me some enemies but it also made me friends among the audience. Most people could recognize the repeat callers and were fed up with them too, and they wanted rid of long-winded bores as well.

I still recognize a lot of the old regulars I wouldn't let on the air. "Go Away!" I'd yell, off the air. "You were on yesterday. Get the hell out of here. You're not getting on again."

I remember once slipping badly. It was difficult to hear a man who was phoning in one day because of a dog barking in the background. As a flippant aside, I quipped: "Sir, would you mind asking your wife to keep quiet." Media Watch rightly complained about that embarrassment. I guess they didn't have my sense of humour. I pleaded guilty.

But there were regular complaints to the Canadian Radio-Television and Telecommunications Commission about me banning repeat callers. But I wasn't censoring, I was editing as I went. There is no point in having a talk show program among five people and one moderator. Everybody else will switch off.

I remember one man who drove me crazy. I banned him. I went on the air the next day and every phone line was plugged by someone who waited until I answered and then left the phone off the hook. I learned later from another caller that this guy had gone up to the Unemployment Insurance office, handed out dimes and told people to call my number and not hang up. I was frantic for a moment, but fortunately I had a taped interview I had recorded the previous afternoon and I was able to throw that on until the lines cleared.

You had to be brutal sometimes in your selection. No people with incomprehensible accents. It wasn't that I was trying to be unfair or racist—who am I to talk about incomprehensible accents?—but I just could not put them on the air because listeners couldn't understand what they were saying. If I couldn't understand, then neither could the listeners.

Although I sometimes made a mistake there too. I reckoned that I could always tell when someone was drunk. And one day a guy came on and spoke very hesitatingly. Rapidly losing my patience, I said, "I wish you wouldn't drink before you phoned me."

"I'm just recovering from a stroke," he replied

In the early days, $1.49 Day at Woodwards was tricky. A lot of my listeners shopped on that day and I had to make sure I had an interview or a pre-taped program. Otherwise the calls were so sparse I would nearly go crazy.

But those were just the little problems.

There were the obvious programs to be done on politicians, controversial pieces of legislation, public figures, sports stars or entertainers. There were oddball subjects, those that couldn't really be classified as news, sports or entertainment. You tried to present a mix of material every day so listeners wouldn't be bored.

I tried to avoid using astrologers, psychics or motor mechanics. You can put any nut on the air and the phones will light up like mad. A famous Dutch psychic, Peter Herkos, came to see me and after fifteen minutes of his bloody nonsense, I said, "From now on we'll do them one at a time. I'll do one and you'll do one."

I made listeners as happy with my predictions as he did. I could often tell from a woman's voice how old she was, whether she was married or separated and how many kids she had.

My favourite light-hearted guest of all time was James H. Boren, a wonderful Yankee whose in-laws lived in Burnaby. He was a portly, dignified, humorous gentleman who wrote a series of books, the first of which was *When in Doubt, Mumble*. It was based on the credo: "When in charge ponder, when in trouble delegate, when in doubt mumble." Boren had been an assistant undersecretary for foreign affairs in the American government but had become so fed up with the bureaucratic nonsense that he quit and became a comic philosopher.

One morning when he showed up for coffee, I was stuck for a program and put Boren on air, identifying him only as an anonymous official from the federal Anti-Inflation Board. He gave an incredible performance, spewing out economic double-speak and bafflegab.

He said there was a new formula being developed that would help defeat inflation. Every time the cost of living goes up a point, civil service salaries will go down a point, he said. After about twelve minutes of this hoax, I took a break and came back with more double-talk from Boren. Then we went to the phones.

"Hello," said the first caller, "I wonder if I might ask Senator Perrault a question."

He had tuned in late and believed that local Liberal politician Ray Perrault, affectionately known as Senator Fogbound, was on air giving a bona fide interview. Even Ray laughed at that.

Talk Radio forced those of us who considered ourselves reporters to be actors, larger than life characters, protagonists as well as narrators of our stories. You had to be an antagonist against all governments; you had to stir the pot; go on crusades; broadcast your arguments with ordinary people. The more unpredictable the program, the better. I ran the gamut.

Sixties counter-culture hero Jerry Rubin and I had a noisy dust up on the air in the days when he was still a long-haired Yippie and not yet converted to capitalism. It opened with him yelling: "This is the first time I've ever been on radio with someone who's drunk."

"I'm sober as a judge and you know it," I retorted.

"Well take your tie off," he said. "It'd probably be the first time."

"Trade for trade," said I. "Take off your Vietcong flag."

"Oh no. It means a lot to me. What does that tie mean to you?"

"It's a question of nice appearance, respectability, one of the squares, a member of the establishment, proper dress. What does the Vietcong flag mean to you?"

"It means I love the Vietcong. My brothers are the Vietcong and the Vietcong flag says a lot more than a tie that sort of sticks you up at that adam's apple so you can't say anything. Those are pretty ugly colours."

We did nothing but insult each other. I made fun of his political buttons, his hair, his attitudes. And he made fun of mine.

"The Youth International Party is going to overthrow the government of the U.S.," he said.

When I continued to scoff, he started yelling again: "You're drunk!"

"No, I'm not in any way shape or form and you won't get me on that way. You might get me on other ways, but not like that. I am not drunk," I said scolding him in mock outrage.

"What do you have against alcohol?"

"I've got quite a lot against alcohol," said I in the best, moralistic, stentorian tone I could muster. He just howled and laughed.

"I'm high!" he said. "I'm high! I took LSD before I came on the show and you're quite a trip."

"You look all right to me."

"LSD is an internal trip," he said. "You've not taken acid?"

"No," I replied.

"You have not lived," he said and began yelling again. "We've got to overthrow all these menopausal old men like Jack Webster who don't take dope, and don't know what it's like to be high, and who are filling our airwaves with bull."

"You're a gem," I said.

"Take drugs and blow your mind," he advised. "Jack, your breath, you're drunk as hell. Anyone out there wonder what makes Jack tick? It's liquor."

Rubin was outrageous. I couldn't help but laugh at his antics.

He actually convinced me that if Rabbie Burns were alive, he would have been a beatnik with long hair, picketing for peace in Viet Nam. We'd have looked down our nose at him and branded him a social menace, too.

I tried to focus on subjects that truly touched everyday life. I wanted to somehow expand people's horizons by letting them vicariously explore the world with me. Sometimes, that proved more difficult that I expected. Like the time a skipper of a halibut boat, Captain David Rintoul, came to see me and said why don't I come out and see what halibut fishing is like. I said "Sure."

I had a few days off and I figured I could go up and make some tapes. I flew to Anchorage, then onto a plane into Kodiak, Alaska. It may be waterfront but it ain't beautiful. A Canadian fisherman turned and said to me: "Who are you sailing with, Jack?"

"Oh, I'm going out on the *Freeland*."

"Man, you must have a death wish," he warned.

"What?"

"Terrible ship. You should have come out with us."

I left him and headed down to the harbour. The *Freeland* wasn't in so I went and had a drink on another ship while I waited.

When I finally boarded the *Freeland*, I found Captain Rintoul, and a great crew: a couple of Nova Scotians, a couple of locals and a Vancouver school teacher. I thought it was shaping up to be a wonderful experience.

Before we set out, the U.S. Coast Guard came around and told us they would be available if we got into trouble—if they could find us in the fog.

I made the terrible decision to sleep in the fo'c's'le. It hadn't been cleaned in twenty years or so. I threw away dozens of old rubber boots and whatnot. Then, I opened the hatch to air it out and get rid of the stench. What a mistake! The hatch leaked for the rest of the voyage.

The first day was gorgeous, two dolphins on each side swimming along beside us in the late afternoon sun, out in the Gulf of Alaska. Over the next few days, we set twenty-four miles of hooks and lines. Then, the weather came up. I couldn't see waves, all I saw were walls of water coming at us. All the plywood protections for the bait cage were washed away and our lifeboat was battered to hell. As night came, we had to release our lighted lines and jog out to sea.

I was convinced the next wave was going to capsize us. "God save us all!" I screamed. "I've got to have a drink."

They didn't drink aboard the ship, but captain produced a bottle of Chivas Regal and, through the night, I drank it in small sips. It was the only thing that kept me from jumping over the side. I had never been so terrified. Talk about danger. It was worse than the hostage-taking in the B.C. Pen because there was only one apparent end to it—disaster and death.

The next day, it was still rough but we had to salvage what we could of the catch and retreat into harbour. On the return, we lost the use of the boat's LORAN and radar guidance systems in dense, pea-soup fog.

When we finally reached Kodiak, we sat in the pub and ordered a raft of beers. One of the Nova Scotia boys said to the waitress: "Is there no stripper here?"

"No," she replied.

"Well, if there's no stripper," he said, "we're not going to stay."

"You want a stripper?" she asked coyly. She strolled over to the jukebox, dropped in a quarter and chose a song. As the first bars of Scott Joplin's "The Entertainer" tinkled out of the speaker, she turned and said: "O.K., you got a stripper."

And she began to take off her clothes.

There was an unpleasant aftermath of the story, however. A month later the RCMP came to see me in Vancouver. On the next trip out in the gulf, a crewman had grabbed a ground-line anchor, clutched it to his bosom and jumped overboard. He drowned. They found my card among his belongings.

"Did he jump or was he pushed," the Mounties wanted to know.

"He was pretty strung out," I said. "He jumped. I can almost understand it."

I did that trip as part holiday, part program. I never went anywhere without a tape recorder.

Talk Radio was an incredibly powerful vehicle for helping people. It was a pipeline into homes and hearts. I regularly went on crusades to help some little person beat big government or big business. Joe Holz, the forgotten Mountie, was one of my all-time favourite victories as a hotline-show crusader.

The 29-year-old Holz lived with his wife, Irene, in Burnaby. He had been left partially paralyzed after doctors removed a brain tumour. Despite seven years of service, three in the security and intelligence section, the Canada Pensions Commission refused to pay his disability allowance. They claimed the tumour was the result of an infection Holz contracted while he was a child in wartime concentration camps. That rendered him ineligible for a disability pension.

For six years in the 1940s, Holz and with his family had been confined in a Yugoslavian concentration camp because they were Germans. When they were released, they moved to Italy where his father found work making culverts. From Italy, the family emigrated to Osoyoos, in the south Okanagan, where his mother's relatives were tree farming.

After Grade 12, Holz signed up with the RCMP and underwent the requisite extensive medical tests. As a fledgling 20-year-old Mountie he was posted from Ottawa, where he was trained, to the Saskatoon detachment. Several years later, he began suffering headaches and dizziness.

"The sergeant finally told me to go to the hospital and find out what was wrong," Holz told me. "After three weeks of tests they found out that I had meningitis, so they tapped some fluid from my back and relieved the pressure in my brain. I went right back to work."

Holz went back to Saskatoon and joined the plain-clothes security unit, still plagued by headaches and dizziness. He was transferred to Toronto in 1968. "One day, off duty, while I was eating dinner I passed out."

Doctors found a brain tumour and operated. The surgery left his right side paralyzed. Holz was forced to walk with a brace and to talk with a slight hesitation.

Still a salaried member of the force, Holz lived for a short time with his mother in Vancouver then moved back to Toronto where he stayed almost a year with family friends before he was discharged from the force in September 1969.

That's when the pension battle began.

Holz applied for a disability pension, claiming his medical problems stemmed from a meal of bad pork he had while on duty in Saskatchewan. The commission refused the pension, arguing that it was unlikely that spoiled meat had caused the tumour. Instead, the commission said that it was likely Holz's affliction could be traced back to the privations he suffered in Yugoslavia.

Meanwhile, Holz, with the aid of his wife, was undergoing rehabilitation treatment at the G.F. Strong Rehabilitation Centre in Vancouver. They were kept out of debt by his now-widowed mother, who sold the family farm.

"But things are still tough," Holz said.

He appealed for the pension through his doctor and was again refused. Every door had been closed. He came to see me and I enlisted the help of Art Laing, a local member of Parliament and veterans affairs minister. Laing was shocked and told me to leave it with him.

For my part, I did several programs pounding away at the

government over this inequity. Finally, Laing telephoned Holz from Ottawa with the good news: he had been awarded a $10,000 lump sum payment and a monthly pension.

People sought me out with their troubles. Some people were obvious frauds and layabouts, some were beyond help, but many I tried to help.

I tried to dispense on my talk shows information about abortion, divorce, education, welfare, health, policing and just about every other issue that touched people's lives. My show focused public opinion, which several times brought about major changes in public policy. The most important to me personally was convincing the government to respond to the plight of severely handicapped children in B.C.

Institutional care for severely retarded children during the 1960s was non-existent. Families were broken apart by the strain, and admission to the appropriate institution was nearly impossible. Time and time, they told me on air about their plight. After an intense campaign, helped along by well-placed material in the hands of opposition politicians, the government was forced to create a special ward in a Victoria hospital and to airlift the children to it.

One wonderful "handicapped" woman I helped was Nova Bannatyne. She was suffering from cerebral palsy and came to see me after she had exhausted every other avenue trying to find a job in Vancouver.

It was obvious the 21-year-old woman from Kimberley, B.C., was physically impaired. She trembled and had to drink through a straw. But she wanted to work and she didn't think her physical infirmities should prevent her from getting a job.

She had destroyed many myths over the years. School authorities had said no one with cerebral palsy could function in a regular school. Nova did. She went through high school and was graduated. She learned to ski, ride a bicycle, type, swim and even drive a car. She had also held part-time jobs before moving to Vancouver.

Arriving on the coast, Nova applied for work at B.C. Tel, Cominco, B.C. Hydro, Vancouver General Hospital, MacMillan Bloedel, City Hall, Central Credit Union, the provincial government and many, many others. No one would hire her.

Upon hearing her story, I took up her cause and leaned on the highest people in the province. I arranged an interview at the Insurance Corporation of B.C. through MLA Pat McGeer. I pressured the human resources ministry. I complained to Canada Manpower.

She phoned me one day euphoric: "Jack, I got a job, I got a good job!"

Nova was to start at the University of British Columbia library and was as happy as lark. So was I. We were both to be disappointed. A few days later, she got a phone call saying there had been a misunderstanding. A laid-off union member with seniority had to be hired instead. Someone had made a mistake.

Everyone was full of sympathy and warm compassion. But that wouldn't pay Nova's rent.

"You bet I'm bitter!" Nova told me when I put her on air. "You cannot tell me that these companies have not been hiring since I've been there. I can't believe that. I'm not trying for a position in the key punch area. I could have done book stacking at the library. I could do a file clerk's job. I could do a mail clerk's job. I can type thirty words a minute. I couldn't be your number one secretary, but I could type letters, invoices, anything that doesn't require speed typing."

"You can't sign your name, though," I said.

"So what! I can sign it! You just can't read it!"

She was living on her own and refused to give in and collect a handicapped pension of $265 a month.

"I could do what I'm supposed to do, go sit in a corner and

don't go out in public. Where handicapped people should be, right?"

"I thought some of our big important friends could have bent the rules a little because up in ICBC there must be attrition of staff," I told her, but there was no legislation requiring businessmen to employ the handicapped. "What are you going to do now?" I asked.

"Keep trying," she said. "Keep bugging you. Keep bugging the companies. Kimberley is a small town and if I go there I will go nuts. No offence to Kimberley, but it's not a town for a person like me to live. I'm happy here in Vancouver, I know I could do a job if given that chance. If. Gee that's a big word if you've been through what I've been through."

I could see her eyes well with tears. She was getting $96 a week on unemployment. "It will run out pretty soon. Then I'll be on Granville Street singing, begging for pennies."

She broke down and cried. I finally got her a job through the federally funded Local Initiatives Program. I arranged it through Vancouver alderman Bruce Eriksen who successfully applied the grant for a project in the downtown east-side. Later she landed a union job sorting mail for the Greater Vancouver Regional District. Jack Campbell, mayor of Coquitlam, got her that job. She's married now, has two lovely kids and still works part-time.

My intended audience over the years in Talk Radio was always the man in the pub and the housewife at home. I wanted to reach them. Like the pamphleteers of the seventeenth and eighteenth century and the men who founded the first newspapers, I saw my preferred haunt as the coffeehouse and the currency of my trade as gossip and good conversation.

Every day I asked myself the same questions in deciding what subjects to tackle: What are ordinary people talking about?

What will I do as a stand-by? Can I get the microwave link to Victoria? Am I going to do that local political story again? No Nicaragua, thank you very much! Goodbye to El Salvador! Leave those stories to the big boys. I wanted to do stuff that people talked about.

Talk Radio was a great equalizer. It put people on the same level. When Mr. Smith came home at night, his wife could say: "You know what I did today? I spoke to the Prime Minister and I told him what I thought of him. What do you think of that?"

I made my career championing the underdog. *Time* magazine called me a paladin of the poor, the powerless and the oppressed. I would investigate genuine complaints and steer sincere callers towards help. I stopped the sale of coffins door-to-door after learning about a swindle. I exposed a demolition contractor who was paying new immigrants with NSF cheques. In that case, I showed up at the man's door with the five workers in tow. I held out the NSF cheques, stuck a microphone in his face and demanded to know why he wouldn't pay the men, and broadcast it live from the radio transmitter in my car.

They never did get their money. The contractor was truly bankrupt.

The trade unions were among the first to realize the clout they could wield by telling their story, unedited and in detail, over the airwaves. Employers were slower to respond, but were eventually forced into it.

The medical and legal professions were among the last to subject themselves to the scrutiny of the public. They demanded their members only appear anonymously and then tried to use "self-advertising" prohibitions to restrict their members' appearances.

Once I had a psychiatrist, due to be interviewed next, walk out of my studio after witnessing a blow-up between me and the preceding guest. "I'm not going to stick around to be interviewed by that paranoid egomaniac!" he muttered as he bustled away.

Complaints about lawyers were always good meat for open-line shows, especially before the advent of legal aid and public legal education.

Many complainants had files six inches thick, some involving unsuccessful lawsuits ten years old. My advice was normally straightforward: "Ma'am, you are fighting a lost cause. You failed in your first lawsuit, and you have lost your appeal. Take my advice and forget about it or you will become paranoid."

I will not forget the case of one woman who was billed $8,000 for a badly handled divorce. More than one of the charges in the itemized bill read "for attending at the office of the opposing lawyer for six hours and not finding him in, $160."

The bill was patently outrageous. After some persistent public nagging the Law Society forced the lawyer to settle the bill for less than $1,000.

The legal profession in those days had good reason to hide in shame. I saw a deaf-mute refused legal aid and forced to plead his own case by sign language and grunts in the B.C. Court of Appeal. In the same court on the same day, a middle-aged criminal, already under sentence of preventive detention for life, was forced to handle his own appeal.

He told the court he wasn't competent to plead his own case and complained that he had been denied the help of a lawyer. One judge told him brusquely: "You have not been denied the right to retain counsel, provided you can pay for it. We are not going to ask anyone to give you free legal aid."

That both men had weak cases is beside the point. Even with the most expensive counsel in the land, the deaf-mute would probably still have lost his appeal against a three-year sentence for dud cheques. Little people, challenged by all the resources of the Crown and the police, had to rely only on their untrained, panic-stricken minds. The profession seemed unable to accept the proposition that not every prosecutor is scrupulously fair, not every accused is guilty.

Lawyers had no reason for the smug self-satisfaction they

were wont to show in those days at Bar Association meetings when they prattled on about "free legal aid" supplied by members. I called it charity legal aid because it had the same stench as charity medical care in the nineteenth century.

The qualifications for "free legal aid" varied across the country then. In Vancouver, a criminal record within the previous five years disqualified an applicant. The situation made the Canadian Bill of Rights a patent piece of double-talk that I suggested should be amended to read:

"No Canadian accused of a crime shall be deprived of equality before the law—provided he has a bank balance of at least $5,000 reserved for lawyers' fees."

There was a link, too, between the injustices of court treatment and the simmering unrest in the jails. The prisons were full of underprivileged characters who were refused legal aid. And behind the walls of the penal institutions, punishments were being carried out that verged on the barbaric.

Somewhere between St. John's and New Westminster on any given day back then, a man was being paddled in the name of prison discipline, then placed on a punishment diet of bread and water in a lonely cell, in the name of 'temporary disassociation.'

Thankfully, those days are gone.

The governing maxim in Talk Radio was: Broadcast *good* information and callers will respond with good questions. You could always raise the level of the telephone participation by broadcasting intelligent, germane material. I maintain that had Belfast had Talk Radio since the early 1960s, much of the violence and inter-community hatred that rent Northern Ireland would have been dispersed in the air. Talk Radio let people blow off steam. It's a release valve that prevents the dangerous build-up of societal pressure the same way a good drama gives vent to our emotions. Talk Radio acts as a catharsis.

But because of the incredible power Talk Radio represented,

I had to exercise a lot of responsibility. The changing complexion and make-up of the Canadian mosaic was always the diciest subject to handle on open-line radio programs. Especially in the wake of any influx of immigrants.

When the first flush of Germans appeared, postwar Robson Street became mockingly known as Robsonstrasse, but it was quickly accepted as a European-style shopping area and not the haunt of hunted Nazis. The Asian immigration of the 1970s and 1980s created similar tensions.

On air, I refused to let anyone discuss ethnic or racial issues except as they pertained to an individual problem. I would not allow generic comments. I quickly hit the seven-second kill button the moment I detected even a hint of racism. I felt some days you could have whipped up a race riot in a moment. Just the tenor of the calls made chills run down my spine.

I don't call that censorship. I call it common sense. Even though I'm dead set against official multiculturalism. New Canadians such as myself object to seeing millions of federal tax money spent on multicultural grants. If people want to keep their distinctive culture after migrating to Canada, by all means encourage them to do so at their own expense. All too often in recent Canadian history, ethnic groups have been bribed or frightened into voting in a bloc for the government that admitted them to the country.

But fortunately it doesn't take new Canadians very long to realize that there is a secret ballot in this country. I still shudder at the thought that some federal government might bring in an official multicultural language commissioner whose aim it will be to have Canadians of all cultures served by the federal government in their own language.

Talk Radio isn't a panacea for society's woes, but it helps give ordinary people a bit of clout. And it helps generate the momentum needed for social change.

CHAPTER 8

"He's right about British Columbians not understanding what's going on beyond the mountains. You've got a hell of a story and you don't even realize it!"

MARJORIE NICHOLS

• In the early 1960s, besides my radio work, I began doing more and more television. I served as the west coast correspondent for This Hour has Seven Days, the landmark weekly newsmagazine program on CBC–TV. I was a natural choice because of the vast amount of work I had already done for the corporation, both locally and nationally, since the early 1950s. To be honest, local Vancouver CBC bosses blacklisted me for five years because of a vicious comment I made about a provincial cabinet minister. I was too controversial for them!

But the national CBC-network programs continued to hire me. Aside from the current affairs shows that used my interviews, I was also a regular guest panelist on Front Page Challenge.

I'll never forget one night in the green room of CBC Studio Four on Yonge Street in Toronto. I'd had supper with Pierre Berton who had innocently asked me if I'd seen our fellow panelist Gordon Sinclair on this trip. On the previous trip I had appeared on a local Toronto interview show and when asked what I thought of Gordon I had said: "He's an old man whose one claim to fame is having had his picture taken in India with the head of a tiger he'd just shot." And, on an earlier show when we'd narrowed a challenger down to the last century, I had quipped: "Gordon will know. He was in his prime then."

That night, when Gordon walked into the green room, he reamed me out: "Who the hell do you think you are, Webster, you west coast upstart. I've done more reporting than you've ever heard of—and don't ever call me old again because to be old is to be near death, and I'm not."

He was apoplectic about my cheap shots behind his back. I apologized. It was over. I didn't do it again and we became good friends. As a guest on my west coast open lines he charmed the listeners out of their socks.

Working for Seven Days was like riding a roller-coaster. I was always under enormous deadline pressure because we had to record the programs on Saturday morning and get the tapes onto the noon flight to Toronto so they could be edited for airing Sunday night. It was always a mad panic partly because my producer, Douglas Leiterman, was a perfectionist. Whereas I was always ready to say, "Oh, that's good enough!" Lieterman demanded I re-tape an interview again and again until he was satisfied we had elicited the best answers from the subject.

This was a big change for me, coming from live radio where you had to be spontaneous, roll with the punches and, at all costs, avoid the dreaded silence of "dead air." One of my first taped television interviews was a round table affair for a show called *Sunday,* in which other reporters and I confronted the politician of the moment—Prime Minister Trudeau. Not realizing that the show was to be edited, I leapt in with question after question when it seemed to me that my fellow journalists had been struck mute. After a few minutes of this, reporter Larry Zolf coughed and said sarcastically that, if I was quite finished, he and the other questioners would like to have their chance.

The one interview I ever did in my life that leaves me chagrined, I did for Seven Days. It involved George Victor Spencer, a slight man dying of cancer who was fired from his job as a postal worker after the government accused him of spying for the Russians.

The story began in November 1964 when two Russian diplomats were expelled from Canada because the Department of External Affairs said they were spying. Then in May 1965, the government announced that two Canadian citizens had been involved in the spy ring. One of the Canadians had cooperated with the RCMP, but the other had refused to to say anything when confronted, according to External Affairs. The men were not named and, although no charges were laid, the government insinuated treason. Spencer was quickly identified as the man who refused to talk.

The government said he "was paid thousands of dollars to gather information and documentation, the purpose of which was to assist in the establishment of espionage activities in Canada and other countries, and to perform economic intelligence tasks, including the provision of detailed information on the Trans-Canada Pipeline system in Western Canada."

Spencer, a mail sorter in the Vancouver Post Office, was subsequently fired and went into hiding. Reporters scoured the country for him.

I found him through my old friend and professional antagonist, radical lawyer Harry Rankin. He called at eight o'clock on a Saturday morning and offered me an exclusive interview. Spencer was broke, Rankin said, and would do it for $1,500. "No problem," I told him.

Today's journalists frown on the practice of cheque-book journalism, but in those days I didn't give it a thought. Besides, Spencer had nothing. He was a nowhere man who was being persecuted by Big Brother.

True, he was drawn to the country's Communist ideology. Spencer had become interested in Socialism in the 1930s. He was living in B.C.'s coal-mining and logging camps doing anything he could to find work. Most of the men were only working a day or two a week and the conditions were difficult.

"I felt that was something that needed to be changed," he said.

I felt the same way growing up in Glasgow, and as far as I could tell he was no more James Bond than I was.

My biggest problem was getting a camera crew together. I had to roust them at home because it was a weekend. The interview had to be filmed and the package put on the six o'clock plane for Toronto that day. Otherwise they wouldn't have time to edit it for broadcast on Sunday's program.

Spencer compounded the problems when he arrived at my Hotel Georgia office because he was terrified. Although he had duly signed the contract and accepted the money, he balked when it was time to go to the television studio. "I can't do it," he said.

"What do you mean—you can't do it?" I asked.

"I can't do it. I'll have to get permission from the RCMP."

"Don't be stupid!" I snapped. "You've just signed a contract, I'll sue you."

As I said this, Spencer began to cough violently. I was sure he was going to die on the spot. But he recovered and I coaxed him out of the Hotel Georgia and over to the CBC building where we would tape the television interview. When we got to the CBC, he began to panic about being identified on television. "They'll recognize me!" he yelled.

"Don't worry about it," I said to calm him. "Just keep your head down." I thought that would be more dramatic. That's show biz!

Inside the studio, once the cameras started to roll, I forgot any empathetic feeling I had for Spencer. I bored in on him, desperately trying to get him to admit he was a spy. It was the meanest interview I have ever conducted. It took about two hours with producer Leiterman interminably insisting I ask the question again because of Spencer's evasions.

"Mr. Spencer, the first question is simple and direct: Were you a spy for the Russians?"

"No," he said.

"Did you or did you not take $8,000 from the Soviet embassy for creating phony passports for Russian spies?"

He put his head down: "You'll have to ask those in charge of national security."

"Face the camera," I bellowed, "and tell three million people: Did you or did you not?"

Here was this poor man dying of cancer and I kept hammering away at him. "Where does George Victor Spencer stand in all this furor and hubbub?" I shouted.

"It's something I wouldn't like to speak about."

"Why did they fire you from the Post Office?"

"I think the fault lies within myself. It's my own mistake."

"You are a small 's' socialist, a Marxist-Leninist, and you presumably are very conscious of your rights and privileges. If you don't feel your rights have been violated, then all the actions taken by the Justice Minister and the RCMP and the reporters who have been hounding you have been justified. Is that not correct?"

"There's nothing in this life perfect," Spencer said with the utmost equanimity.

"Did you give information to the Soviet Union of any kind?"

"That is something in the hands of the people that's in charge of my case. And it is not up to me to divulge anything at all. I don't know anything. I know about as much as you."

"I don't think so," I snapped. "But would you betray a country whose medal you accepted."

"I don't think I've betrayed my country."

He was adamant.

"But Mr. Spencer, you've been named as a spy, nabbed as a

spy—you're kept under surveillance and you'll be kept under surveillance for the rest of your life. . . . Surely you must feel outraged?"

"No, strange to relate, I don't feel outraged."

"Do you feel that your rights have been violated, as a Canadian citizen, and a war veteran, a decorated war veteran. Have your rights been violated?"

"No."

I pressed him again and again using loaded questions, but he would admit nothing.

We went around and around. I kept trying to break him, to make him confess. He evaded each time. "How can I accept that you're an innocent man?" I said at one point. "We arranged this interview so we could sit and talk frankly. I was fully convinced when I met you at first that a 62-year-old postal clerk with lung cancer was a man who could not conceivably be involved in a James-Bond-type operation with the Soviet diplomats being deported from this country partly because of his actions. Now I'm not so sure. Why, you leave doubts in the mind of a fair-minded reporter."

"That I can't help Jack. I can't help what the other man thinks."

"You helped the Russians, didn't you! I want to make you talk! Make a clean breast, make a clean breast of it instead of kowtowing to the RCMP officers who say, 'Don't say a word, or you'll be in trouble.' This is a free country, come on!"

At the end of a two-hour grilling Spencer had admitted nothing.

Three weeks or four weeks later he was found dead in his tiny east-end room, a broken, poor, pathetic soul. Among his possessions was an audio tape of our interview. It was his last moment of glory.

I saw it as my nadir on *Seven Days*.

Overall, though, I was enormously proud to have worked

with the calibre of journalists who worked on the program. I was disappointed when it was cancelled.

The big difference between television and radio is the difference between talking to someone in person and talking to them on the telephone. My rasping, brattish voice, with all its inflections and sneers, is tempered in person by the sparkle in my eye. People were surprised that I sometimes sounded so amazingly nasty on radio but in person I was far less intimidating. The camera revealed that I usually ask a nasty question with a little bit of a sparkle in my eye, or a little bit of a smile. You can get away with murder if you do it with a smile on your face and a twinkle in your eye. I must have libelled a thousand people with tone of voice, but it's very difficult to sue on tone of voice.

I was always a bit of a ham, and that made me a natural on television. I came by that honestly. Old Grandpa Webster was always mugging about and as kids we had to perform at every family function. Everyone in the family was an extrovert. There was touch of Irish in us, although I try to keep that a secret. Some of my mother's people came from Armagh, in what is now Northern Ireland. Glibness, the gift of the gab, is also a good thing to have in television. And I always had that—it was inherited!

I was no fan of Prime Minister Pierre Trudeau in those days, but I blindly supported to the full his suspension of civil liberties, the introduction of arrest and search without warrant, and the use of the army to search out and destroy the kidnappers of the British diplomat and the Quebec cabinet minister. I flew to Ottawa to cover the crisis.

The Front de Libération du Québec first came on the scene in 1963 with a spate of bombings. "FLQ is no different from liberation movements of Palestine, of Vietnam, of Black Power," proclaimed its spokesman, Charles Gagnon.

The violence wasn't much of a surprise to anyone who had been following Quebec's economic development.

For more than a century, Quebeckers were the pool of cheap labour for British and American capitalists, and they were repressed by a Church hierarchy which kept Quebec a closed society—clerics and lawyers were the aristocracy. Quebec was kept out of the twentieth century in wages and living standards until the mid-1950s when a group of young rebels—including Trudeau—exposed the graft and corruption and led what then was a "quiet revolution."

In the following ten years, Quebeckers got up off their knees. Then came French President Charles de Gaulle and his celebrated taunt in 1967 to insult his Canadian hosts: "Vive le Québec libre!"

The federal government declared him persona non grata—but the damage had been done. De Gaulle, with what I believe to be malice, gave momentum to the terrorists' movement, and over the following three years, bombings, dynamitings, raids on armouries became endemic in Montreal. Seven people were murdered. De Gaulle was the spark that ignited October 1970s terror.

Montreal police had managed to infiltrate the old cells of the FLQ and, they thought, smashed them successfully—until the kidnappings. British diplomat James R. Cross and Quebec labour minister Pierre Laporte were both snatched.

Those weeks were perhaps the tensest moments in Canada's national life since the Second World War. I arrived in Ottawa, took a hotel room at the Skyline Hotel and began working the phones to get an interview.

Trudeau, who sometimes sat in the House of Commons with a rose between his teeth, was a man of mystery in those days. He was disdainful of the Press. Newspaper publishers had weakly accepted his dicta that his world travels for skiing and skin-diving must not be spied upon. He told me during an interview that Canadians could "like or lump" his policies, and that if he met head-on opposition in his Cabinet he might walk away and never come back.

Despite the rose in the teeth and the glamorous image, he was a tough guy. Declaring the War Measures Act was the toughest decision any western politician had made since the Cuban missile crisis. It also established that Trudeau was prepared to fulfull his self-appointed mission to prevent Quebec separation at any cost.

Quebec alone got half a billion dollars a year from other provinces, notably wealthy Ontario and British Columbia. Unhappy rumblings were heard about the millions being committed to bilingualism in the federal civil service. Many key jobs in the country were being filled by French Canadians.

Trudeau's inner Cabinet was entirely French Canadian— brilliant men, but with little feeling for the rest of the country— which then numbered six million French Canadians and fourteen million others. I wanted to talk to one of them because I knew they could offer some insight into what was happening in Quebec.

Ray Perreault, who was then the member of Parliament for Burnaby-Seymour, a suburban Vancouver riding, and parliamentary secretary to the minister of labour, helped me get an interview with regional development minister Jean Marchand.

Marchand said he would come to my hotel room and we could tape it there. He arrived accompanied by a Canadian soldier brandishing a submachinegun. It was then I realized just how seriously the government felt the crisis had become.

A nervous and jittery Marchand began by saying that neither I nor anyone else who lived on the other side of the Rockies truly understood what was happening in Quebec. Partly, he said, that was because the FLQ was supported by only a few thousand Quebeckers.

"If there were 25,000 or 50,000 FLQ members in Quebec,

well, everybody would be aware of it," he said. "But they are not so many. The problem is that they have had the training very important to insurrection and they have sympathy outside."

Marchand told me that the Liberals invoked the War Measures Act because the FLQ was really attempting to disrupt the municipal elections in Montreal to benefit a local civic party called the Front d'Action Politique. The party was known by its acronym, FRAP, and Marchand said it was merely a front for the terrorists.

"We had good reason to believe that the FLQ wanted to disturb the election by explosions of all kinds and by further kidnapping or even shooting people," he said gravely. "It was very dangerous."

He went on to say that one of the most outrageous demands of the kidnappers was that the government identify police informants operating within the separatist organizations. They wanted the undercover agents' pictures printed in the papers. It didn't take a genius to realize that the informers would be quickly executed by the FLQ. No government could meet this demand, let alone their others, which included the freeing of twenty-three convicted criminals, half a million in gold and a plane to freedom. It would have been laughable had lives not hung in the balance.

The immediate causes of the kidnappings were two-fold as far as I could see: One, follow-the-leader Palestinian-style ransom demands. (Some of the FLQ terrorists were trained in Jordan. Others were Frenchmen who escaped to Canada after fighting in Algeria where they had become old hands at sabotage and torture.) Two, the 1970 Quebec elections gave the separatists led by René Lévesque a whopping twenty-four percent of the popular vote in their first time out. But they only got ten percent of the seats—patently unfair and a legacy of the gerrymandered Quebec electoral system. The mainstream separatists publicly disowned the FLQ, but the fringe elements screamed that the only way for justice for Quebec was by violent overthrow of the Anglo-Establishment.

Marchand saw a pernicious conspiracy at work.

"We know there are about two tons of dynamite that have been stolen in Quebec," he said. "Presumably they [the FLQ] are in control of them. There are more than 100 rifles that have been stolen from a ship, a Japanese ship, in Montreal and other guns which have been stolen elsewhere. So how much arms they have we don't know but we know very well that they have enough dynamite to blow up the heart of Montreal!"

"How many of them are there?" I asked, becoming more and more alarmed.

"I don't know," Marchand said. "It might be something between 1,000 and 3,000. Now, all members of the FLQ are not terrorists. But there are enough to create a lot of trouble and a lot of killing and this is what we have tried to prevent. . . . It is not the individual action we are worried about now. It's this vast organization supported by other bona fide organizations who are supporting, indirectly at least, the FLQ. This is what we have been told by the police."

"They might be wrong," I said.

"We couldn't afford to take that risk," Marchand assured me.

"Should we thank God we had a gang of French-Canadians in Ottawa who knew the score and are able to deal with them?"

"Yes," Marchand said smugly. "I think the municipal elections in Montreal on Sunday will show that we were right."

I left the interview thinking I had recorded the same story cabinet ministers were spreading all over town. How wrong I was!

In the parliamentary press gallery, I met a young reporter named Marjorie Nichols. Fresh faced and eager, she was a vacuum cleaner when it came to information. It took her only a minute to ask to hear the tape of my Marchand interview.

"Sure," I said, I was in no particular hurry and was completely oblivious to the import of Marchand's remarks.

Marjorie was astounded at his remarks.

"He's right about British Columbians not understanding what's going on beyond the mountains," she said. "You've got a hell of a story and you don't even realize it!"

I didn't.

Marchand's inflammatory remarks made headlines across the country the following morning. Transcripts of my interview were published verbatim. FRAP, of course, denied it was a front for the terrorists and the government never did provide any proof to substantiate its charges that a larger conspiracy was afoot in the land.

In the end, the FLQ was exposed as little more than few dozen extremists. Cross was eventually freed but Laporte was found strangled with his own gold chain, tied to a wooden stick and twisted round the back of his neck.

As a macabre sequel, years later, on my phone-in show I asked Sir John Ford, British Commissioner, if he still had the armoured Rolls Royce purchased after the Cross kidnapping.

"Yes, old boy," he said. "Matter of fact it is for sale."

"Good show," says I, "how about adlibbing a thirty-second commercial. No charge."

Quick as a wink, he responded—"Rolls Royce, in excellent condition, one of a kind, armour plated, little rust perhaps, but a bargain. Upset price—$60,000."

In the next few days we created a "commercial," accompanied by the music of "Land of Hope and Glory" and found a buyer within an hour.

It was the adrenaline-rush I got from covering hard news events that kept me from home more than I should have been.

I started my days at 6:00 A.M. By seven, I was downtown having the first of fifteen coffees. By 8:30, I'd done the mail, answered a dozen calls, read the papers, taped an interview, lined up the show, emptied the first of five packs of cigarettes and was on the air. Between 8:30 and 9:30 was crucial because that's when most people were listening: 186,000 of them by 1972.

At noon, I'd nip over to a private club for some racquet-ball. Back to the studio, a quick sandwich, phoning, talking, reading and interviewing until the evening. During one week, I interviewed in person or on the phone twenty-three people including two federal cabinet ministers and a senator. On average, there were four interviews a day in the three hours I was on air and scores of calls. And then there was my commercial and television freelancing!

Mainly I only won little battles. Never big ones. I never won an election, for instance. The Social Credit government of W.A.C. Bennett survived for two decades despite my tirades. In the end, my annual victory list—I kept one each year to review at the end of December—enumerated achievements such as: rental problems solved, private hospitals cleaned up, harried the government into rebuilding bridges, forced private insurance companies to capitulate and investigate delays in claims, helped settle a waterfront strike. . . .

It was always a feeling of satisfaction when a talk program caused instant action. Like the woman who phoned to complain that an FBI agent had come to her door in a U.S. consular car to question her son. After I aired the story and complained to the Prime Minister's office about this violation of Canadian sovereignty, no more did FBI agents question Canadian residents without an RCMP officer accompanying them.

One time, Vancouver lawyer Neil Fleishman brought a private eye to me and the investigator detailed on my program how he had bugged a union meeting for a rival labour organization. The disclosure sparked an immediate provincial commission of inquiry that led to the B.C. privacy act.

I enjoyed embarrassing the police when they were on a wiretap binge by identifying the phoney B.C. Tel truck the force used. Or being lucky enough to be in the right place at the right time when a U.S. airliner was hijacked and landed in Vancouver. For five hours I relayed negotiations between the skyjacker and United Airlines and police—by chance the only broadcast frequency the man could receive in the cockpit was the station for which I worked.

I was a workaholic, broadcasting interviews, commentaries and advertisements. I covered everything — from labour disputes to night club acts, from court cases to politics. It was the last, politics, that came more and more to be my forte.

CHAPTER 9

*"How dare you suggest that any cabinet minister of mine would
do anything wrong or corrupt. Get out of this room, Webster,
you horrible person!"*

W . A . C .   B E N N E T T

● One of my prized possessions is a ninety-five-year-old player
piano I keep at a farm I bought on Saltspring Island, an idyllic
retreat in the Strait of Georgia. My family has hammered on it
for years and it has given us more fun and joy than any other toy
we have ever had. It is the world's greatest exercise bicycle. But
I also got the surprise of my life when I needed to have it tuned.

The man who arrived to tune it was Robert (Honest Bob)
Sommers, the only cabinet minister in the history of the British
Commonwealth to go to jail for corruption. Tall, rangy and still
handsome in his mid-sixties, Sommers had spent twenty-eight
months in Oakalla prison for accepting bribes. I was among the
leaders of the pack who hounded him from office and yelped at
his heels until he was jailed.

Sommers shook my hand and bore no apparent bitterness.

"There's no use whining," he said as he stepped inside the
farmhouse.

I hadn't seen him since he had been imprisoned nearly a decade before.

The Sommers story began in the smoky confines of the
Terminal City Club, the private enclave where timber barons,
industrialists and government ministers wined and dined. It was

there the wealthy and powerful pressed the flesh and made their back-room deals.

Political reporting had been beyond my reach when I was a junior in Glasgow. It became my forte in television. But if I didn't cover many political events as a young reporter, I was certainly shaped by them.

The famous Clydeside Red orators spoke every Sunday night in St. Enoch's Square in Glasgow. There would be a couple of horse-drawn coal carts bearing the blind, the crippled, the lame and the poor—the victims of industrial exploitation. The Communist Party, the Independent Labour Party and a host of other strange political groups such as the Christian Communist Party would all be represented by a speaker or a banner. The slum conditions in the inner city bred radicalism. And nobody was more solidly socialist at that time than my own father, who had been a union shop steward in the Clyde shipyards for many years.

The political speeches were filled with fire and fury. Jimmy Maxton of the Independent Labour Party, for instance, could have taken a collection of Brian Mulroney's Conservatives and turned them into raging radicals with his sulphurous denunciations of the capitalist system in Britain.

The abuses of B.C. Premier W.A.C. Bennett's Social Credit administration, an amalgam of conservatives, Christians and capitalists, re-awakened my political consciousness.

The Socred victory in 1952 had been a fluke of the province's bizarre, second-choice-ballot election system. B.C. allowed voters two choices—their second vote was counted if they initially picked a candidate who hadn't received a clear majority.

The Liberal and Conservative Parties had formed a coalition in the province before the Second World War to prevent the popular left-wing Co-operative Commonwealth Federation from gaining power in the normal three-party race. An ambitious small-town merchant, Bennett orchestrated a take-over of the Social Credit organization when his aspirations within the government were thwarted. It allowed him and his backers to offer voters the chance to change the government and "keep out the godless socialists." Bennett's narrow victory was a result of his party's success as the second choice.

Bennett's great propaganda and strategic success was in creating a near hysterical climate in which those who supported the free enterprise system felt forever at risk because it was essentially a two-party system. It was always "us" against "them," a conservative Christian democracy versus a godless socialist dictatorship. He kept businessmen and the wealthy too scared to support an effective, middle-of-the-road party that could have challenged the Socreds.

I was still at the *Sun* when I first met them all, and what a collection of characters they were. I grew to have great disdain for many of them because they didn't measure up to high standards of public morality. Whether on radio or television, I saw it as part of my job to monitor their behaviour as a public watchdog.

Robert Sommers was appointed minister of lands, forests and mines after the election. Like the rest of the primarily neophyte politicians, he was as surprised as anyone to suddenly find himself in a position of power and influence.

Born in Alberta, the son of German immigrant, Sommers was a 41-year-old elementary school teacher when he was elected. He had lived most of his adult life in the grain-growing steppe of the northern Peace River country and in the valleys of the Kootenay Mountains in the southeastern corner of B.C. He played the trumpet and spent his summers in charge of a forest fire crew in the Interior. He was particularly unsuitable for a position of high-office, especially given his penchant for drinking and gambling.

Sommers had earned his cabinet post by beating the coalition's minister of health and welfare in his home riding of

Rossland-Trail. When questioned about his suitability, he also assured Bennett that he had beaten his personal problems. He lied.

In the 1950s, a provincial member of the legislature needed a second income. Sommers was broke from the moment he arrived in Victoria and he dug himself deeper into debt with his habits.

Sommers borrowed mainly from one of his friends, H. Wilson (Wick) Gray, president of Pacific Coast Services Ltd., a small logging company. The money went to cover Sommers's mortgage and to pay for his daughter's wedding. But at the Terminal City Club, the air was filled with whispers and innuendo. Rumours freely circulated that for the right sum of money Gray could guarantee anyone a forest management licence. It was insinuated that Gray had Sommers in his pocket.

I heard the rumours and began to sniff around the story.

The coalition government had established a licensing system after the Second World War in an attempt to properly manage the Crown-owned resource. The licence gave its bearer a swath of the province's forests provided the holder paid a set fee for each tree cut and agreed to whatever other conditions the government deemed essential to protect the public's interest. The first Forest Management Licence was granted in 1948, and eleven others had been issued—covering more than two million acres of virgin forest—before the Socred victory.

In theory, the system ensured the renewal of the forest resource while providing a guaranteed supply of timber to forest firms so they could attract long-term investors willing to spend the huge sums of money that were required to develop the province's forests. In practice, the licences were a ticket to an instant fortune.

The Liberals and then the Socreds in power found themselves the recipients of large campaign contributions from those who wished a licence, and forest ministers were courted because of the largesse at their disposal. The system threatened to eliminate small logging companies and thoroughly corrupt the political process.

When Sommers gained office, the potential for abuse was enormous. One of the companies pressing for a licence was B.C. Forest Products Ltd., a subsidiary of E.P. Taylor's Toronto-based Argus Corporation. The Canadian millionaire met with Bennett, Sommers and a few others in 1953 to lobby his case.

Before long, the province was buzzing with reports that Taylor had received not only an assurance that he would get the licence he wanted, but also he would get a bonus patch of forest already promised to a small group of local smaller loggers.

Gordon Gibson, a local legend who had built a family fortune from logging before becoming a Liberal MLA, knew from the inside how susceptible the system was to abuse and he knew independent loggers were being pushed out. He himself had flipped the family's forest licence to a larger firm, pocketing a sizeable profit. Gibson heard the rumours about Taylor and confronted Sommers.

Gibson claimed that he urged the minister during a private dinner to change the licence system. "They're wrong," he said. "I wish that you would put your foot down firmly and not issue one more until you know more about them."

"That's one thing I won't do," Sommers replied. "They're all pretty well committed, and I know where they are going."

"If you're short a lousy five or ten thousand dollars, I'll lend it to you," Gibson said. "But don't put your neck out here or you'll be ruined. I'm just the man who will do it. I know what you make and I know all about your poker games in the Empress, the men who are playing there, and that they are losing intentionally, and you know that they are. So just quit now!"

Sommers told Gibson to mind his own business. But Gibson couldn't.

Gibson had incredible habits and they were forever getting

him into trouble. He liked a drink as much as Sommers. Gibson could consume a bottle of rye for lunch in The Empress hotel, rise in the Legislature at 2:15, begin a sober-sounding speech and, by the time he sat down, would be slurring his words and generally displaying the effects of his liquid lunch.

Gibson stewed about the Sommers' matter. He wouldn't let it rest and when Premier Bennett himself told him to mind his own business and forget about it, he made his accusations in the Legislature on February 15, 1955. The man they called "The Bull of the Woods" ran rampant through the china shop of parliamentary privilege. "I firmly believe that money talks and money has talked in this!" he bellowed in the ornate chamber, accusing Sommers of taking a bribe.

His colleagues were stunned.

Gibson charged Sommers and the government with fraud and corruption in the handling of the forest management licences. He demanded the matter be immediately referred to the Legislature's forestry committee for investigation. Pandemonium erupted in the House.

There was so much screaming and yelling back and forth, the Speaker adjourned the House.

I was as surprised as anyone at the vehemence with which Gibson attacked Sommers and at his refusal to withdraw his remarks when the Legislature reconvened. He was ejected from the chamber. It was great theatre and marvellous fodder for my radio shows.

Gibson was allowed back into the House despite his anemic apology and continuing insistence that Sommers was guilty of fraud. All of us in the media loved the story. And I for my part encouraged Gibson anytime I saw him. There were big, black headlines, editorials and I hammered away on radio. If Gibson thought there was dirt there, the government would have to do better than stand behind parliamentary decorum to prove it was clean.

Bennett summoned me to room 913 of the Hotel Vancouver, his regular suite, to talk to me about my coverage. I went up full of trepidation. He was a teetotaller and he didn't mingle with the press much.

"Mr. Webster," he began, "what's all this nonsense you are going on the air with about with Mr. Sommers?"

"Mr. Premier, in my humble opinion you should suspend him from his cabinet position until or if he is cleared."

"How dare you say that!" he snapped.

"Come on, Mr. Premier," I continued, "there's enough stuff around."

"Are you suggesting," he hissed, "that I would appoint anyone to my Cabinet who was less than scrupulously honest?"

"Well," I said, getting less and less sure of myself, "you could have made a mistake."

"How dare you suggest that any cabinet minister of mine would do anything wrong or corrupt," he said. "Get out of this room, Webster, you horrible person," he added with a wave of his hand. It was as close as he came to cursing.

Chastened, I turned on my heels, dropped my head and left.

The government couldn't dismiss the clamour quite so easily, however, and Attorney-General Robert Bonner appointed a one-man commission of inquiry to investigate the accusations.

Judge Arthur Lord conducted the inquiry over three days in March 1955. The fear of a lawsuit made Gibson cautious and he refused to make his charges to the inquiry because he wasn't covered by the parliamentary immunity he enjoyed while speaking in the Legislature. Only one witness actually appeared before Lord, C.D. Orchard, Sommers's right-hand man in the ministry.

Orchard laid down the government's whitewash. Before Lord's inquiry had convened, Sommers went over Orchard's testimony with him. Sommers and the Cabinet had wanted to approve the B.C. Forest Products' application for a licence over

the objections of ministry officials. The minister wanted Orchard to doctor the files and testify that he had recommended
approval of the licence. Orchard said he wouldn't go that far in
helping cover up the political embarrassment, but he wouldn't
blow the whistle either.

Orchard's muddy testimony caused Lord to dismiss Gibson's
charges as groundless and conclude there had been "no impropriety on the part of any person in connection with the issuance
of any forest management licences."

Fortunately, Gibson was too proud to let the matter die.

He resigned his seat to make the issue the subject of a byelec-
tion. But when he lost on September 12, 1955, even that didn't
deter him! Despite the humiliation, Gibson went looking for
dirt on Sommers with a vengeance. He spent a fortune turning
over rocks looking for evidence to use against Sommers, and he
found it.

Wick Gray had asked Sommers to sign notes for the loans he
had received. Those documents had passed through the hands
of Gray's accountant, Charles Eversfield. Worried about being
caught up in a scandal, Eversfield had consulted a lawyer, David
Sturdy, before leaving the country for Los Angeles once Gibson
started his public witch-hunt.

Gibson learned about Eversfield's role from Sturdy, a Liberal
soul-mate. Dipping into the family fortune, Gibson paid Sturdy
to help orchestrate his revenge. Sturdy flew to Los Angeles and
persuaded Eversfield to return to B.C. and spill the beans. Gibson paid his expenses and salary for lost time at work.

On December 7, 1955, Sturdy took Eversfield's affidavit and
copies of the notes and other documents to the attorney-
general's office. He charged that Sommers had been receiving
bribes from Gray and that they had conspired with several other
parties to establish a system of bribes in exchange for ministerial
favours. Bonner refused to deal with the charges. Instead, he
told Bennett and Sommers about the incident.

Sturdy went public with his documents and story on December 16. But Sommers continued to deny any wrong-doing and the Socreds backed him.

Sommers filed a civil lawsuit against Sturdy for libel and slander, although it was simply another attempt to shut up those of us in the media. It was to become a standard Socred ploy: file a libel action the moment a scandal breaks so the media can't talk about it as it's before the courts; once enough time has passed, drop the lawsuit. It was an effective strategy. No one is interested in a warmed over controversy. As long as Sommers's civil suit was before the courts, no one could publicly discuss the substance of the charges against him. Public interest usually wanes long before any lawsuit makes its way through the clogged court system and gets before a judge.

During the following Legislative session, the Opposition raised Sturdy's charges again, demanding to know what Bonner was doing about them. He shrugged. Bennett too dismissed the clamour. "Fluff, fluff and bluff," he snorted. "A smear campaign. Propaganda."

When the storm of protest continued, Bonner asked the RCMP to investigate. On March 14, the Mounties blew Summers' protestations of innocence out of the water. The investigators said there was "definite indication of wrongdoing." But Bonner ignored their findings!

As long as the RCMP report wasn't public, it wasn't a problem. The government was in no hurry to deal with the allegations.

I was flabbergasted when I heard what was happening. To me the Socreds were trampling on the very essence of the democratic system: the right of the people to know how the government is conducting their business.

By August, the libel action still had not come before a judge and the government continued to ignore the RCMP's findings.

I was apoplectic. The Socreds had prevented the press from

discussing the issue by hiding behind the courts and had suppressed the police report by ministerial fiat.

With the scandal securely under wraps, Bennett called a provincial election. Sommers campaigned on the slogan, "Honest Bob." Bennett and the Cabinet stood four-square behind him, campaigning on his behalf and promising his riding a new bridge across the Columbia River. They were shameless.

The opposition parties tried to make the charges into an issue but were unsuccessful. Honest Bob and the government were easily re-elected. Afterwards, Sommers continued to have the civil case deliberately delayed and Bonner continued to reject the media and opposition requests to see the police report.

In October, with every tactic for stalling and delaying exhausted, Sommers's libel suit was thrown out of court in the face of overwhelming evidence supporting Sturdy's statements. Sturdy filed the documents with the Vancouver court registry and the stonewall so artfully constructed by Bennett and Bonner collapsed. The scandal exploded onto the airwaves and the pages of the newspapers. Summers fled the country, sure that criminal charges were imminent.

The government tried to sweep the dirt aside by appointing another inquiry, but that was quashed after a constitutional challenge. The attorney-general's office had no choice but to lay criminal charges. On November 21, 1957—nearly two years, 707 days, after Bonner had first heard Sturdy accusations, Sommers was charged. I editorially excoriated Bonner for his behaviour on numerous programs, emphasizing again and again the unconscionable delay in dealing with the most serious of charges against a cabinet minister. I savaged him for his procrastination.

Sommers, who had returned to B.C. when his family refused to join him in exile, was accused of bribery and of conspiring with Wick Gray, Charles Shultz, B.C. Forest Products, Pacific Coast Services, C.D. Shultz and Co., Evergreen Lumber Sales

Ltd., Hector Munro and divers other persons unknown to assist
or favour B.C. Forest Products, C.D. Shultz and Co. and its cli-
ents in the transaction of government business. The others were
charged too; most faced multiple counts.

The trial had moments of farce. The information that was put
before the jury was so convoluted, it was difficult for anyone to
make sense of it.

Sommers had no money but he was represented by one of the
most expensive lawyers in town, Angelo Branca. No one, not
even Branca, would say who paid the fees—but it wasn't Sommers. Similarly, no one would say who repaid the $8,000 Som-
mers borrowed to re-pay Wick Gray. And Hector Munro, head
of B.C. Forest Products, died before his role in the scandal
could be probed.

I always felt that Sommers probably would have been acquitted had he not taken the witness stand. His testimony was too
incredible to be believed.

He admitted borrowing the $8,000 from the Canadian Impe-
rial Bank of Commerce in Victoria on Bonner's advice.

"What happened to that loan, Mr. Sommers?" he was asked.

"Well, some months later I walked into the bank and asked
to see the manager." The manager came to see him and Sommers related how he had said: "Tell me Mr. Manager, how's my
loan? The manager said, 'What loan?'"

"The loan of $8,000 I borrowed here some months ago and
on which I've made some payments," Sommers replied.

"I'm sorry," said the manager according to Sommers,
"You've got no loan here."

"Well what happened to my loan?"

"It's been paid off."

"Who paid it off?"

"I'm sorry, I can't tell you."

Sommers testified that at that news, he left the bank office.

It was such a farfetched story, I used it whenever I spoke to service clubs. I always got a laugh when I told audiences about walking into my bank in Burnaby and asking, "How's my loan?"

"You still owe $452," replied the clerk.

"What do you mean? Has my loan not been paid off? It seems other people's are paid off at other branches. I demand to know why my loan hasn't been paid off."

Sommers's loan was repaid out of a Socred party slush fund, according to the best information I could dig up. Though, that was never clearly established.

On November 1, 1958, Sommers was convicted; Wick Gray and his companies were, too; B.C. Forest Products was acquitted of three charges and a fourth was stayed. The jury couldn't make up its mind about the others involved.

"I do not enjoy hitting men when they are down, as both you men are," Judge J.O. Wilson told them during sentencing, "but this is an exceptional case, and requires comment. The jury, not I, has found you both scoundrels. The evidence on which that finding must be based reveals that both of you have befouled the political and moral atmosphere of this province over a period of many years, resorting to every sort of shabby device to conceal your iniquities. The harm you, Sommers, have done to our traditional respect for government will I hope be slight, because, thank God, the sort of behaviour of which you have been convicted is not just exceptional but unique in our political history."

Judge Wilson sentenced both Sommers and Gray to five years in jail and fined Gray's companies almost $20,000.

There were serious disagreements about many of the facts in the case. And in the end only Sommers and Gray carried the can for the whole thing. BCFP went on to great success. Sommers served two years and four months before being paroled in July 1961.

While in prison, he told me, he learned to tune pianos. That's what brought him to my farm that day.

The Sommers case revealed a lot about B.C. and about W.A.C. Bennett.

People like me screamed at the time that the forest licence should have been lifted. But that would have had such a devastating effect on the company I could understand why the government was reluctant to act without a finding of criminal guilt. But in my books, that was simply moral cowardice.

Gibson for all his bravado and loud talk does deserve credit for being the only guy willing to blow the whistle. In a large part, it exposed the split in B.C.'s establishment, between the old guard Liberals and the Socreds. Bonner used to joke that they'd beat them at the polls but meet them at the bench. The federal government, which remained under Liberal control, appointed dozens of defeated Liberals to various courts.

Gibson was always trying to expose Socred malfeasance, although he put his foot in his mouth as often as he hit the mark. I got a phone call from his brother Jack Gibson on one occasion. "We're up shit creek again with more allegations of corruption," he said. "Gordon has just said in the Legislature that 'every time he lifts the corners of the Social Credit carpet he finds that dust and corruption has been swept underneath.' And Bennett called him on it—'Prove it or else.' The last time Gordon opened his mouth and said 'money talks', it cost us $55,000. We've got to get a speech together for Gordon to get us off the hook. Will you do it?"

"Why not?" I said.

I told them it was going to be very difficult to get Gibson off the hook given the nature of his charges. He didn't have any proof, only suspicion. "But I'll do my best."

Gibson made his charge on Friday and I had the speech written by Sunday night. In writing the speech, I had Gibson back away from his specific charges but muddy the waters by attacking the overall sleaze that seemed to characterize many of the Socred ministers, especially Highways Minister Phil Gaglardi. "It's no good," Gibson said when he'd finished reading it. "It doesn't say 'money talks.'"

"Gordon," Jack said, "you damn well better learn it, because you're going to read every word of it—and it ain't going to say, 'Money Talks!'"

Gordon read it and got off the hook; I got $1,000 for my help.

Sommers was the first sleazy act of the Bennett government but it wasn't the last. It did make me realize that W.A.C. was afflicted with the Nelson touch, the habit of putting the telescope to his blind eye when he didn't want to see long-distance signals bearing bad news. It was as if Wacky, as we called him, had a personality defect. The moment he put the mantle of the Bennett touch on a person, that man was sacrosanct. He could do no wrong. He had a blind spot for anyone he trusted.

Bennett told me in an interview later that he had asked Sommers when the allegations first surfaced: "What's all this nonsense I'm hearing about you Mr. Sommers?"

"It's not true," Sommers told him.

"What do you mean it's not true?"

"I give you my word of honour that it's not true."

"Mr. Sommers, if I have your word of honour, I believe you. I will back you all the way."

After that, Bennett refused to consider that Sommers might be on the take. Wacky refused to admit he'd made a mistake in judging character:

"History will show that Sommers was an honest man," Bennett maintained. " He was stupid and foolish perhaps, but honest. Foolish to surround himself with certain people and to borrow money from them. But you tell me one person who in one period of their life somewhere, did not do something that was stupid and foolish—that person can still be a good and honest man. Sommers made some bad decisions, but he gave no special concessions to anybody, anywhere. That's the reason the courts never proceeded against these companies about any special concessions—because there were none. I think history will vindicate Sommers."

It was because of such obviously human sentiments that I came to warm to and to like W.A.C. despite his government's failings. He came across arrogantly at first. I still remember a series of questions I fired at him at a major press conference. Four in a row!

"That's enough from you," Bennett said testily. "Is there nobody else here to ask questions?"

Pregnant pause. Thirty seconds. "Oh," he says. Pause. Forty seconds. A sigh of submission. "You might as well continue, Webster."

Once he called me while I was on air discussing a major bank's organized run on provincial parity bonds—the unique and somewhat quixotic ious by which the province financed its treasury. "You're a liar, Webster!" he thundered, and then angrily hung up without waiting for my response.

I grew to admire him, but only after he was out of office. While he was in power—which was for twenty years—his government outraged me. Ironically, he finally fell victim to his own dictum: that governments are destroyed from within, not from without.

His administration became riddled with rot.

To me, Phil Gaglardi's conduct was the most abominable. He mesmerized himself every time he opened his mouth. He once told me on air, "If I tell a lie, it's only because I'm convinced I am telling the truth."

In my most generous state of mind I'll accept that as a true statement of the man's confusion. His behaviour was often an insult to democracy. When he resigned his seat on March 21, 1968, Gaglardi said he was being plagued and persecuted by the press. For good reason!

Sure he spent sixteen years building or rebuilding every major road in the province, preaching on Sundays and telling us he worked around the clock. But the fact is the Bible-thumping-preacher-turned-politician spent just as much time fending off allegations of impropriety.

In 1959, Union Contractors, which had a highway contract, ran into financial problems. The court issued on behalf of a money lending company an order forbidding the company from receiving any money from the Highways Department. The money was to go instead to a court-appointed receiver. Shortly afterwards, the department sent the company more than $75,000 via a U.S. bank. Gaglardi was cited for contempt of court and fined $1,000.

Gaglardi was severely criticized regularly for the way his ministry dispensed construction contracts to Socred-supporting companies or individuals. One man, Ben Ginter, a friend of Gaglardi's, won so many contracts that political opponents claimed road-building in the province was controlled by a triumvirate—Ginter, Gaglardi and God! Gaglardi once proudly boasted: "I'm a minister of the Crown and a minister of the King of Kings."

On several occasions, Flying Phil as he was called was convicted of speeding, of driving without due care, and his licence to drive was suspended.

He used the government jet flying his family hither and yon. Gaglardi dismissed his constant and capricious use of the plane with a quip: "There are no Mounties up there."

I regularly attacked him for his conduct. But most of the time it was a waste of breath. I confronted him one day about charges that he had bought pews for his new church in Kamloops with a bit of creative financing. He denied, denied, denied. "If what you say were true," he told me, "I'd jump out the window now."

Nodding at the landscape ten stories below, I smiled at him and said: "There's the window. Why don't you jump!"

Of course, he didn't! And I was never able to prove that Gaglardi was anything other than an unctuous little man whose personality grated on me and whose politics infuriated me.

Not long after he was driven from office, he was back. Like a bad smell. "Fella" he liked to say, "the smell of pollution is just the smell of money. Out here in British Columbia we make 'em strong. A little pollution never hurt anybody."

He more than anyone made me dislike Social Credit. But it didn't matter how much I aired that view, the party kept waltzing into power. Upon seeing my exasperation once, W.A.C. Bennett quipped: "Jack, every knock from you is worth another five votes!"

After 1963, every major election in B.C. was fought on the open lines. The provincial government used to tape my programs and conduct training sessions on how Webster operated. They decided the best strategy was to keep talking, talking, talking. Every minister was given the same advice: "If you keep talking, Webster can't ask questions."

I had a heck of a time trying to butt in and ask a question without sounding as if I was jumping all over them.

Once, I got hold of a script that was being used to train rookie ministers and New Democratic Party leader David Barrett and I read it on air. It was a very silly script and at one point it called on me as Webster to say: "Well, that's a very good answer, Mr. Brown, but your fly is open."

Without missing a beat, and completely unrehearsed, Barrett adlibbed: "Not to worry, dead birds don't fall out of the nest!"

My preserve was mainly provincial politics, and I hate to admit that we have allowed the level of public debate in British

Columbia to deteriorate into sycophantic swill. I hammered away for years about the bloody Bennett government, but it didn't matter on election day.

W.A.C. Bennett will be remembered for his power policy and the massive development he spearheaded. When I arrived in 1947, B.C. was just entering the industrial age. It was as if the province was populated by a group of prospectors who lived in a tent. They had piles of gold but they didn't have running water, sewers or roads.

Bennett changed that physically. He provided the infrastructure that allowed the province to flourish. His Achilles heel, however, was that he understood natural development and capital investment but not social development.

To try to convince him that there was something beyond highways, beyond power megaprojects, beyond the physical things you could build with bulldozers, was impossible. The Social Credit government didn't promote anything its members couldn't have their picture taken beside at election time. They had an edifice complex. They didn't understand things like fair expropriation laws, day care or drug treatment centres. There was no human face on the government.

Talk about patronizing!

The government functioned without Hansard, the official written record of the Legislature debates, without a set sitting period and without a question period. It met at the whim of W.A.C. Bennett. He limited its sessions and restricted members' expense allowances so the Opposition would be reluctant to employ any tactic that would extend the sitting. And he forced them to sit all night it they were obstreperous when it came to passing one of his bills.

I tried to help drag the province into the modern era by dripping the poison about Social Credit's failures for years. The NDP victory in 1972 was a great triumph. I was overjoyed. Euphoric.

I went to the Coquitlam Sports Centre for Barrett's victory party and some of the things I said on the air were partisan beyond belief. "Where are you now Bob Bonner?" I taunted. "Where are you now Gaglardi?"

I went through the entire Socred list. It was one of the few times I would admit being on the air with a couple of drinks in me. I went from there to the Vancouver Golf Club. There were maybe twenty or thirty of its well-heeled members in the bar. "Victory for the workers!" I shouted. "Who wants a drink?"

But no one would take a drink from me. They were that upset that the NDP had won the election.

The great thing about the Barrett government was that it was the first human government in B.C. But in the recent NDP leadership race, Barrett failed to convince the delegates that he should lead the federal party into the 1990s. Pity.

Hansard was established as well as a set question period, social legislation was introduced at a tremendous rate, public service workers were given bargaining rights, teachers and school administrators had their lot in life improved, a Rentalsman Office to solve landlord-tenant disputes was created, the Insurance Corporation of B.C. was established and vast swaths of the province were protected from development in the Agricultural Land Reserve.

Barrett had a host of good ideas, but his administration was sloppy and made careless, needless errors that brought it tumbling down only three years later. His handling of Mincome, a plan to give $160 a month to everyone over 60, was an example of his propensity to move too quickly. As a leader, he often moved too fast for his followers. They lost him.

Barrett came on my program to promote the plan and during the course of the interview admitted on air that it didn't matter how wealthy you were, as long as you were over 60 and didn't have a job or other income, you could draw the $160. Barrett said if you had relatives who were over 60, they could fly to B.C. to begin collecting the pension instantly.

I was incredulous.

"You mean to say I can fly my old granny over from Scotland or Pakistan or Portugal tomorrow and that they can apply for and get Mincome?" I asked skeptically.

"Certainly," he replied.

"Come off it now, Mr. Barrett! In no time at all you'll have hundreds of people flying in to get $160 a month because of somebody's old granny."

Even if you had $50,000 in a safety deposit box, as long as it wasn't earning interest, Barrett maintained you were still eligible for Mincome. "I want our old people to be able occasionally to be on the beach in Hawaii," he told me.

A couple of months later they had to change the legislation as the repercussions of the policy sank in. As I recall, 183 people had flown to B.C. and got the $160 in Mincome without residential qualifications.

The Agricultural Land Reserve Bill had to be amended, too, after Barrett appeared on my program because its sloppy draftsmanship was exposed. I asked him how the appeal process would work if someone wanted his property kept out of the reserve. Barrett asked Attorney-General Alex Macdonald who conceded they'd forgotten to include an appeal process.

The NDP were in such a hurry to get things done, they stepped on toes and created the impression that they were erratic. That was how Barrett did things. He wanted to do too much.

I believe his government's most import social move was establishing the Insurance Corporation of B.C., which was denounced as sacrilege by the free enterprisers in the province. But let's face it, people here were sick and tired of the private insurance industry's rip offs, expensive premiums, long-drawn out settlement periods and risk plan.

Barrett's ICBC has been a boon to the provincial treasury and a benefit to everyone.

But the Barrett regime was all human face and no edifice. There was a warmth and ebullience to his style. But poor Barrett had nothing to have his picture taken beside. And his government was an aberration: 1972 was the last time more than two parties seriously contended for power in a B.C. election. In a two-party race, the Socreds were always favoured because they represented a coalition of Liberal-Tory voters. It was only when the Socred Party veered too far to the right and alienated the middle-of-the-road voter, the party's Liberal component, that the NDP were a serious threat.

Barrett was defeated because the establishment parties ganged up on him and big labour abandoned him because of the back-to-work legislation he unhesitatingly employed when faced with a major strike. The NDP administration's handling of the economy and labour even had me hammering it for incompetence. I was so vitriolic at the end, I received a neatly typed death threat in 1975 warning me that if the NDP was defeated I would die.

That was one of the few threats I received over the course of my career, and I took it seriously.

Back then, my studio in Gaoler's Mews was too exposed to take a chance. There was no escape from that office. My secretary was in the anteroom and me in the studio behind a piece of ordinary glass and a door. I called police and obtained a permit to carry a pistol—a .32 Savage semi-automatic I kept in my briefcase.

In the days before the election, and in the days following Barrett's loss, police scoured my office building and the building opposite. It took me a few weeks after the campaign to relax. I turned the pistol in a few years later. Nothing I hated more than having a gun lying around!

When I look at what W.A.C.'s son Bill Bennett did as premier between 1975 and 1986, I am disappointed. He created a climate of confrontation that lasted for years. His stewardship was disastrous for British Columbia.

Aside from Bill Bennett's pernicious fiscal restraint policies and tax-draining megaproject binge, his administration set a dreadful standard for civil conduct. Even the scandals of the W.A.C. Bennett government didn't generate the moral stench that emanated from Victoria during his son's tenure.

Bill Bennett was an amateur when he used his father's political legacy to win the leadership of the Socred party. He was totally inexperienced and his regime will be remembered for its bungling. His attempt to ram twenty-six bills through the Legislature in July 1983 brought me back from vacation early and provided days of volatile programming.

It was an attempt to re-write in neo-Conservative twaddle the social contract of the province! And neither Bennett nor his ministers could cogently explain why such a sweeping attack on public sector employees as well as the provincial medical and education systems was necessary.

Bennett's attempt to restructure the economy and transform labour relations took B.C. to the brink of a general strike. Unprecedented social unrest racked the province for almost a year before a modicum of common sense was restored. If the B.C. Government Employees Union and the loosely bound Solidarity Coalition of social and labour organizations hadn't reached an eleventh-hour settlement with the government, this province could have been crippled. As it was, B.C.'s international reputation was tarnished.

Bennett seemed to have learned only two things from his father: how to polarize and how to turn a blind eye to his supporters' sins. It was outrageous that a cabinet minister was not fired for appearing on television sporting a black-eye, admitting he was beaten up by his cuckold. His cabinet colleagues would also have been turfed for getting involved with a morally repugnant escort service that was a front for prostitution. I don't understand why Bennett didn't suspend them or remove those men from Cabinet immediately.

The new morality, I suppose.

There were other examples of ethical controversy involving other sitting Socreds involved in policy decisions despite blatant conflicts-of-interest and party workers who engaged in election dirty tricks. Bill Bennett didn't seem to care. Then again, the public reaction was similarly pallid. Did anyone really care?

At least Barrett had the guts to axe a cabinet minister when he lied about being caught with a girl in his limousine. That required nerve. But then maybe that's just my political stripe showing.

Unfortunately, Bill Bennett's successor, Premier Bill Vander Zalm, is showing exactly the same predilection as his predecessor. Minister after minister has resigned after allegations of conflict of interest.

I believe Bill Reid, the former tourist minister, should have been fired and charged after the allegations that he channeled Lottery funds to his friends. It isn't a good enough excuse to say that lawyers consulted by the government opined that the odds were against Reid being convicted. To me, the test is not whether any lawyer consultants decide on the odds of a conviction. Only a judge should decide.

Whenever there is a prima facie case for trial, especially one involving a public official, it must take place in public. Sure the Crown has discretionary powers as to whether or not to lay charges based on the evidence. But when a public official is involved, it must be put before a judge. Justice must not only be done, it must be seen to be done.

But then again what is to be expected of a government led by a man who can't see his own conflicts?

After Vander Zalm won the leadership of the Socred Party, I

pointed out that he was in a serious conflict of interest because his immediate family firm owed millions to the government's principal banker—the Canadian Imperial Bank of Commerce. "Is $5.7 million the amount of the debt?" I asked him. "Wouldn't that make the interest payments alone about $60,000 a month?"

He claimed ignorance. He didn't know the details, he told me. I told him bluntly: even the appearance of a conflict of interest cannot be tolerated in the premier's office. He looked at me quizzically. He really didn't seem to understand.

I lectured him on the need to be lily white in his financial affairs now that he was the man in charge. Those who make decisions involving the government's lucrative fiscal business are financial diplomats: they must not only act properly, they must appear to act properly.

Vander Zalm did have the good sense to relinquish the finance portfolio after he won the provincial election campaign. But his inability to really grasp the concept of a conflict-of-interest would rack his administration again and again.

But it was a predictable performance when you saw how the Social Credit Party power brokers acted upon Vander Zalm's ascension. It was stomach-churning to watch at the 1986 Socred leadership convention the fawning behaviour and listen to the assurances of eternal fealty and loyalty to a man they disliked from defeated leadership hopefuls. Their professed support didn't last long.

It has become a party without a soul. Its members do more about faces than weather vanes. Few have any convictions, and most of those who aspire to lead it are prepared to out-spend each other with our money to get votes. No wonder people are turned off by politics in British Columbia and the level of public debate is at an all-time low.

I know eastern Canadians like to sneer that we've got the political life we deserve, that we spend too much time sitting in hot tubs going ga-ga over the scenery. Well, what's *their* excuse?

CHAPTER 10

"Dear Mrs. Webster, We have traced your natural daughter. . . . Her christian name is Joan."

K . A N D E R S O N , I N V E S T I G A T O R

• All in all, the 1960s and 1970s were good to me. I became a nationally recognized journalist and had money enough. I began to think I should stay home for my family's sake. But much as I said I wanted to, I couldn't bring myself to rise and go to Innisfree. The closest I came was buying the 94-acre hillside farm on Saltspring. All it taught me, though, was that as a broadcaster I can make a living, but as a farmer I am a national disaster.

It began when I rushed into the purchase because land of one's own is a Scotchman's dream. Not for me the scientific study of the pasture, or even a common sense look at the possibilities (believe it or not) of making a dollar, but just the plunge straight into the cattle business.

By an unhappy coincidence, I had a friend, Guy Rose, who is a big-time cattle breeder in the Nicola Valley of British Columbia. Over a noggin we decided he should ship to me forthwith no fewer than fifteen of the finest range bred Hereford heifers in the Interior to stock the farm.

No sooner said than done. The delivery job was handed to my cattleman friend and my son, Jack Jr., and one sunny afternoon they delivered the fifteen heifers to Glen Falls Divide Farm.

Prior to the arrival of these animals I had expended untold

dollars and hours of labour in splitting with my son 1,100 cedar fenceposts to surround the hill farm, and in stretching the finest wire, topped by two strands of the fiercest barbed.

A simple sighting of this expensive barricade would have convinced anyone other than Field Marshall Rommel that it would have stopped a Panzer brigade, but when the cattleman and my son arrived with the load of heifers they did not count on one stupid stray dog.

As the heifers were being unloaded, the dog spooked the lot. Eyewitnesses tell me the cattle scampered across the fence in approved commando style. They swear that the first heifer knelt at the wire and the others skipped up its back and onto the highway.

My dismay was uncontrolled. First, I had to secure special insurance coverage in case any innocent motorist was impaled on my stray cattle, and secondly I had to find some way to round them up.

I venture to suggest I am one of the few people still alive to tell the tale of the difficulties of trying to re-corral cattle from among the impenetrable logging slash on the hillsides of Saltspring.

Luckily for me, seven of the heifers returned by accident. They just wandered in through the gate. It was seven months before I retrieved the others, and they were worn to skin and bone from emulating the runt deer of Saltspring. My nights were haunted by the fear that the locals would shoot them as such.

My weekends were spent travelling the logging roads high on the mountains, asking stray hippies and others—"Have you seen my cattle?" People there still think I am a weirdo freaked by Herefords, but in my final extremity I hit on a sure-fire plan to recapture the lost herd.

I had seen it done on television, and we reasoned that what can be done on the Serengeti Plain can surely be done on Saltspring Island. Sparing no expense I hired a man from the

Stanley Park Children's Zoo who was skilled in the use of a tranquilizer gun. The plan was simple—knock the cattle out with the darts at close range, tie them up and drag them back to the farm.

The only trouble was that the Herefords did not know they were supposed to go to sleep when hit by the darts. "These damn cattle of yours," complained the frustrated hunter, "can absorb a dose that would knock out a polar bear, and still walk away."

But he did after the expense of many darts and many dollars manage to tranquilize three animals, and we hauled them back to the farm.

The other five? They got fed up with the paucity of grazing on the mountain and "surrendered" at a friend's farm on the Fulford-Ganges road.

It's hard to believe that the five bedraggled escapees were the hard core of the fifteen expensive Herefords that had caused my beard to turn grey.

Next step was to spend a small fortune with Mr. Buckerfield in an attempt to fatten up the returning prodigals. I gave up all thought of breeding a herd from the ungrateful bovines, and shipped them off to the auction, with disastrous financial results.

I stuck with the simpler and less heroic aspects of the agriculture industry after that. I'm very strong on brown-egg chickens. Don't mind the odd inoffensive crop of hay, and as far as livestock is concerned I breed a flock of sheep.

Sheep are a friendlier and more grateful breed. They do not crash through four-foot barbed wire fences. They tend to be a bit more appreciative of free food and accommodation. And we sell them, cut, wrapped and frozen, for exorbitant dollars.

I love it! Margaret and the kids and I had a great time whenever we were there. It was a place were we were able to relax and unwind and escape from the pressures of the world, although I could only stay there for so long before that old fear would grip me: Something's happening somewhere and Webster's not there!

In 1969, Margaret had a bit of a recovery and decided to take a recuperative holiday in Scotland. She had been in poor health before then. She travelled by herself to Stirling, where her old school friend Betty lived. She returned so full of good cheer she said she was going to make it an annual event, and did for three years.

It was quite funny how much money she spent on these trips. "How much did you spend?" I asked once.

"Oh, eight hundred pounds," she replied.

"How did you spend eight hundred pounds?"

"I was taking people out to the Red Lion in Stirling," she said, "and Ferrari's in Glasgow."

Margaret wasn't a person to take people out to dinner normally, especially with her agoraphobia. Yet she claimed to be frequenting the poshest spots in whatever city she happened to be in, running up a healthy tab. What she was really up to, was something I didn't even dream about: the search for the baby girl she had seen for only five minutes at the very most when she was born in the Glasgow nursing home thirty-six years before.

I got the shock of my life in 1972 when I came back from a conference I had been attending in Ottawa to find a letter on my dinner plate. Margaret just stared at me as I read the letter from K. Anderson and Co. Private, Commercial and Insurance Investigators, Stafford St., Edinburgh. It was addressed to Margaret in Stirling:

"We have traced your natural daughter. . . . Her christian name is Joan. I can tell you that the adoptive mother is a widow and is no longer living in Edinburgh but has moved to England where she is living somewhere south of London. For your information, Joan was a pupil of Gillespie School in Edinburgh. Herewith enclosed two extract birth certificates which were loaned for the inquiry. What are your further intentions?"

I was overwhelmed, to say the least.

"Who knows what we are going to turn up?" I said testily. "We have had troubles enough. Let's forget it."

I didn't want to walk into Joan's life and disrupt it.

"No way!" Margaret said. "Unless you do something about it, I will ruin the life of the woman who stole my baby the way you ruined my life."

My blood ran chill and I knew that I would finally have to face the decision I had made more than three decades before.

I wrote back to the detective thanking him. "Go to the place of business of my daughter's husband and tell him who we are. Tell him we would do nothing to disturb the happy relationship between him and his wife, or Joan and her adoptive mother."

The detective wrote back:

"I have to report that I travelled to Essex. It would have been possible to speak to the husband outside of his place of business without having made an appointment. I decided to make my presence known by calling personally at his place of business. I found him to be a very charming and considerate person. I informed him that the reason for my visit was regarding his wife, your natural daughter. He said that information had drifted back to him from relatives I talked to in Scotland and he suspected something of this nature. It was only two weeks previously that he had ascertained that she had been adopted and she herself does not know. He wished a few days to think it over, whether to tell her, and again he wanted to do it at the right moment.

"For your knowledge, your daughter was awarded a degree at the Harriet Watt University College in Edinburgh and is now a full-time housewife and mother. They have a family of three: Angus, seven, Duncan, five, and Fiona, three months. They live in a rural village in a substantial, red brick detached house surrounded by expensive new property. I have seen the location but I did not call.

"The husband said he will make his decision and inform me

of the outcome. I told him that he need have no worry that you will call without previous knowledge. I can assure you that your daughter has a very good and considerate husband and there is no doubt that he is concerned about the knowledge imparted to him and in no circumstances will he have his wife either shocked or upset.

"Immediately after I have the husband's decision, you will be informed."

I responded by reiterating that it was not our intention to infringe on the private lives of Joan and her husband. "But," I said, "it would give my wife and myself considerable freedom of mind to meet our daughter after all these years."

I sent a biography of myself while Joan's husband had me checked through the Financial Times service. Then we waited on pins and needles from early February 1972, through the end of March before we heard again from the detective. He said Joan had agreed to meet us and gave me her home phone number in Essex.

That year heralded the advent of commercial radio in Britain, and Beaverbrook Commercial Broadcasting was host of a conference called Tune-in '72. More than three hundred delegates, including me, were invited to the Grosvenor House Hotel in Park Lane. I was billed as the Canadian expert on commercial radio, open-line talk-shows and I was to give a seminar. Margaret and I decided to meet Joan during that trip.

With considerable trepidation we were on our way to London. I don't know if Margaret was really happy about it or not. My son Jack was in Turkey at the time and I phoned the Canadian consulate in Instanbul. They found Jack and he met us in London at the airport.

Once we got into the hotel, however, Margaret got cold feet. I didn't blame her.

"OK. Margaret, phone Joan."

"No, I changed my mind," she said. " I don't want to go through with it."

"Come on, Margaret," I pleaded. "We've come this far. We're not backing out now."

I picked up the phone, dialled the number. A woman answered and I will never forget the conversation. "Is that you, Joan?" I asked haltingly.

"Yes," she replied. "Is that you, dad?"

I was overcome with emotion.

That was on a Sunday night. We arranged to meet at our flat in Mayfair on the Tuesday night.

My brother Sandy was in town also for the Beaverbrook event in his position as editor of *The Sunday Mail* and a top man in the Associated Newspapers. Sandy was a gung-ho, confident guy who on occasion could make me look like a blushing violet. "We're going to Stone's Chop Shop in Soho," he said. "A bit of a celebration."

We got to Stone's and there was a long queue of people waiting to get in. Sandy barges to the front of the line and says, "I'm Sandy Webster of Associated Newspapers and I have my table upstairs."

We go in and get this beautiful table and I'm terribly impressed. I said, "If we're going out with Joan tomorrow night, we're coming here."

I gave five pounds to the maître d', five pounds to the wine steward, two or three pounds to everyone in the place right down to the doorman. And I told them, "My name's Jack Webster. I'm from Vancouver. I'll be here tomorrow night at 7:30 sharp. I want that table, next to the big ice swan, very special treatment and, please, remember my name."

The emotional strain was overwhelming until Joan and her husband John arrived the next evening. She was the spitting image of me. My looks, my personality. It was incredible. Our reunion went naturally. No one was in tears. No one was in hysterics. Margaret was happy at last.

I had been careful not to have a drink that day because I was meeting the daughter who had not heard of me until only a few months ago. But she came in and we kissed and welcomed each other warmly. Within five minutes, I felt that I had known Joan all my life.

I said to her husband, "I haven't had a drink today, I hope you drink."

He said, "Boy, I have not had a drink either. I've just been waiting till we met to find out if you drank so we could have a Scotch."

We had a delightful reunion and then headed to Stone's. I got out of the car, and the doorman says, "Good evening, Mr. Webster, and how are things in Vancouver?"

We heard, "Good evening, Mr. Webster," all the way through the whole thing and I was sure Joan must have been terribly impressed. Much later when we talked about that evening, she told me she hadn't even noticed.

Margaret found it more difficult to adjust because Joan was a clone of me. She's a delightful girl, she's part of our family. All my kids loved her at once, and she loves them. It was as if they were brought up together, living proof that it's not only environment that creates character, but genetics. I could have spotted her at a hundred feet in a crowded room. My double.

The reunion was the most exciting personal thing that ever happened in my life. I was the one who had rejected her; I was the one who hadn't married her mother; I was the one who didn't want to push the reunion. But none of that mattered now.

Joan insisted we come out and meet our three new grandchildren. So early Saturday morning, Margaret and I drove to the house in Essex and it was really like coming home in many ways. Margaret and myself were both instantly entranced with Joan and our grandchildren.

Within five minutes of arriving at the house, I was playing with the boys. They were climbing trees and throwing fruit at me, apples and plums. We had some great outings.

When I think of all that my wife suffered from 1936 until

1972, with this ghost that haunted her, I was amazed at how well she behaved and stood up to the tension of meeting the daughter who had been "stolen" from the crib beside her. I think that was the first time I understood how Margaret felt for those thirty-six years.

The missing child wasn't something that really haunted me during all those years. I was quite prepared to wipe the unhappy incident off the slate. But not Margaret. For the rest of my life, I'll carry the guilt that I wasn't grown up enough to insist we get married when she became pregnant.

The only question that remains in my mind is whether her subsequent neurosis was caused by that trauma in 1936, or my own lack of consideration over the years for her burning desire to be reunited with her daughter.

I never was smart enough to change my attitude until Margaret, against all odds, traced the baby herself—thirty-six years after it was "stolen." I regret not having made a better effort in 1957 when I went looking for the lawyer.

Joan and I later went to visit some of her adoptive relatives in McDuff, Scotland. It was a beautiful sunshiny day, but so cold you couldn't even get out of the car. We found the farm where Joan had her happiest times as a youngster learning to ride horses.

Joan didn't tell them who I was at first. They gave her a great warm welcome, and when the old man of the house arrived to join the reunion with Joan, he took one sharp look at me and said, "Who are you?"

"I'm Jack Webster."

"You may be Jack Webster, but you're Joan's real father."

We looked like twins. Mind you, I'm not that much older than she is.

During the trip, I asked Joan about her upbringing and whether she ever suspected something was different about her.

"I always thought there was something wrong." she said. "I

never really fitted in and I didn't know why. I didn't really want
to know why because my mother was so unlike me. The looks.
The behaviour. The way she thought. They way she did everything. I just felt I had nothing in common with her. The same
with her husband. What a difference it would have made if I
had known I'd been adopted."

It was a desperate attempt by the adoptive parents to save a
marriage. It hadn't worked.

"I know absolutely nothing about their past," Joan said.
"They never discussed anything emotional. They wouldn't even
tell me where they were born, where they were married, where
they met, or what they did. Anything I knew about them was
from secretly looking through photographs or trying to find out
from various other people. The few friends and the relatives
they did have never seemed to appear. She didn't get along with
anyone at all and she never spoke to anybody. I always thought
there was something funny about that because I spoke to everybody and was happy and jolly while they were miserable and
most peculiar.

The adoptive father left Joan and his wife in 1952.

"He was quite a nice chap," she said. "She was cold and icy.
She looked after me well and taught me a few things, but I never
had any kind of sympathy or empathy with her at all. I never really heard from him after he went away. The next thing I heard,
a woman came to the door calling herself his new wife and just
told us he had died.

"I remember the day, I was papering the bedroom upstairs
and she stood on the doorstep and said 'I've come for the birth
certificate because I can't bury him. They won't issue a death
certificate without the birth certificate.' I remember saying to
her, 'Come in and have a cup of tea.' But she wouldn't.

"We wouldn't give her the birth certificate and she went off.
The next day we went to the hospital where he had died. I remember that day because we had to borrow the money for the
bus. We saw the doctor and he said, 'All right, I'll issue the

death certificate, but you'll have to pay two pounds.' We didn't have that money, and I burst into tears. She said nothing. Eventually I cried so long—I was about 16—he just gave us the certificate and off we went. Then we arranged the funeral.

"I always felt that blood was thicker than water and I always thought I should like my parents, but I thought maybe it was just me. But she'd never kiss me goodbye or anything like that. I'd always thought something funny was going on. I had a really crazy idea that because they couldn't have children, these two friends had me and gave me to them. When I found out about the Websters, it was just the greatest relief to know I had been adopted."

No one ever told the adoptive mother that Joan had been reunited with her real parents. "I don't know why I didn't tell," Joan told me after her death. "She had deceived me all those years. I resented her. She clothed me and brought me up, but she gave me no love. I don't know why I didn't tell her. We didn't tell the children [about my adoption] until five years later. We were afraid they'd tell her. She was quite different from most people. Hard. Not horrible, but hard."

Now I know what a miserable life Joan had in the earlier days. My conscience kills me on that one.

But Joan said, "Let's start from today."

We had some great fun with Joan. In 1984, Margaret and I had our wedding anniversary party on Saltspring with forty or fifty friends. At five o'clock, I said, "Oh Margaret, I forgot something. I've got to run down to the store."

In fact, I had a charter plane waiting at the dock in Ganges and I flew over to the airport in Vancouver where Joan had just got off a flight from London and picked her up. We were back at the house about forty minutes from the time I left, complete with Joan. Margaret was shocked silly. Happy as a lark that Joan had come out for the anniversary. That was our forty-fifth anniversary. It should have been our forty-eighth.

I think I got a little more happiness out of finding Joan than Margaret did because I was more outgoing than she, which was not fair. Sad.

The funny thing is that finding Joan never caused any trouble in our family. But then, when Margaret and I had rows or discussions all the family were involved and everyone gave their opinions. There were no secrets. So when Margaret found Joan, the kids weren't surprised. They were only as surprised as I was that she had gone on these trips to Britain and done it on her own without any help. That was her crowning achievement.

All our children melded together like they had been brought up in the same family from day one. It was quite incredible— and still is!

CHAPTER 11

"I consider myself an artist, a creator, rather than a business-man. I like to go into areas of undeveloped industrial possibili-ties. I consider the west coast of Canada such an area."

HARRY STONEHILL, U.S. TYCOON

● Margaret and I had some wonderful times together over the years despite the radical mood changes that sometimes plagued her. She was a beautiful woman and she could be irresistibly charming. I came home one evening to find her entertaining a smooth Philippine journalist, and the meeting led to us twisting the night away with Ferdinand and Imelda Marcos.

She had a smile on her face when she greeted me that night. "You have a visitor," she said coyly.

"Who?" I asked.

"Esclamado."

It was quite a surprise.

Alejandro Esclamado was the editor-manager of the *Philippine Chronicle* in San Francisco and I had met him a week before. He had appeared in my office at the Hotel Georgia and said: "You interviewed Harry Stonehill."

Stonehill was an American tycoon who had made his fortune in the Philippines and who was seeking landed immigrant status in Canada. "Yes," I said, "for last week's edition of This Hour Has Seven Days."

"Then I want a sworn statement of what Stonehill told you," Esclamado demanded. "And a copy of the interview tape."

"I'll tell you what he told me," I said. "You can interview me, but I don't have a copy of the tape. It's in Toronto."

In those days, the Philippines was a country very much in the grip of carpetbaggers. Stonehill had been the biggest and brashest of them all. The portly, tanned Stonehill, who favoured the *barong tagalog*, the native embroidered shirt, could have passed as my twin brother in looks. In Manila, they called him "Harry-in-a-hurry." It was easy to understand why we got along.

A former U.S. Army lieutenant, Stonehill started working in the Philippines upon his discharge in 1945. Over the next fifteen years he built a corporate empire worth more than $50 million, embracing oil, real estate, machinery and glass-making companies. He founded U.S. Tobacco Corp., whose best-selling cigarette brand was called Puppies, and he was the single biggest taxpayer in the Philippines.

But the American boasted once too often about how he'd bought off the Filipinos, and President Diosdado 'Godgiven' Macapagal was forced to order an investigation in response to the outcry. The probe ended with Stonehill's deportation in August 1962, after one of the main witnesses against him was badly beaten. There was also the insinuation that Stonehill had killed another enemy and dumped his body into the ocean.

In his interview with me, Stonehill discussed his checkered life in the south seas. When asked about the rumours of the slaying, he shrugged: "How can they be investigating me for murder when they haven't found the body yet?"

Esclamado used what I told him for an article in the *Chronicle,* and that was the last I thought I'd see of him. Now he was in my living room, seeking a tape of that CBC interview again.

"I need that CBC tape!" he insisted.

Esclamado and the Marcos forces wanted a copy of the interview because in it Stonehill acknowledged to me that corruption was endemic in the Macapagal regime. In defence of his own conduct, Stonehill quoted from a current issue of the *Harvard Business Review*: "In countries where payoff is as much a part of the economic process as payroll, whose ethical standards are right, the visitors' or the natives'? Is management's role that of developer of wealth and missionary simultaneously; or is it true that better standards of living are prerequisites to 'better' ethics? To win over the opposition do you join them or fight them?"

Stonehill said he did both.

"It is like the sea riding over you," he told me. "It's a way of life. I'm not bragging or proud of the way we were forced to operate there."

Stonehill said he along which his wife, Lourdis, and his four children loved Vancouver and wanted to settle in Canada. "I consider myself an artist, a creator, rather than a businessman," he said. "I like to go into areas of undeveloped industrial possibilities. I consider the west coast of Canada such an area."

Macapagal's attempt to eliminate the Stonehill scandal failed when the American was exposed as his main bagman and most powerful supporter. Nearly everyone in the Macapagal administration was on the take. The Marcos-led opposition was baying for Macapagal's ousting and they believed my taped interview with Stonehill was the smoking gun they needed to finish him.

I told Esclamado that I was going to Toronto to tape a Front Page Challenge show that Tuesday. "I'll see what I can do for you."

He chuckled. Friends again, I thought, and after a few more pleasantries he headed off.

A few days later, I flew to Toronto. I wasn't in my room at the Park Plaza more than two minutes when the phone rang.

"Señor Webster?" said the voice. "It's Esclamado."

"Where the hell are you?" I asked.

"I'm in the room above you."

"Why didn't you come with me on the plane?" I asked mystified.

"Because it would have been dangerous for two enemies of Macapagal to be in the same plane at the same time."

"Me an enemy?"

"Oh yes," he said, "you're an enemy."

It gave me a bit of a shudder. How Byzantine was the world of Philippine politics, I wondered? It didn't take me long to learn that party affiliation was virtually meaningless. It was personal loyalty and graft that fuelled the political machines of the Asian archipelago. The latest turbulence was a result of seven years of in-fighting that began in 1957 with the accidental death in a plane crash of Ramon Magsaysay. As Philippine president, Magsaysay had institutionalized an elaborate system of payola in the wake of the Second World War.

Macapagal had come out on top of the struggle for the presidency in 1961 by running on an anti-graft-and-corruption platform. His program was a manifest hypocrisy, but it didn't seem to matter. Now, Marcos was leading a popular campaign against Macapagal, accusing him of being dirty and promising an honest administration. It was beyond farce.

Stonehill had travelled the world to let the dust settle in the Philippines before arriving in Vancouver in May 1963. The American entrepreneur, who was accustomed to greasing government wheels to get what he wanted, hired Al Williamson to help get landed immigrant status.

The bald, pipe-smoking Williamson was a well-connected public relations consultant who did a lot of work for B.C.'s Social Credit administration. At the time he began working for Stonehill, he was also acting as an assistant, speech-writer and public relations consultant to Bennett.

Williamson introduced Stonehill to ex-*Sun*-reporter-turned-

Prime-Minister's-aide, Hal Dornan, and other Ottawa heavy-weights. Williamson promised Dornan that B.C. premier W.A.C. Bennett would soon send a letter supporting Stonehill's application. Because of Williamson's connections and friend-ships, no one doubted him. And a letter on the premier's statio-nery duly arrived at Dornan's office. "Dear Hal," it began, "Thanks for your interest in the settlement of our friend in Can-ada.

"Investment in secondary industries such as he proposes can be of inestimable value to the economy of British Columbia and we are most anxious to see this type of development," the letter continued.

"I understand his plans have been somewhat delayed due to uncertainty about his future and hope this can be settled favor-ably as quickly as possible.

"I hope you are well and enjoying life in Ottawa."

"Very sincerely yours, W.A.C. Bennett."

Dornan automatically forwarded the letter to the immigration department without questioning its legitimacy. But during the subsequent scrutiny of Stonehill's application, the forgery was exposed.

Williamson, who was a reserve member of the RCMP, was eventually charged with forgery and uttering a forged docu-ment. After a five-day trial, he was found guilty of two counts of forgery.

The 60-year-old Williamson collapsed upon hearing the ver-dict. The judge noted that W.A.C. Bennett hadn't been called as a witness in the trial and suggested that his absence left unan-swered the question of whether Williamson had the authority—as he claimed in his own defence—to pen the letter on the premier's behalf. Williamson was sentenced to six months in jail.

The ensuing controversy eliminated any chance Stonehill had of staying in Canada, although he claimed to have been as surprised as everyone else that the letter was a fake. When I interviewed Stonehill on February 4–5, 1965, Williamson was still protesting his innocence.

Stonehill's fifth child was born in Vancouver on February 11, just a week after my interview aired.

On December 10, 1965, Marcos's press secretary, Jose Asperaz, telephoned me in Vancouver. Marcos had won the election. "Mr. Webster," he said, "the president would be greatly honoured if you and your wife would attend his inauguration as his guest."

"What?"

"He credits the interview with Stonehill that you did for Seven Days in Canada for exposing the corruption in the Macapagal regime. You helped in a major way to win the election."

The tape of the interview had been broadcast over and over again—seventeen times, I was told—on the Philippine radio and the television network owned by the family of Don Ferdinand Lopez, Marcos's vice-presidential running-mate. It had become the focus of the election.

It was one of the best trips Margaret and I had in our lives. We were treated like royalty. She was supplied with a personal hairdresser and dress maker, to be fitted with a Mantilla gown for the celebrations.

But Manila was a very strange place.

It was a city of nearly a million and a half people encamped on both sides of the Pasig River, a sludgy, slimy sewer. Its northern waterfront was a maze of alleys snaking through a warren of mud-floored huts and hovels built from packing cases and gasoline drums. Many of the streets were riddled with pot-holes; rats scurried in the alleys, and children choked the main boulevards, hawking all manner of geegaws and knick-knacks.

There were roughly 9,000 murders that year—more than occurred in New York. Citizens owned more weaponry than the military and police forces combined. Most clubs had signs on their front doors: "Check your firearms before entering."

Opulence and overwhelming poverty were everywhere side by side. Gorgeous homes and shanty-town barrios. The images were hard to forget as we attended the glittering reception in the Malacanang Palace, swaying with Bayanihan dancers.

I interviewed Marcos during the trip.

"What are you going to do to wipe out corruption?" I asked

"I shall promise you this is going to be the cleanest government southeast Asia has ever seen," he told me. "The last time we got a billion dollars of war reparation money from the United States and only $100 million reached the people. That will never happen again.

"The Filipino has lost his soul and his courage," Marcos said, and to be honest, I found him sincere. "Our people have come to a point of despair. Justice and security are as myths. Our government is gripped in the iron hand of venality, its treasury is barren, its resources are wasted, its civil service slothful and indifferent. Not one hero alone do I ask, but many."

Afterwards we all went out to dinner and I danced the twist with Imelda until the wee hours of the morning.

In 1968, we were invited back to the Philippines for Vice-President Lopez's fiftieth wedding anniversary.

At the airport on the way to Manila for that trip, Margaret was asked about the gift-wrapped wedding gift she was carrying. The American customs officer wanted her to open it, but she adamantly refused. They argued for a minute, but she refused to open the parcel. "It'll spoil the wrapping," she said stubbornly.

The frustrated customs man looked to me for help. I think he recognized me, because he simply sighed, smiled and said, "O.K., ma'am," and waved us through.

In Manila, we mingled with the exiled royalty of Europe and Hollywood film stars such as Burt Reynolds. The champagne didn't so much flow as bubble endlessly from fountains. You dipped your glass into the sparkling pools whose effervescence was occasionally revitalized by a servant who would pour in another six or so bottles of Dom Perignon. The vice-president's house was so big there was a full-size American-type bowling alley with ten lanes.

The chasm between rich and poor still had not been bridged and throughout the islands, tensions were high and the poor angry. The compound was guarded by casually dressed men brandishing submachineguns. Beyond the ten-foot wire fence, hundreds of hungry Filipinos milled.

Shortly before Margaret and our son Jack, Jr., then 16, went on a rafting trip down Pagsahan Falls, Marcos's men had engaged in a firefight with guerrillas intent on seizing hostages from among the VIP guests.

I went to Baggio during that trip and interviewed the so-called psychic surgeon, Tony Agpawa. He was surrounded by the usual schizophrenic, paranoid, middle-aged people, all of whom said he cured their internal afflictions. They reminded me of members of a brain-washed cult, each gleefully told me ad nauseam how he had operated on them with only a touch of his fingers, pulling bloody tumours and other pernicious growths from their bodies without ever making an incision.

Nonsense!

He refused to operate in front of a sceptic like me.

But the paranoia was pervasive during that trip and I've not been back to the Philippines. During one dinner, a top Marcos crony said to me: "Mr. Webster, I'm very pleased to meet you. But you should know, when you were here three years ago you could have been in real trouble for upsetting the graft and corruption in the Macapagal government."

Marcos hadn't been interested in changing anything, only in

creating the illusion that he wasn't as dirty as Macapagal. The man's comment was the beginning of my enlightenment about Marcos.

At the same dinner, my son Jack came to me with a Philippine politician. "Come on, Senator, tell my dad what you told me," Jack insisted.

The man was reluctant and embarrassed. "I just told him that not only is your driver armed, but you have personal security everywhere you go, even if you don't see it," he said.

"It's a nervous society," I said.

"Well," the man said, "you're not as well liked as you used to be. You're not as well liked as you were three years ago when you helped elect Marcos. And if I had met you three years ago, I'd have shot you."

The man was convinced I was a pawn of Marcos who was clearly just as dirty and crooked as the rest.

Before we returned from that trip, I received a sub-rosa phone call. "Mr. Webster, maybe you could come up and see me?" the male voice said.

"Who are you?"

"I'm an American, I live in Forbes Park. I'd be very grateful if you come and see me."

"I'll bring my wife."

"No! Don't bring your wife."

He was anxious that I come alone. I agreed and went over to the Forbes Park compound and met the man who said he was from the U.S. information office. "What's the problem?" I asked.

"The American manager of the Sheraton Hotel was pistol-whipped today and thrown out of the country with his family."

"So?"

"They made him travel economy and he couldn't take all of his baggage. Would you take his baggage home to Hawaii for him?"

"No!" I said. "How do I know what's in the baggage?"

"You are a VIP, you can take what you like out of this country," the man said. "Besides, I'll guarantee the baggage is O.K."

I was still worried, but I relented.

When we left, I took the man's bags with me to Hawaii. I met him in the Royal Hawaiian Hotel. He was sitting dejectedly, bruised and battered. They'd beaten him because he wouldn't let his kitchen staff sell the hotel's edible garbage to local pig farmers. I gave him his bags and he fled with nary a thank-you.

He wasn't that pleased to see me even though I'd brought his baggage all the way from Manila. He didn't want to be associated with anyone however slightly connected to the Marcos regime.

I thought about the problems of the Philippines during a wild interview I had with Allen Ginsberg, the poet. The discussion, which was to be about the censoring of an irreverent, alternative Vancouver weekly newspaper, reminded me about how important free speech is in maintaining a democracy and preventing abuses of power. Yet the interview began with Ginsberg singing a stirring rendition of a William Blake poem.

"Ladies and gentlemen!" I said when he'd finished. "This is not a Salvation Army meeting at Carrall and Cordova! This is not a revival meeting! This is Allen Ginsberg, who is regarded in the United States as a kind of Apostle of the Peaceful People, the Apostle of Peace."

Ginsberg, who sat stroking a magnificent beard, had flown into town to join the *Georgia Straight* newspaper's struggle to continue publishing after a savage attack on a local magistrate. The Vancouver weekly regularly featured a mixture of movie reviews, acerbic attacks on politicians, pornography and nonsense.

But Ginsberg, I suppose, was the man who really started the modern battle against censorship with his publication of HOWL in San Francisco in 1956. He was only too happy to bring the fight here. And underneath his antics he had an important message.

"I'm just interested in the question of freedom," he said.

"Total freedom?" I asked.

"No, a free press."

"But a totally free press?"

"A free press," he said. "Like they have for you. You can speak your mind on the air. The mayor of this town tried to say that the *Georgia Straight* couldn't publish its paper. That's really carrying things a bit far."

"I agree," I conceded.

"And then the courts went along with that too and started to fine them a lot of money so they can't continue. So that I gotta come from 3,000 miles away to defend the poor old free press of Vancouver, B.C."

"Ah," I said, "but you gotta bring it into perspective, just give one itsy-bitsy bit. They committed an offence: they held the judge up to ridicule and contempt. That's against the law."

"You can find a technicality to take this program off the air if you want, you know."

"Somebody can take me off the air?"

"Sure. And if they did you sure would start screaming."

"Yes, but. . . ."

"Well, I'm screaming!" he yelled.

"Scream more!" I shouted.

"Well, I don't have to now. So let's continue with the music: 'Piper, sit thee down and write. . . .'"

"No, no no!" I yelled.

"No?" he screamed. "No?"

"You're a great poet, but you're an abominable musician!"

"I was in Prague in 1965, and I was elected King of May by the Prague students, the same students who were in trouble with the authoritarian police-state government. As a result of being elected King of May, I was bounced out of Prague by the Committee of Ideology and the Minister of Education who found technicalities to bounce me."

"Because you were a free soul?" I asked.

"No. They said, 'You have violated the laws of Czechoslovakia.' Exactly what laws they didn't quite say, and they would have had a hard time really proving it in court. Just as in the long run probably the *Georgia Straight* will win its case technically."

He was forceful and articulate, but in the long run there was always something about his argument—be it about censorship, imperialism, Viet Nam, the peace movement or free press—that repelled me. I didn't think the anarchy of the Hippies was any better an answer than the jack-booted order imposed by Marcos.

"Tell me Allen," I said finally to him, "do you give all the rest of us who haven't joined your active peace movement, do you give all the rest of us up as hopeless? Do you think we're all so hide-bound and reactionary that we can't appreciate the nuances of some injustices against people like the *Georgia Straight?*"

"No, I'm sure the people of Vancouver are beginning to become aware."

I told him that maybe we were using the police to dispense with social problems we'd rather not face instead of real crime. For instance, Vancouver police regularly used John Doe warrants to arrest dirty, bearded men on the courthouse steps, but respectable looking vagrants were allowed. "This," I said, "was an obvious misuse of authority."

"Right," Ginsberg said. "They might have gotten Jesus Christ there without knowing the difference."

Not a bad point!

A free press is essential in preventing the misuse of authority. That was one of the problems in Manila — there was no really honest political debate going on. It was simply one armed thug elbowing aside another. That was one of the lessons of the Mulligan Probe. The use of the courts by the Socreds to block debate about Sommers was another example in which public debate was curtailed deliberately by heavy-handed authority much to the detriment of the body politic.

Sweeping scandal underneath the rug and hoping it will vanish is a dangerous game that saps the public's faith in the administration of justice. I made a point of always investigating complaints of corruption, graft or police brutality throughout my career. I don't believe there are more potential sadists and crooks among the ranks of politicians and police officers than exist in any other group of people. But the potential for abuse is so great in those spheres that any suggestion of impropriety must be rooted out.

I remember one man, who had a hook for one hand, came to me with a broken nose and fractured wrist. "I've been beaten up by the police," he said.

"I don't believe you," I replied.

"Well, I was in hospital with a police escort," he said. "They've taken off the escort, and I haven't been charged with anything."

I investigated.

He'd gone to a nightclub on Main Street, got into some trouble and was arrested. He said the police beat him so badly they got worried in the city lock-up and took him to hospital. I went to the station to corroborate his story. When I looked at the charge sheets, I saw that an entry had been erased. Cover-up!

Acting on my gut instinct, I put the man on the air. Then I refused to let the story die. I aired the man's complaint seven or eight times until two police officers were charged. They were convicted, but beat it on appeal. They suffered so terribly as a result of the publicity and the tarring, one on them quit the force.

Surprisingly, I met the other policeman years later at a Vancouver Police Dept. Pipe Band Burns supper. I was doing the Webster walk-about, full of charm and grace, when I came up to a giant of a man. "Hi," I said smartly, "I'm Jack Webster."

He looked down into my eyes, took my proffered hand, and began to squeeze. And to squeeze, and to squeeze, and to squeeze. "I know you're Jack Webster," he said as I began to cringe. "You're the reason that I've been a constable for twenty-odd years!"

He was just about breaking my hand when one of my police buddies came up and elbowed him in the ribs. "Stop it for God's sake! Mind your manners."

The burly policeman let go just as I was about to burst into tears of pain. I apologized for what had happened and we agreed to let by-gones be by-gones. We sat down and had a drink. But he had obviously hated me for years. And who could blame him?

The incident was just another example of how I forgot or ignored the unforeseen and unavoidable repercussions caused by the spotlight I focused on people. I forgot about the people for whom I'd caused trouble. Mulligan's wife, for instance. I'm always ready to say, "Hi, I'm that great fellow Webster!"

On one occasion a woman on a ferry snapped at me: "Oh, it's you Webster, you're getting fatter and uglier all the time! You owe the people of Mayne Island an apology."

I couldn't even remember what the issue was, I had done so many broadcasts over the years. I just ignored her and continued on my way. She followed along barking insults at me until I finally I turned around, covered the side of my mouth with my hands and, very quietly, so that only she could hear, whispered: "Go away!" (or words to that effect).

She vanished never to be seen again.

That was the only time I can remember when I had to resort

The negotiations between hostage-holding prisoners and the authorities during an aborted escape attempt and riot in 1963 at the B.C. Penitentiary went on for hours and hours. I was exhausted from acting as the mediator and this picture was taken during a brief lull in the crisis.

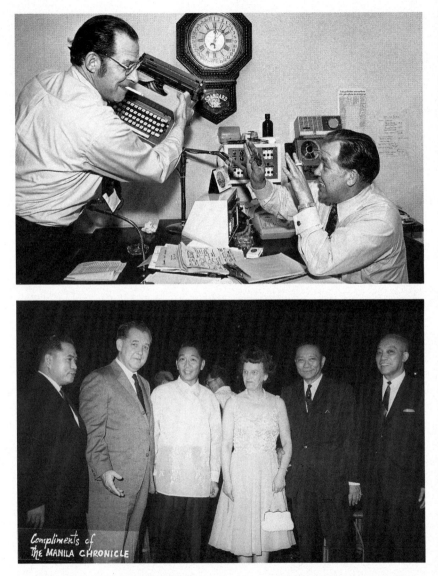

TOP: *Jack Wasserman and I lived in each other's pockets for thirty years. We shared office space and information. This was us mugging it up for the photographer in the late 1960s. (Credit: Don Le Blanc Studios)*

BOTTOM: *From left, Alexandro Esclamada, me, the late-Philippine president Ferdinand Marcos, Margaret, Don Fernando Lopez and someone else whose name I've forgotten, at Marcos' December 1965 inauguration ceremony. (Manila Chronicle)*

TOP: *Every election in B.C. since 1963 has been fought on the open-line shows. The press and the politicians didn't always get along but that didn't mean we were uncivil. Here, from left, me, Premier W.A.C. Bennett, his aide Bill Clancy and Wasserman share a joke after a press-conference encounter.* (Credit: Jim Ryan)

BOTTOM: *Pierre Berton is a close friend. Here, the Vancouver gang—from left, Allan Fotheringham, Pia Shandel, Berton, Juliette and Webster—help him celebrate book no. 25:* The Wild Frontier.

TOP: *In 1976, one of Vancouver's legendary newspaper editors, Himie Koshevoy, front and centre, retired. These were a few of the journalists who came to wish him well: sitting, from left, Hal Straight, Wasserman, me, Paddy Sherman; standing, from left, Harry Filion, Ed MacPherson, Merv Moore, Cliff McKay, Bill Forst, Reid Moir, Allan Fotheringham, Art Jones and Jim McKeachie.*

RIGHT: *Talk Radio meant a gruelling daily marathon of fielding calls and thinking on your feet. Here I ham it up a bit during my City Mike days.*
(Credit: Franco Citeralla)

TOP: *Bill Vander Zalm, his wife Lillian and I celebrate my last radio show in 1978 when Bill was better known as a gardener than the premier who lives in a castle in Fantasy Gardens. We have never been close politically, mainly because I don't care for the political company he keeps.*

LEFT: *Much of my life was spent making the rounds picking up tidbits of gossip and information. There was always a regular gang of us. Two of the most prominent at least in the 1970s were Herb Capozzi, ex-Socred MLA and businessman, and Umberto Menghi, Vancouver's most famous restaurateur.*

The 1984 election campaign had one highlight for me, Tory leader Brian Mulroney's refusal to answer questions on Webster! Prime Minister John Turner, in the background, tried to pump a little momentum into his foundering campaign with this T-shirt when he appeared. It didn't help.
(Credit: Brian Kent)

TOP: *Fotheringham, Patricia Carney and I at the Webster Foundation journalism awards dinner. The three of us have been a friendly media triumvirate for years.*

BOTTOM: *One of my warmest memories was introducing Prime Minister Pierre Trudeau to my daughter, Joan, who happened to be visiting Canada in 1982 and was on the set for that morning's taping of Webster!*

ABOVE: *Labour leader Jack Munro has been a close friend for years, always there when I needed him.*

RIGHT: *Prime Minister Brian Mulroney doesn't like live talk-shows. But as this picture attests, he projects an incredibly affable front, chatting up the crew and anyone else who's in the studio or the immediate vicinity of the set. Just don't ask him to answer the phone!*

to insult to get rid of someone. Generally, I didn't make enemies. True, W.A.C. Bennett's wife May would leave the room if
she saw me. But he didn't hold any personal animosity towards
me. He once told me, "I always get more out of a press conference if you are there than if you're not."

Margaret complained that I never did any happy stories, that
I only got enjoyment out of seeing somebody screwed. She preferred my pieces with Mohammed Ali, James Garner, Milton
Berle, Jane Russell, Jack Benny, Steve Allan, Jayne Meadows,
the Smothers Brothers, Rolf Harris, Uri Geller. . . . She loved
the programs I did about entertainment figures and good-news
stories.

Maybe she was right. They were always a giggle and often a
surprise. Jack Benny without a script was a disaster; Jane Russell
was actually larger in life and Sophia Loren was as cold as an ice
cube if you dared even hint about her divorces. Bob Newhart
left me in stitches when he told a caller who asked if he could
bring the kids to see the comic's nightclub act, "Sure, by all
means. The first show finishes at half-past ten and you'll be able
to take them home and tuck them in drunk."

Margaret thought I didn't do enough bright pieces, that I was
too negative, too cynical all the time.

I plead guilty. That was ultimately the difference between us.
I truly cared about how public life was conducted. Hers was a
intensely personal universe, mine incredibly public. She admired those who made people laugh; I admired those who made
history.

I'll be the first to confess that I can sometimes be a little too
personal or a little cheeky. I once asked the glamorous Mila
Mulroney on air: "How do you keep your weight down? How
heavy are you?"

"One hundred and thirty-nine pounds," she replied, slightly
perturbed.

"How tall are you?"

Five feet nine and a half inches."

"You're maybe five pounds overweight," I suggested.

"Do you also want to know my age?" she said snidely. "It's 32."

"Are you five pounds overweight?"

"I think so," she replied sheepishly.

Later, Ottawa reporter Mike Duffy helped patch things up by prodding me into apologizing to Mila outside of the Pan Pacific Hotel during another visit. "You're forgiven, Jack," she said, kissing me on the cheek.

C H A P T E R   1 2

"Oh, don't tell anyone he's dead. They've got to get their money's worth."

L I B E R A L   D I N N E R   O R G A N I Z E R

• I never really thought about dying until April 6, 1977. It was the death of my friend Jack Wasserman at the age of 50 that made me really think about slowing down, perhaps retiring to the farm to spend more time with Margaret.

My mother died in her mid-fifties and my father lived until he was touching 80. I felt their loss, but their death really didn't make me consider my own mortality more seriously. In fact, on his deathbed, my father had my brother Sandy telephone me in Canada to tell me to cancel the plans I had to fly over to be by his side. "Tell Jack not to waste his money," Wullie Webster said. "I'll be dead in the morning."

And he was.

But the events of the day Wasserman died are seared into my memory. We had had an argument that afternoon. Wasserman burst into my studio and yelled at my secretary Linda: "Get us some coffee and leave us alone."

Born in Winnipeg, Wasserman had studied law at the University of B.C. before getting interested in newspapering. He and I met in 1947 when he started part-time at the *Sun*. Later, I gave him his first column. When I joined CJOR and needed a new studio, it was Wasserman who told me to get an office next to his in Gastown. That piece of advice alone allowed me to keep my finger on the pulse of the city for years. And he was a faithful friend to Margaret.

His biggest coup was in October 1959, when he got the exclusive and dramatic account of Errol Flynn's last moments in the apartment of a Vancouver doctor: "Movie swashbuckler Errol Flynn died on the bedroom floor of a West End apartment Wednesday with his young blonde protege desperately trying to breathe life through his pain-twisted lips."

Wasserman's story went on to detail poignantly the events leading to Flynn's collapse and the 17-year-old starlet's attempts to resuscitate him. Wasserman also helped negotiate the release of a woman hostage in 1972 during an incident at Oakalla prison.

When he and I were office neighbours in Gastown, it was a great stopping-off place. People would come and see me in the daytime, and see Jack at night. We fed each other items all the time; we used each other brutally. He would fly kites, I would develop the story. I'd feed him items, he'd give me ideas. I picked up the daytime gossip and he picked up all the nighttime rumours.

I'd come in in the morning sometimes and check to see whether he was asleep on his couch and whether or not he'd delivered his column. I'd go around town with him once a month. But he didn't get along well with Allan Fotheringham, who was then a senior editor at the *Sun*. Fotheringham had come from the sports department and Wasserman looked down on anyone who hadn't cut his teeth as a real hard-news reporter.

"What the hell's the matter with you?" I asked that April day in 1977.

"You're interfering in my business again," he said.

"What do you mean interfering in your business?"

"You went to Fotheringham to get my deadline changed."

"Yeah, doing you a favour."

The *Sun* had moved Wasserman's column deadline ahead from six in the morning to 11:30 at night. I had phoned Foth and said, "You're going to kill him. He can't write his column by 11:30 at night. You've got to give him a later deadline."

Foth had it changed to 3:30 A.M., but Wasserman had somehow learned of my meddling.

"Don't you ever do that again, you son-of-a-bitch!" he shouted.

"O.K.," I said. "Sorry."

We made up over coffee, but he was still simmering as we headed up to the CBC to tape Hourglass, a nightly current affairs program on which Wasserman was a regular interviewer. I jumped into a question right off the top and began to hog the first part of the show when Wasserman burst into a coughing fit. It was so bad they had to stop taping and start again. As they were rewinding the tape, Wasserman turned to me and snapped: "It's my program and I'll ask the first question!"

Chastised, I shrugged and we began again.

Frances Russell, who was ending a tour of duty with the *Sun's* Victoria bureau, and the CBC's Bob Gillingham were also on the show. Afterwards we went to the dinner, a $25-a-plate roast of Gordon Gibson, Sr., the Bull of the Woods, at the Hotel Vancouver where Wasserman and I were both scheduled to say a few words.

"Why am I speaking first and you're second last?" he asked.

I needled him: "Because they save the best for last."

Herb Capozzi, a local millionaire, former Socred MLA and an old pal of ours, was the principal after-dinner speaker.

We ate some wonderful prime rib and then Wasserman began the festivities. Relaxed and seemingly in fine form, he warmed up the crowd. With a glance at the head table, he remarked that if they ever bombed the Teamsters Union headquarters in Washington, D.C., "We've got a good group here to fill in."

"After they dressed us up in these leis," he continued, "I decided we looked like a bunch of professional mourners at an Italian funeral.

"I heard the roasters rehearsing their little speeches beforehand. Very soft, gentle nice remarks about Gordon Gibson. It's no use fellows, the will is already made up. You're not in it and he's not going to change it!

"I see we're favoured tonight by the presence of Herb Capozzi. Somebody referred to him as a professional roaster. I wrote an item one day, I said Herb has a business card, 'Have roasting pan will travel.' He's the Julia Child of the banquet circuit.

"You know what a roast is? That's when friends gather to pay their respects in one way or another, to rip and to tear and to bludgeon the guest of honour and it's all in good fun. Until tonight.

"You know as a reporter I recall the time Gordon Gibson stood in the Legislature alone. Amassed against him was the might of the government of the day. But Gordon Gibson was right and he stood alone. The government thundered and it roared. But Gordon Gibson did not quaver, he did not waver. Gordon Gibson was right and he stood alone.

"You know sincerity is a very important thing. It's next to religion. Gordon is not a very religious man. But he went to a lot of churches during election campaigns. He even turned up at a Catholic church one Sunday and they took up a collection for the poor of the parish. One of his constituency workers gave him a nudge and said, 'Gordon, give $10.' He gave $10. Then there was a collection for the orphanage in the diocese. Another nudge, 'Gordon, give $25.' Gordon gave $25. Then they took up a collection for the missionaries to Rhodesia. 'Gordon, give $50.' Gordon gave $50. As everyone is filing out of the church, the priest at the door said, 'Gordon how did you enjoy the ceremony?'"

Wasserman paused for the punchline. His speech was going so well, I thought, it will be difficult to top it. Then I heard the *thud*!

Wasserman had pitched forward in what from a distance seemed to be a deliberate punchline collapse done with the timing of a comedian. He then tumbled backwards, disappearing from view, with a resounding crash.

I knew the moment he hit the ground he was dead. Three doctors in the audience rushed forward and began pounding on his chest. Even when it was announced an ambulance had been called, many thought they were watching a skit. Then the stretcher bearers and an inhalator crew arrived.

They put him on the stretcher, my best friend, a man I had been close to for God knows how many years, from 1947 to 1977. Thirty years in each other's pockets. As I'm leaving one of the Liberal officials said to me, "What's happened?"

"He's dead," I said. "You'll have to cancel the meeting."

"Oh, don't tell anyone he's dead," he said, "they've got to get their money's worth."

The organizers continued the event, saying Jack would have wanted it that way. Hogwash!

Later, they announced his passing: "The sad news, ladies and gentleman. Jack Wasserman didn't make it."

He left his second wife, Patricia, and a daughter Jana, who was a product of his first marriage and who lived in California.

I went off considerably distraught. With the assistance of Len Lauk of the CBC we sent a car to bring Pat to St. Paul's Hospital.

We stood around for what was a horrifying fifteen or twenty minutes in the hospital waiting room. A fireman came out and said to me,

"It's the funniest thing, you know. Every time we pick up one of these heart attack victims he always has a package of Tums in his pocket."

We collected Jack's personal belongings and headed over to his house. Wasserman's neighbour was a doctor and he cared for Pat. I got into the liquor cabinet and we had a good drink. Then the phone began to ring, and ring, and ring.

The first important phone call I got that night was from a gentleman who asked to speak to Mrs. Wasserman. I said she couldn't be disturbed, she's been sedated. "Who are you?"

"I'm the undertaker for the Jewish community. I want to see about Jack's burial in the faith."

This was during Passover.

"I've got bad news for you," I said. "He's going to be cremated. That's what Jack wanted."

"Oh," he said, "that's impossible."

"Very sorry," I said, "but that's the score."

I hung up.

Minutes later the phone went again. "Webster? I'm the chief rabbi for all of British Columbia. What's this about Jack not being buried in the faith?"

"Look," I said sharply, "these are my instructions—he is to be cremated."

"That's wrong. That cannot be. This must not be allowed to happen. He was a prominent member of the Jewish community. We're all buried in the same manner. We're all from the same place."

"Sorry, rabbi. Nothing I can do about it. That's what is going to happen."

I stood there thinking, what the devil is going on here? More calls came in, all kinds of people called to express condolences. Then the coroner called. "Webster? This is Glen McDonald. You can't have Wasserman's body for cremation in the morning."

"Why not?"

"Because he died under suspicious circumstances. He could have been poisoned. I'm holding the body back for an autopsy."

I told him he was wrong, that Wasserman had reported pains

in his chest to his doctor after he had had trouble a few months before in Montreal. "You're not getting the body until after my inquiry," he said, and hung up on me.

I had another drink to keep my spirit from flagging. Fotheringham called and said I must come down to the *Sun* to write a piece. Hugh Pickett, Vancouver's first and foremost impresario and the doyen of the downtown social scene, was a good friend of Wasserman and I. He had come to the house to offer any help he could. He drove me to the newspaper office.

Just after I arrived at the Pacific Press plant, Margaret called in near hysterics. She was upset because McDonald had just called her too. He wanted to talk to me again. I called him back and he said: "Well, I have your friend's body in front of me. I've confirmed that he did die of a coronary occlusion and you can have the body in the morning."

I'll felt sick as I began to type. It was a little like writing my own obituary. One key at a time. J-a-c-k W-a-s-s-e-r-m-a-n w-a-s one-of-a-kind. His sort of newspaperman may never come down the pike again—and more's the pity. I worked with him—and against him—for my thirty years in Vancouver. I was there when he died. I hope I go as well as he did. . . .

Wasserman was unique. He was a reporter who never lost the craft. It's hard to believe that Vancouver can get by without his ear eternally to the keyhole. It was dangerous to whisper a hint to Jack. Two more telephone calls and he knew the full story.

Not all his contacts were friends. But let me step back a pace. Perhaps my only claim to prescience over the years, was that I assigned him that column—two nights a week—After Dark—for which the paper paid him an extra $20. It was only the beginning of an illustrious career.

But, as I was saying, not all his contacts were friends. Though he mixed with the high and the mighty, the proud and the powerful, he got much of his journalistic meat from the people at the other end of the scale. It was a dicey business.

Sometimes I'd say to him: "Why do you do it?" Jack would

shrug his shoulders and say—"So what? They wouldn't touch me." There were times when I wouldn't have bet on it.

It would be fair to say that Jack Wasserman lived on recognition. He was a character and he knew it. I used to josh him that he had a secret code whereby he entered a public place—and, in less time than it takes to tell—he was paged on the loudspeaker. True or false, it was a good device.

Together we covered murders and fires; rape cases and political trials. He was a terrible golfer; he hit the ball either 200 yards or 200 inches. There were no half-measures. It was the same with his putting.

One afternoon at the Vancouver Golf Club, I was in a sand trap to the side—out of sight. I pitched the ball out to within two inches of the pin. His reaction was instantaneous. He called to his partner—"Check Webster's fingernails for sand." He had that kind of devastating wit.

I finally got to my own radio studio at half-past eight the next morning, considerably shaken. There were about twenty-five people crowded around who wanted to say their bit about Jack on the air. I told them no, did my own ten-minute piece and left it at that.

Wasserman's funeral was held the following Saturday, the last day of Passover, in a Unitarian Church. In the middle of the service, a woman jumped up and shouted: "If he hadn't been making fun of the Roman Catholic church in his speech, he'd be alive today."

Len Lauk grabbed her by the arm and hustled her outside.

Wasserman's wife Pat asked us to look after his ashes, and a couple of days later those of us who were his closest friends decided to have a little ceremony at the Malkin Bowl in Stanley Park where Wass had sold programs as a boy.

I called Herb Capozzi and told him to bring some wine. All Wasserman's close buddies went and stood around in the rain, had a little ceremony, drank wine and spread the ashes around the rose bushes. *Sun* columnist Denny Boyd took some and later sprinkled them under the statue in front of the Pacific Press building. Capozzi took some, too, and placed them in Wasserman's favourite nightclub.

He was a great loss to journalism in British Columbia and no one in the media has succeeded in filling Wasserman's shoes as the definitive source of street-level stories. His contacts, his savvy and his legwork were that good! Whereas I became in many ways more and more of a performer over the course of my career, Wasserman remained first and foremost a reporter.

CHAPTER 13

"Jack, I'll make you a deal. You and I retire together, O.K.?
When you get out of this game, I'll get out."

PRIME MINISTER PIERRE TRUDEAU

• By the spring of 1978, I was ready to call it a day and move to
the farm. I had been in the media business for forty years at the
time and I'd been one of the highest paid broadcasters in Canada for a long time. I didn't want to end up like Wasserman, dying on my feet at some podium performing for people I didn't
really know or like. I also wanted to spend more time with Margaret.

I was also beginning to wonder whether I was losing touch
with a population whose demographics demanded broadcasters
appeal to a younger and younger audience. Figures compiled by
the Bureau of Broadcast Measurement, which monitors audience size for radio and television stations, indicated that eight
out of ten of my listeners were over the age of 50. The attitudes
of my generation seemed to be more and more out of step with
the times. And to make matters worse, rival hot-liner Gary Ban-
nerman, who was holding forth on CKNW, had nearly as many
listeners as I did.

I wasn't sure what I wanted to do: get into the trenches to secure my place as B.C.'s most-listened to journalist or to retire
while still on top. I felt a little like an aging boxer wearily sizing
up the latest wave of young contenders.

Then Ray Peters, president of the local CTV affiliate, BCTV, asked me to move to television. He was convinced I could be a hit. The offer was lucrative and provided four months off during the summer—the sort of vacation time that was becoming harder and harder to take on radio because of the intense competition.

I nervously made the deal to start on October 2. But I inserted a clause in the contract that allowed either side to walk away after six months if we didn't suit each other. Bill Elliot, the station's executive producer, predicted I'd have 100,000 viewers by Christmas. I did.

I phoned CJOR owner Jim Pattison after signing the television contract and told him about it. During the conversation I said, "Jimmy, there's a slight problem I want to talk about."

In the contract I had with Pattison was a provision that guaranteed me $25,000 a year for five years if I quit working for him provided I didn't compete against his station "on radio." "In effect, I'm going to compete against you," I told him, "but not on radio."

"What does the contract say?" he said.

"Competing on radio."

"You're competing on television—you get the money."

I left CJOR in June 1978 and, true to his word, Pattison paid me the $25,000 over the next five years as promised.

I had the same nightmares when I started at BCTV as I had when I started in radio in 1953. What's an old man like me doing? I should be sitting in front of the fire reading a dirty book instead of performing on the far-side of prime time.

The physical transition involved in my move to full-time television from radio was difficult in itself. The set for the Webster! program was smack in the middle of the BCTV newsroom, which was forever buzzing with action as Cameron Bell and his Newshour staff put the show together.

I was used to having my own space, and after a show the staff of the program and I would sit around and hold story conferences or impromptu bull sessions about what was working and what wasn't. The noise we made drove the reporters and Bell up the wall and he once came raging over to bark at me: "Is that all you've got to do with your time—upset my news room?"

But we learned to grudgingly accept each other as time went by. I couldn't help but admire that together with Keith Bradbury, Tony Parsons, Bernie Pascal and a host of talented young journalists Bell had created a newscast that had the best market penetration of any program in North America!

As time went by, I also learned that the difference between TV Talk and Talk Radio was like the difference between a formal church wedding and a civil ceremony. Talk Radio at its best was a shirt-sleeve operation that followed breaking stories when possible. It was a three-and-a-half-hour marathon every day, but you could rely on listeners to provide a constant source of bright fill, and often their on-air tips produced the best stories. Television demanded more of you. It required that I not only be alert and prepared, but also that I appear to be. Still, I felt I wielded ten times the clout on television.

What kept my interest from flagging was politics. I turned to Prime Minister Pierre Trudeau for help in kicking off my initial television broadcast. Although besieged at the polls and on the verge of defeat, he made time for me. He always did.

The best I ever did with Trudeau, who is only a year younger than I, was break even. Maybe once I had him on the run. He was such a cold, Jesuitical debater that I eternally had to remind him that I was asking the questions. I wasn't going to answer his questions. But he was the only man I was ever truly nervous about interviewing in all my years in radio and television.

Early on, I regarded Trudeau as the most arrogant, supercilious SOB I had ever met as a politician. But he became my one true political guru even though our first meeting was nasty, brutish and short.

Trudeau only entered national politics in the mid-1960s and was chosen Liberal Party leader, thence Prime Minister, because the backroom boys had to find a television personality. They didn't know what or whom they were promoting.

He was frankly lukewarm about the monarchy, Commonwealth and other Canadian-Anglo-Saxon articles of faith when he gained power. He sauntered around the official residence barefoot, attended official receptions in sandals and cravat, and delicately sniffed roses while seated in House of Commons debates.

Trudeaumania swept Canada. Men and women literally fought to touch the hem of his garments. He undoubtedly had a charisma which enveloped even this hard-nosed reporter who told him on television coast to coast, "You'll either be the best or worst prime minister Canada has ever had."

Trudeau was not pleased with my attitude because he had little time for nosey reporters and basically distrusted the press—with reason when one remembers his part in fighting press monopoly in Quebec in the early 1950s.

I disliked Trudeau after our first meeting when he was only a cabinet minister. He was so god-damn arrogant.

We were at a press conference in the social suite of the Hotel Vancouver. Jack Wasserman and I were there together and we took offence at all the Liberal hangers-on who joined the press conference. Wass and I put our feet down: "Get all these flacks out or there ain't going to be any press conference," we said.

We won our point.

During the ensuing questions a young student said to Trudeau, who was then minister of justice and running for the Liberal leadership: "If you become leader of the party will you withdraw from NATO?"

He gave an answer.

The young U.B.C. kid said, "In other words, you'd pull out."

"That's not what I said," Trudeau replied.

I said, "Let me try Mr. Trudeau. IF YOU BECOME PRIME MINISTER WILL YOU PULL CANADIAN TROOPS OUT OF NATO?"

He gave me an answer. I said, "See, the U.B.C. kid was right. You gave me the same answer you gave him and I interpret it the same way."

So our first meeting was a little bit abrasive.

Our second meeting, in a small room at the Bayshore Hotel, wasn't much better. He was still minister of justice. And at that press conference, sitting in the front row, were newspaperman Doug Collins, Wasserman, Pat Carney, at that time a journalist, and me.

An aide got up before Trudeau arrived and said, "O.K. this is the drill for today's conference. One question from national newspapers, one question from local newspapers, and no questions from weeklies or broadcasters."

Well, I was in the front row and I'm radio and this flunkie figured I was going to sit back and not ask a question. I jumped in the moment Trudeau began taking questions. I asked one, then another, then a third. A non-stop, quick-fire interrogation. Finally, after a fifth and sixth question from Wasserman and Collins, this little guy says, "That's enough! Give someone else a chance."

I turned to Trudeau and asked, "Who's running this press conference? You or your P.R. man?"

Trudeau gave the flack a baleful look and the aide left the platform. It was at that press conference I asked Trudeau if he had used marijuana. "Under the system of justice we have I don't have to make any statement on that kind of thing," he said.

He smiled his coy little grin and conceded that he knew "the smell of pot." I barked at him: "Have you ever smoked marijuana?"

"Under Canadian laws I don't have to incriminate myself by answering that," Trudeau replied haughtily.

And they all began to laugh. The national reporters, the cameramen, the hangers-on, everyone from the East began to laugh.

So we locals bored in after him on it. We weren't going to take that kind of supercilious answer and the treatment we gave him shook him a little.

I went back to the studio and I picked out the clip where everyone was laughing about the marijuana and played it. And played it and played it and played it. Over and over and over again, until finally one of the Liberals phoned me up and said, "For God's sake, you've had your pound of flesh. Please, stop it."

I guess I had the last laugh on that one.

Trudeau could not have been aware then what a hard line I had come to take on drugs. If a drug trafficker was jailed for seven years in prison, I'd be on air saying the court was soft—he should have got seventy! I did a program on the toll it was taking in Vancouver by interviewing forty families who had lost sons and daughters to heroin addiction.

I believed smoking marijuana should be a firing offence in the schools. I talked to one 17-year-old kid potted out of his head. He had no money, no hope and no future. He told me he came from Kamloops and had become hooked because of the glamorization of the drug culture by the Beatles, the Rolling Stones and other rock groups.

Trudeau eventually clarified for me his stand on the issue in a subsequent interview. "Decriminalization, yes—in the sense that we don't want a person condemned for mere possession to have a criminal record that will follow him or her for the rest of his or her life," he said. "Decriminalization in that sense, yes.

Not in the sense that it will no longer be an offence of any kind to possess and use marijuana. There will be some restraint, but it won't go into your criminal record or result in a jail sentence."

I pressed him: "But you would expect a big increase in the use of marijuana among young people who say, 'Oh, it's decriminalized; it's legal. It's not a danger.' That doesn't worry you too much, marijuana?"

"It would worry me if I was smoking it or I saw my kids smoking it," Trudeau said. "I think the effects on the mind are not determined any more than the effects of alcohol and a lot of other drugs. I think if you can stay away from it, it's better."

"And if you can stay away from all of them, so much the better," I added.

"So much the better," he agreed.

I always took a hard line on drugs. In the beginning, as far as I was concerned, junkies should be quarantined until they died or kicked the habit. Later, I came to see addiction as a more complex problem that was deeply rooted in prevailing social conditions.

Trudeau never did change the law.

In the early days, all Trudeau and I ever seemed to do when we met was argue. I would accuse him of trying to censor press conferences; he'd accuse me of attempting to hog all of the questions. Touché!

After one dust-up, I overheard him say to an aide as he left: "Why does that man hate me?"

"Webster doesn't hate you," the aide replied.

"But he's always yelling at me," Trudeau said.

"Webster's always yelling at everybody."

After some years in government, Trudeau lost his early socialist fervour and became a fairly orthodox Liberal in many ways. He would probably describe himself as a pragmatist. He appeared from nowhere at a time when it looked as if the nation might well be split apart by French Canadian separatist influences, and he may well be the man of the century for keeping this nation in one piece for as long as he did.

Quibbling about Trudeau's mannerisms and peccadilloes goes out the window when you realize he was the only Canadian federalist at the time who could talk equally to six million French Canadians and fourteen million non-French. He was so bilingual he wrote poetry in both languages. He rode Anglo-French feelings with the touch of a master. He coped, too, with political potentates who controlled ten provinces, from wealthy British Columbia to the underprivileged Maritimes and touchy, sensitive Quebec, where one wrong move brought outrage from the rising tide of separatists.

Trudeau was the first Canadian Prime Minister since Glasgow's John A. Macdonald a hundred years before who was brutally frank on major issues facing Canada. I'm sure Trudeau made the White House shudder at his frankness.

To his shame, Trudeau did move Canada away from the traditional British Parliamentary system. He increased his personal staff vastly and in many ways is to blame for the problems that plague us today. But Canadian governments for the previous twenty years had been filled with an awful lethargy. It was wonderful to have a swinger with such a vast selection of glamorous girlfriends as Prime Minister instead of stodgy diplomats and mouthy politicians.

Remember Eva Ritting-Hausen — a jetsetting blonde he lunched with in London? She left telling everyone it was "love at first sight." The next night he was out with a brunette. "I don't feel snubbed at all," insisted scorned Eva. "I think he should enjoy himself."

We were willing to take a chance on Pierre, married or single. I grew grudgingly to respect and finally to admire the man.

We had several memorable exchanges over the years on radio. One in particular was the way he dealt with an ambush I planned. I arranged for a man who was manipulating the unemployment insurance plan to call and embarrass the government. "I just called to thank you for your generosity over the past year," the fellow began.

"Does that have a sting in it or is that sincere?" a wary Trudeau asked.

"It's got a bit of a sting in it actually, I've been collecting $85 a week UI for the past ten and a half months."

"You'll be cut off soon and have to go back to work," Trudeau said.

"No, I'm in a special category, I can carry on until January 26th to be exact. But my wife has been earning $500 a month and we've been living extremely well in the West End and I hope something positive can happen for me in a job sense. I've been looking for work, honestly looking for work, and I've been through the Canada Manpower grind. I even took the psychological tests to see if I'm a sane, all-Canadian boy. Which I am. They recommended I go into sculpting or pottery. I have a wife and a child to earn a living for. I'm 27, I graduated from high school in 1964 and I have two years of university."

"Don't give me all the details," I interjected, "but what are you going to do with the money you saved on UIC?"

"We just got back from San Francisco and we're planning to go to Hawaii at Christmas time," the caller said proudly.

"Have you refused any jobs Manpower offered you?" Trudeau asked obviously irritated.

"Yes," the man replied, "I refused two. I refused to load bricks on a lorry at $1.95 an hour and I turned down a job for $400 a month as a delivery boy."

"There's a lot of guys getting a free ride on unemployment insurance and we're cutting them off at a very high rate," Trudeau warned sharply. "So if that's your case I'd be very interested in having your name. Please send it in. I guarantee you a job within ten days and if you don't take it, I guarantee you'll be knocked off. And if you go to Hawaii, it'll be as a bum."

I gave Trudeau the man's name after the show and I learned a few days later that he had been offered and accepted a job at the Post Office.

Trudeau and I got along because he wasn't afraid to speak his mind. He was honest and he didn't mince words, or gestures. His attack on B.C. Supreme Court Justice Tom Berger during the manoeuvring to repatriate the Constitution was a typical example of his blunt, no-nonsense style.

Berger had authored an article in *The Globe and Mail*—whose publisher publicly opposed Trudeau's package—headlined: 'Steps that'll give Canada a fairer form of constitution.' Among several points, Berger argued that Trudeau was "repudiating native rights" and "this is wrong."

To its credit, the federal government later modified its package to meet some of the complaints. "Do you think Berger will be happy now that you've put back the aboriginal rights clause even with 'existing' rights in it?" I asked Trudeau.

"Well, Jack," he began quietly, "that's a pretty sensitive subject. I'm not sure what was the intention of Justice Berger to enter the public debate on a resolution which is before Parliament. The judges are very sensitive when politicians criticize them."

You could see the glint in his eye as he zeroed in on the principle Berger had transgressed: judges had no role in political debate. "I do not think it's the purpose of a judge to get in and discuss an accord that was reached or a bill before Parliament and I take strong exception to that. If he had wanted to do this I wonder why he didn't support the bill when it was there and when it gave Quebec the veto and it gave the Indians aboriginal rights."

The original constitutional reform bill proposed by Trudeau—and supported only by Ontario and New

Brunswick—contained the contested aboriginal rights clause and a proposal to give Ontario and Quebec a permanent constitutional veto over any constitutional amendment.

"Berger didn't support us then," Trudeau said, insinuating that the judge had discarded his judicial cloak of impartiality to dabble in partisan politics. "He saw fit to get off the bench and enter the political arena at a very inopportune time. I just regard that as the judiciary getting mixed up in politics. I hope the judges will do something about it."

Berger quit the bench soon afterwards.

There was one Trudeau-Webster exchange, however, that the eastern media and Trudeau-bashers will always hold against me. It was when I asked him when he would retire on February 20, 1981. He gave me that famous Cheshire-cat grin and said, "Jack, I'll make you a deal. You and I retire together, O.K.? When you get out of this game, I'll get out."

I just laughed. A lot of people told me I should have accepted the offer, including the editorial board of the *Globe*: "We trust the eminent west coast broadcaster Jack Webster does his bounden duty and retires forthwith."

They were sure the country would be better for it. I'm not so sure.

Trudeau met my daughter Joan in the studio just before he retired. He looked a little surprised when I introduced her. I said, "Someday, I will tell you the really human, dramatic story behind my daughter Joan."

"No you won't," he said shaking her hand. "I'd rather hear it from Joan."

Trudeau was really the only prime minister for whom I've had much of a warm spot. Joe Clark was a non-entity by comparison. Trudeau was five-foot-ten and looked six-foot-one. Clark was six-foot-one but looked five-foot-ten. While I always addressed Trudeau as Mr. Trudeau, or Prime Minister, with Clark I'd psychologically slip and unhesitatingly refer to him as "Joe."

Still, Clark was always gracious.

Prime Minister John Turner? Well, what can one say about Turner? At least he, like his predecessors Trudeau and Clark, appeared on my program prepared to answer questions from the people. Which was something his successor, Brian Mulroney, wouldn't do. Mulroney always carefully chose his appearance times, leaving nothing to chance.

My relationship with the Mulroneys has always been cordial, perhaps because of his blatantly manipulative style. I first met Mulroney in 1980 at the Ritz Carlton where he encamped to mastermind his assault on the Tory leadership. He sent a bottle of champagne to my table as if I were his long-lost love!

He was more than cordial when he finally entered the arena of public debate.

During the 1984 campaign, then-Prime Minister Turner appeared at the studio with a t-shirt bearing the message, "I'm not afraid of Webster." It was a dig at then Tory-leader Mulroney's refusal to face me and handle calls on the open-line.

Mulroney hid from the people of British Columbia during that election! There were guards hired so I couldn't ambush him when he appeared in the BCTV studios to tape the CTV network current-affairs show, Question Period. Mulroney's policies were a pig in a poke and his campaign a series of glorified photo oportunites.

I was assured by his office that he would appear and answer questions during the campaign and I was infuriated at what I saw as a double-cross when he refused. I attacked him for three consecutive nights on the BCTV six-o'clock news, which has a larger audience in B.C. than Question Period has across the country, for refusing to appear on my program. He bypassed me, I'm sure, simply because he likes to carefully orchestrate and manipulate the media. I have always railed against that tactic.

"Please forgive me, Mr. Mulroney," I fumed in the editorial that led the first newscast. "But this is the only way I or anyone else can seemingly talk to you. I just have a simple question: Why won't you talk to us? We just want to ask you in public for the people of British Columbia some simple questions and get some straight answers. And I promise I won't even mention the stench of patronage, which followed from the Liberals to your regime; won't even mention your backtracking on the old age pension de-indexation; won't even mention all of the problems.

"I trust you will be nice to us and speak and say, 'Oh, hello British Columbia, have you any questions to ask?' Maybe next year if you are still around we'll be allowed to talk to you, because you are here on our expense account. You might as well have stayed in Ottawa. It wouldn't have made any damn difference at all."

I got a call from one of Mulroney's aides later saying he wasn't amused and that I should apologize. "I'll do you a favour," I told the flack, "and forget you ever called."

When Mulroney arrived at the studio for Question Period, he didn't come anywhere near my set. Even when the taping was delayed for thirty minutes, leaving him nothing to do but twiddle his thumbs, he sat stonily silent rather than walk across the room to my set. I sat behind my desk, across from an empty chair and fulminated to national reporters.

Mulroney sent a hand-written note on August 26, saying, "I was sorry that an unusually heavy schedule precluded my appearance on your show. It is my hope that we can do it at an early moment—I've always enjoyed appearing on Webster and look forward to doing so again. Mila sends her best regards."

Photo-opportunity campaigns without interviews will be the death of democracy!

I sometimes have the gravest doubts about how we pick prime ministers in this country. There was a time when the prime minister was picked by the largest group elected in the House of Commons—as Britain did for a hundred years. A nice simple system.

Along comes Pierre Elliot Trudeau and we edged, it seemed to me, towards the U.S. presidential system with a large and powerful executive but with none of the checks and balances built into that country's constitution. Today in Canada MPs have been reduced to mere nobodies, meekly submitting to the party Whip's instructions while calculating when their handsome pensions become due if a crisis should develop. Twice in recent years we have seen unelected people gain power solely through the nomination of a group of privileged party delegates.

The only difference between Canadian and American politics is that in the U.S. they cater to rich establishment figures with billion-dollar bagmen. Here, the bagmen deal only in million-dollar denominations.

I think we have a duty, especially older geezers like me, to point out very bluntly where our politicians are failing us. And Mulroney is failing us when he acts like some feudal overlord, some suzerain born to reign over us! Mulroney did sit down with me in his hotel suite for a twenty-minute interview after the election. But again, he refused to take questions from callers, who are often the most telling political interviewers. That's why I attacked him on a newscast, and I'd do it again if I had to. Politicians must be accountable to the people.

I remain convinced that if he had ventured out of Ottawa and sold the Meech Lake Accord directly to Canadians on open-line shows, it might have passed. His uneasiness at being questioned by real people has bred the feeling that he is hiding something.

Still, I shall always wonder if I could have coped with political office, a cabinet post, no matter how minor. The paucity of aggressive reporters unafraid to cross swords with those in positions of power has, more than anything else, kept me from becoming a politician despite offers from every major party.

As an incorrigible critic, I doubt I could have survived in a world so full of compromises. Maybe that's why I've always found a reason to say no whenever a political party has approached me—and they all have.

I had breakfast with Bill Vander Zalm just before the Socred leadership convention in 1986. As we sat in the White Spot, I said to him: "You know Willie, you probably have a chance of getting it. But be careful what you say. Don't do this 'walk away from everybody calling your cabinet colleagues gutless' like you did last time."

"Would you like to run with me?" he asked.

"Only if you make me Attorney-General," I said joking.

"Well," he said, "that's possible."

"No thanks," I said. "I ain't going to run with you anyway."

When my friend Pat Carney stepped out of politics, I found myself being courted to run in her place in the federal riding of Vancouver Centre. Initially, I laughed.

I'm not a Tory, never could be anything other than a maverick who would find it tough to be lashed into line by the party Whip. But Prime Minister Mulroney himself even called—and he's a difficult man to refuse. One of his senior party henchmen temptingly whispered that if I accepted, I could be sworn into Cabinet before the nomination meeting.

I sweated over that for a couple of days, dreaming of grandeur and instant political clout. But I would have put P.C. after my name forever if I had won the seat. I turned it down.

My friend Carney held three major posts—energy, international trade and treasury board. She was the most powerful woman in Canada. She negotiated the Atlantic accord, deregulated the oil and gas industry and stickhandled the free-trade agreement.

But I know her frankness was never appreciated by the chauvinists in central Canada. Just look at the insinuations in the stories about her fight to win her son—she's a single parent—the right to use the free spousal airline ticket given to every sitting MP! And she was unfairly lampooned for a Christmas holiday she took in Hawaii—where she was spending a few brief days with her family instead of remaining perpetually in Ottawa to handle every minor crisis!

Think of what they would have done to me! Besides, who needs the jetlag, or the headaches!

CHAPTER 14

"By the way Jack, I met a man the other day who wanted to kill you. . . . John Farris!"

PREMIER BILL BENNETT

• I've always seen myself as a gadfly. I wanted to expose scandal and fight for what was right, not for what was politically palatable. After all the years I covered public life, only one incident remains like a burr under my saddle. I remain outraged at how both federal and provincial politicians handled the John Lauchlan Farris scandal. It is a perfect example of how the system favours the establishment over the common man, and why people like me must continue to battle for the little guy.

Farris was one of the top judges in Canada. Yet, he consorted with a hooker whose boyfriend was deeply involved in the underworld heroin trade. His disappearance from public life was the most embarrassing scandal in the judicial history of British Columbia.

In 1973, John Farris was appointed directly from the ranks of the legal profession to the lofty position of Chief Justice of the B.C. Court of Appeal. He was a man with an impeccable record in the courts. His appointment was received publicly by paeans of praise, and properly so for his legal brilliance and pedigree.

Farris was from a well-heeled, Canadian establishment family. A Farris sat in Canada's first Parliament, another was a cabinet minister in New Brunswick; his father was Vancouver's first prosecutor, a former attorney-general and a labour minister in the provincial government before the federal Liberals made him a senator.

Farris himself graduated from U.B.C. and earned a Harvard law degree before practising at his father's firm. He worked at defence headquarters in Ottawa during the Second World War. Afterwards, he taught commercial law at U.B.C. and became a senior partner in the family firm, Farris, Farris, Vaughan Wills and Murphy. Farris had also served as chairman of the board of Crofton House, one of the city's posh private schools, and been a director of the Toronto-Dominion Bank, B.C. Telephone, Loomis Corp., and the Sun Publishing Co. before becoming chief justice.

The appointment of the tall, distinguished, white-haired lawyer to the province's high court, privately raised eyebrows all over town. After his resignation people would say, "It was only a matter of time."

Farris had had a skeleton rattling around in his closet for years. Then, in September 1978, he made a fatal telephone call to an attractive prostitute named Wendy King. He phoned her at the wrong time on the wrong day. Farris didn't know there was a wiretap on the line. Police were monitoring the calls as part of a lengthy undercover investigation into a Hong Kong heroin deal involving King's boyfriend. They normally ignored the bawdy house calls but the presence of a top judge could jeopardize their investigation if he was on the take or susceptible to blackmail.

The story broke when George Peden, a Devonshire Hotel detective, boasted that he knew of a provincial court judge who was hiring downtown prostitutes, and he had also heard that a Supreme Court judge was also dabbling in the underworld. Peden sent letters to the attorney-general and the media saying such conduct was appalling. He also appeared on open-line shows (not mine!) hinting that the senior judge had been caught on a police drug wiretap, but was being protected. That forced government officials to act.

The provincial court judge, who said he was an alcoholic, confessed almost immediately. He admitted that he had hired a 19-year-old prostitute. But it was a one-time moment of weakness, he said, caused by drunkenness and the stress of caring for his crippled wife who suffered from multiple sclerosis. He claimed Peden spotted him the only time he had ever succumbed to a street-walker's solicitations.

The provincial judicial council, which governs judges' conduct, accepted his explanation and labelled his behaviour a "single moral lapse." The judge spent a year on leave of absence, still receiving his full $35,000-a-year salary, and returned to the bench.

But he was the small fish. Everyone wanted to know about the senior, federally appointed judge who was consorting with hookers.

On November 8, 1978, nearly three months after Farris was identified by police on the wiretap, Ottawa confirmed it was investigating the conduct of B.C.'s top judge. The following day, Farris submitted his resignation.

His letter was circumspect to say the least. "I have been advised that certain allegations against me (not of a criminal nature) have been preferred to the Canadian judicial council for investigation," Farris wrote. "I consider that the mere fact that these allegations have been made, regardless of their substance, has so impaired my usefulness as Chief Justice that it is in the public interest that I resign."

And, because from the moment he resigned he became a mere private citizen, not from that day to this has there been any investigation into the strange circumstances which caused him to flee his job.

It has always bothered me that Farris's conduct was never investigated to establish whether or not the administration of justice had been corrupted as a result of his extra-curricular dalliances. It has also never been adequately explained why was he appointed Chief Justice in the first place, especially since his deviant sexual appetites had been the subject of common gossip for the previous decade!

Farris's predilection for prostitutes became known when a well-known madam, Diana Frew, was arrested in 1960. During the raid on her apartment, police seized nine books listing her customers and their preferences.

Frew's lawyer, the late Nick Mussallem, who was famous for his shabby, tattered legal gown, led reporters on a merry dance during that trial. One week he would titillate our interest by promising to call a flock of big-name witnesses and open the books to the public. The next he would say, "It's going to be guilty pleas. No witnesses, no books, no names. Sorry, boys."

In February 1961, finally, Mussallem marched into court with his client and pleaded guilty. The nine books were entered as exhibits but not read into the court record. Frew got eight months in jail. She later launched a court action in an effort to obtain an income tax deduction for the bribes she claimed to have paid over the years to city and police officials. The court ruled that she could claim the deduction only if she identified those who accepted her bribes. She wouldn't.

After Frew was convicted, I asked if I could see the books containing the customers' names. "Mr. Webster," the magistrate said, "I must warn you that your name might be in the book."

I bristled.

He smiled and said: "Surely, you could see how any astute madam might put names like yours or your colleagues in her records as a form of protection against publication of any names."

He smiled at my bemusement: "You may look at the books. They are public documents but I would appreciate it if you did not tell that to the public, or half the women in town might come down here to check on their husbands' extra-marital activities."

The first name I searched for was my own. It wasn't there.

Farris's was. As a customer, along with many others, but none was as prominent.

Thirty years ago the media was not so bold about broadcasting or printing names in those circumstances. In any case, I was advised against using Farris's name by the station's lawyer. But it's fair to say that after the Frew trial almost every policeman, many lawyers, judges, men about town, rounders and reporters were aware of what can best be described as the colourful sexual preferences of John Farris. He thereafter became the butt of many smirks and jokes.

But Farris crossed the line in September 1978 when he stumbled into the midst of the drug stake-out. The narcotics agents normally paid no attention to the calls for girls in the bawdy house. They were concentrating on the smuggling conspiracy. Then, they heard the call from "John—white haired John."

Later, they watched Farris park his brown cadillac and enter King's apartment building. Police raided the apartment after Farris had left and seized King's address and telephone book.

What followed were a series of urgent meetings involving top-level police and justice department officials in Ottawa. What to do about Farris? His involvement, no matter how innocent, could not be ignored once the drug bust occurred. When the drug trial started, defence lawyers would certainly expose him.

King, an attractive strawberry blonde, a 30-year-old better known as Heather Fortune, Candice Simmons and Wendy Buchanan, was charged with keeping a bawdy house nearly three months after the phone call and raid.

Justice minister Marc Lalonde accepted Farris's resignation and said that ended the investigation into his conduct and marked the end of the case. Lalonde pointed out that sexual relations with a prostitute was not a criminal offence, and that there was no evidence of any criminal involvement on the part of the disgraced judge. B.C. Attorney-General Garde Gardom said the province wouldn't investigate the matter because it was a federal responsibility. The Canadian Judicial Council considered the case closed too, citing its lack of jurisdiction to investigate Farris now that he was a private citizen.

There was no public investigation into Farris's conduct!

All well and good, those who agree with Lalonde's logic might say. But the question to be asked is whether Farris's sexual conduct left him open to blackmail or whether a fear of exposure over the years might have influenced his exercise of judicial discretion?

Is a lesson to be learned, in the public interest, from the Farris case? The authorities told us time and time again that the moment he resigned and became a private citizen the judicial council had no jurisdiction to penalize him or investigate the matter. But I have since learned that the attorney-general of B.C., who rejected a probe because the matter involved a federal judge, argued privately that a proffered judicial resignation not be accepted until a decision is made for or against a public inquiry. Then, the public could see that justice had been done.

Not only was there no public inquiry into Farris's activity, but when Wendy King eventually pleaded guilty to the bawdy house charge, the judge ordered that both her little brown notebook, containing about eight hundred names, and the wiretap warrant be sealed.

I can tell you that there were many sighs of relief in downtown business offices that day because I myself had been asked a half a dozen times by individuals who had been customers, if I knew whether their names were in the book.

King was fined $1,500, placed on probation for nine months and ordered to complete two hundred hours of community service, preferably among senior citizens. It was her first offence. In the associated drug trial, her boyfriend was sentenced to seventeen years in prison for his role in the $4-million heroin conspiracy that began in January 1976 and ended with the seizure of four pounds of the drug.

On my morning program on BCTV—where I ran a persistent campaign for a full-scale probe—I found it next to impossible to get B.C. lawyers to go on the air to discuss the case. No one from the B.C. Law Society and no one from the B.C. Branch of the Canadian Bar Association was willing to talk about it.

The only two lawyers who did appear and discuss the issues with me frankly were John Fraser, MP, now Speaker of the House of Commons, and Stuart Leggatt, MP, now a B.C. Supreme Court judge. Bless them.

One other factor which still disturbs me is that after Farris resigned from the bench he applied in January 1979 for re-admission to the Law Society, which was granted without any inquiry. A lawyer to be a member of the society must meet two criteria: he must possess a valid degree and be of good repute. Farris's re-admission violated those requirements. I hope it would not happen today.

A chill ran down my spine one day when Premier Bill Bennett came to my studio not long after Farris quit. He said to me: "By the way Jack, I met a man the other day who wanted to kill you."

"Who might that be?" I asked innocently.

"John Farris!"

Farris practised law in the back-room of a big law firm until he died. I was fairly naïve in the 1960s and it was a shock to learn of such a prominent man's bad habits. But there was no excuse for his appointment to the British Columbia Court of Appeal. There's no doubt in my mind that he was shielded for many years because of his stature and position. The authorities knew about his sexual peculiarities and his perversions when he was appointed. If I knew, they knew. And they did. They simply turned a blind eye.

Farris was a black mark on our system of justice. Had the me-

dia not hammered away at his conduct, he might not have resigned.

For me, morality comes first in public life and in private. You
do what your conscience dictates and damn the consequences.
Yes, maybe sometimes I do come off sounding like a Victorian
prig. But I have no time for hypocrites or those without a moral
spine. Especially in public life.

I gave up doing lucrative commercials for the real-estate firm,
Block Brothers, when the New Democratic Party government
began debating the Agricultural Land Reserve. Dropping Block
Brothers cost me $20,000 a year!

Later, when my ownership of a tax shelter in a pulp company
was questioned during a debate on logging in B.C., I divested
myself of those shares too—at a loss.

It is perhaps because of my screaming insistence over the
years that anyone in public life not just be clean, but must appear to be clean, that I became so upset at my friend Allan
Fotheringham.

Years ago, he christened me Haggis McBagpipe, the Mouth
that Roared and, worst of all, Glasgow Fats. It was as if he believed I was some kind of kilted, claymore-wielding invader!
And embarrassingly, he forced me to corner the Saltspring Island market on one issue of *Maclean's* magazine.

I had happened to be in Ottawa for my sixty-fifth birthday,
and invited a few friends up to my room for a drink. It was a
great party. The star performers as a singing duo were Charlie
Lynch and Webster. Hundreds came, it seemed. I spent most of
the night ordering drinks and clubhouse sandwiches, cut into
very small portions. The room-service bill was $887!

At 5 A.M. when the smoke cleared, two guests were left in the
room: a famous broadcaster attempting to give mouth-to-mouth
resuscitation to a woman passed out on my bed. I rescued her
and escorted her home.

Foth was not at the party, but he duly reported it in one of his back-page magazine columns, complete with caricature of me holding a sheep. I learned of the forthcoming article and grew worried about Fotheringham's description of the events and Margaret's reaction to them.

Maclean's is delivered on Wednesdays on Saltspring and, as the store opened, I was on the doorstep to buy all fourteen copies. The story was only a trifle embarrassing. It accurately quoted my room service bill and attributed to me the thought, "Here I am at 65 trying to get a woman out of my bed instead of into it!"

I showed it to Margaret. She forced a smile.

Fotheringham, whose ability with words I greatly admire, is forever using his friends as grist for his column. But that isn't what bothered me. It was his attack on my involvement in the Clifford Olson case.

In his book, *Birds of a Feather*, Fotheringham accuses the publishers of the *Sun* and the *Province* and me of being part of a conspiracy at the request of Attorney-General Alan Williams to suppress information. While Olson was on the loose, Fotheringham claimed, the Mounties had a deal with him that he would be paid money for information leading them to the burial site of the child killer's victims. "The longer he bargained and the more he killed the more money he got," according to Fotheringham. "It was to Olson's advantage to kill more before he was taken in. . . . "

Garbage!

What idiot would make a deal to allow a murderer to remain free to kill children and earn $10,000 a body? No one! And no one did! Fotheringham not only got the year of Olson's killings wrong, he misconstrued other facts, too! A simple phone call to any of us involved in the discussions with Attorney-General Williams would have clarified the situation for Dr. Foth.

Olson was arrested in August of 1981 and police had no evidence against him or any information tying him to several killings and disappearances save the fact that one victim's name was written into his telephone-address book. After a week of intensive interrogation, Olson offered a deal. Police accepted in the hope that they would be able to trick him and solve the killings. At no time was Olson free to kill after his arrest. At no time while he was free, did the media or anyone else agree to suppress information!

Yes, the attorney-general asked me and the publishers of the two major newspapers to keep the deal secret after it was struck. But all we agreed to do was remain mum until Olson's right to a fair trial had been respected. After the sentencing, we were free to publish or broadcast all that we knew.

That's the way it was.

Over the years, I think I was only guilty of one libel—when I inadvertently during a broadcast allowed a guest to label a lawyer a drunk. Afterwards, I grovelled all over the floor apologizing to the chap but he wasn't amused.

The station's lawyers were very slow in attempting to settle the matter with him and it hung over me like the sword of Damocles. The station offered him an insulting $1,200 settlement. I finally asked a friend to go see him and ask how much he wanted.

"$10,000," came the reply.

I had the documents prepared and paid the money out of my own pocket.

Whenever I was wrong, I hope I corrected it promptly. After all, such was the conduct I demanded of politicians and other public figures.

I guess that's why of all the journalists I have known, Marjorie Nichols remains my favourite. From the moment we met during the FLQ crisis, through her years in B.C. as the most trenchant provincial political columnist, she was indomitable.

Marjorie's moral fibre is unbending. There is no grey in her book, only black and white. I think that's why she and Margaret got along so well. Margaret was much more moralistic than even I am. For years, she and Marjorie would talk on the telephone no matter where Marjorie was in the country. She was one of the few friends I had after Wasserman died with whom Margaret could still relate.

I always appreciated that.

Even today, under the stress of ongoing cancer treatments, Marjorie amazes me. She continues her column, chastising and admonishing those politicians who sacrifice principle to expediency. Her outrage remains fierce, her damnation eternal.

I remember David Barrett, while he was premier, emerging from the Legislature and calling her a "venomous bitch!"

Where I would simply have replied in kind, Marjorie remained calm, went back to the press gallery and bashed out a column that excoriated Barrett for his bush-league behaviour. I don't think she ever forgave him for his rude, ill-tempered remark. When Barrett ran for the federal NDP leadership years later, she was only too happy to remind voters of his flaws as premier of B.C.

That's what I like about Marjorie. She has character. And more than anything else, that is how I measure people, be it Trudeau, Mulroney, the highest public official in the land, or those I call my friends. It is how we act, how we decide what is right and what is wrong that matters. And it doesn't take a genius or a Jesuit to figure that out: all it takes is just a bit of common sense, a dash of decency and a dollop of fairness.

CHAPTER 15

"The petitioners call upon this House to make sure that Mr. Webster's personal vendetta against native rights and environmental groups . . . is brought to his attention."

NDP MP JIM FULTON

● Jack Munro has been my closest friend since Wasserman. That was why I was relieved to see him the night Margaret died. I can't think of anyone else to whom I could have unburdened myself. We have been friends since the mid-1970s when he came to the coast from the Interior of B.C. as a vice-president of the International Woodworkers of America.

We sat until just before dawn that night in 1985, and he listened to my stories. I have a few regrets, but none that can eclipse the incredible richness and joy that has punctuated my life. Munro and I reminisced about the moments we had shared and how quickly time passes.

Munro and I cemented our friendship while I was still in Gastown working for CJOR. Tom Fawkes, the union's press advisor, and I had chatted the day before a show on which Munro would be appearing. "This program is only half an hour, Tom," I told him, "and we haven't got time to get Munro warmed up, so what can you tell me to get him mad right away? If he's mad, we'll have a better program."

Fawkes let me in on a couple of issues that would incite Munro, which assured me of an anything-but-boring broadcast. But, unbeknownst to me, on the way to the studio, Fawkes warned Munro.

The broadcast began and Munro launched into me, saying he "wouldn't take any more BS from a haggis-eater." I was dumbfounded. I was prepared to confront him with a little speech and was caught completely by surprise. Since then, we have become close friends.

"I was a little afraid of you, Jack," Munro told me the night of Margaret's death, "so I had Tom come with me to help me out. He knew that I was worried about the show and a little insecure."

"Come on, afraid of me! I never intimidated anyone in my life."

"You beat the hell out of me two or three times when I'd come on."

No wonder Fawkes let him in on the ambush—Munro was the guy who signed his pay cheque!

I laughed.

During one of our confrontations, Munro had stood up on the set, towering over me. "Stand up Webster, you little pipsqueak!" he bellowed. "People think you're as tall as me. Stand up and let them see what a midget you really are!"

Munro is nearly a foot taller than me, an imposing six-foot-four, and he weighs some 265 pounds. But we both looked the same size on television when we were sitting down behind a desk.

"I think both of us being Scotch gives us this natural affinity," Munro told me. "When you first came to this country you put out the *Lumber Worker*. So there was always an affinity there. You came to our conventions and always had time to talk to the local presidents, tell them how to improve their media relations. You knew the IWA, knew it from the inside, knew how it worked."

I'll never forget the day we were fishing at Port Alberni, just after a big plant had been closed in New Westminster. A boat came alongside and a guy leaned over and yelled: "Let's see what you can do now, Webster! I've just been laid off. I've got twenty-four years' seniority in the IWA, but there's no way I'll get another job as long as I live because of the job loss brought about by technological change."

There was nothing I could say to the man. He was right. The union in the last decade has seen its membership cut in half. And those are the people I worry about. I don't worry about the Yuppies and the up-and-ups. I don't worry about them at all! It's the average guy, the man with a regular job, a wife and a couple of kids, who is trying to make ends meet. It's him I care about.

"That's what the IWA always appreciated," Munro said, as we talked the night away. "You didn't take cheap shots at us because we were 'Big Labour.' Your show was a vehicle for us, really the only one we had to get our position out, to tell our side of the story. We went through some tough times and Webster was an important part in getting the workers' side across. And I think you helped me get recognized by a lot of people. Everywhere I go in this country people still know me from the Webster show, even on the east coast of Canada where they only received the show on satellite."

It bothers me that everyone wants a white-collar, government job. Who has the best pensions and benefits—MPS and civil servants! Plus, they get enormous expense accounts to hire staff and researchers. It's incredible when you compare it to the life of the ordinary person. You never see a row in the House of Commons or the Legislatures about MPS' increases. One of them will make the grand gesture and he won't take it. But they're living high off the hog. It's bloody awful.

Munro once said to me: "Sometimes I get really put off with you when you have Trudeau on," he said. "You let him give you a hard time. He's responsible for the mess the country is in yet he's the only guy that gives you a hard time in an interview."

I plead not guilty.

Munro and I shared a lot of good times. We were both invited to dine with the Queen in 1983 on the royal yacht *Britannia*. It was one of the worst meals I ever had, over-cooked, tasteless English cuisine. I think the main course was canned boneless turkey. It was hard to tell—everything tasted like it had come out of a tin.

"You were in your glory, though," Munro said. "You arrived at my house an hour and a half before we needed to leave and you were so excited and nervous about being late we had an hour and fifteen minutes to kill by the time we got downtown. We went for a drink at the Hotel Vancouver and the first thing you said to the bartender was, 'Give Munro one single drink. *No more.*'"

It was one of my great heartbreaks that I was never able to take Margaret. Knowing how she felt about the royals, she would have loved it. But her mood swings were so frequent, and they occurred without warning, that I didn't want to take the chance that the invitation would trigger another bout of instability.

Despite the food, I loved state dinners. I attended one dinner as the date of former federal cabinet minister and close friend, Patricia Carney. She was the official federal escort for the royal couple, so at dinner we sat very close to her majesty and the Duke of Edinburgh.

I was on my very best behaviour. "By the way, sir," I said to Prince Phillip when the appropriate moment arrived, "did you know we are about to choose a bird emblem for British Columbia?"

"Interesting," Phillip, a wildlife lover, dryly replied. "What choices do you have?"

"We're thinking of the Steller's jay, the peregrine falcon or the raven."

"Surely not the raven," he said. "That's a garbage bird. Choose the falcon."

I told him politely that the raven was particularly important in B.C. because of its mythological place in the province's aboriginal culture. "Besides," I said brightly, "I've lost more newborn lambs on my farm on Saltspring to ravens than I have to falcons!"

As they readied to leave the table that night, the Queen turned to Phillip and said: "Where's my handbag?"

"There on the floor," he said a little too curtly.

"Well pick it up!" she snapped. And he did. Just like any of the rest of us would have.

Munro's been over to the farm more than a few times to help me out. "That was where I saw you most frightened," he told me the night Margaret died. "You were giving your two little grandchildren, Bobby and Jessica, a ride on that John Deere tractor, rolling along in low gear. You tried to change gears on the hill and it began to roll out of control.

"I watched the damn thing roll down the hill, going faster and faster, running down that trail alongside the gulley, high above the creek. I was sure it was going to be a disaster." The tractor went over the edge, hit a tree and careened into another. If the bucket hadn't slammed into a stump and flipped the tractor, it would have gone over the embankment. "It was a bloody miracle the kids weren't killed along with you, Webster."

Munro was right. I still have the scars on my shins, and I'm still thankful someone was watching over me that day. I guess because we'd shared moments like that, I was happy to see him at the hospital that night. He was someone I could talk to, with whom I could share my feelings. We sat long into the night, reminiscing.

"I regret not having retired in 1978," I told him. "I could

have spent more time with her. I always expected we would retire to the farm."

"Jack, you can't think like that," Munro said. "You're being
too hard on yourself. You did the best you could in the circumstances. Everyone has a regret or two."

He's right. When you look back, everything seems so much
clearer, the right road is clearly marked, the pitfalls patently obvious. I made a few mistakes, but I hope I learned from them.
Certainly the reunion with my daughter Joan in 1972 was a personal revelation that changed how I saw my wife and our relationship. If I had been selfish in the beginning, I did the best I
could to make her last years happy.

Margaret's funeral was conducted in the Presbyterian Church
in West Vancouver. It was a nice service. My daughter Linda
wrote a piece so the minister would get it right. Margaret was
buried in Capilano View Cemetery where we had bought two
plots years ago. My old friend, Ian Millman, of the Vancouver
Police Pipe Band, played "Amazing Grace." Then, we all went
back to the house.

I lost some of my enthusiasm for work with Margaret's death.
I could still get excited about big stories, but it was harder and
harder. I like to think I was always a plain reporter with colourful opinions, possibly known to give them sometimes. But in the
public's eyes I had become a bigger celebrity than most of the
people I was interviewing. And, my style and attitudes were becoming more and more out of step. Shortly after Margaret's
death, the climax of the controversy over logging in the Queen
Charlotte Islands brought that home to me.

Munro got me involved in that issue, but it was too late to
save the jobs of his members. The best we could do was win
them a stay of execution. Munro elicited my help at the end of a
television program. He handed me a letter from the IWA local in

South Moresby and urged me to open it and read it on air. I did.

The letter from the loggers said they were about to lose their jobs because the Social Credit government would not give their company, Frank Beban Logging, the cutting permits needed to harvest the trees on Lyell Island.

The island was the flashpoint in an ongoing debate about the future of that misty archipelago near the Alaska Panhandle, off B.C.'s northern coast. The Haida Indians wanted logging halted because they claimed the land belonged to them. Environmentalists were against logging because South Moresby was cloaked in virgin forest and the Queen Charlotte Islands were an Eden on earth. The forest companies protested that they had been granted licences to harvest the timber on Lyell Island, had been harvesting it for more than seventy years, and were dependent on that wood supply for economic survival. The provincial and federal governments were wrestling with the quandary and had simply let the cutting permits expire, leaving the lumber company without legal authorization to harvest the wood in the southern third of the archipelago.

I promised to come up and look at the situation.

"That was just great for us," Munro later told me. "Not just for the guys on Lyell Island, but for a hell of a lot of workers throughout the province who thought, finally, here is a guy willing to put physical effort into something a lot of people just talk about: protecting jobs. The great sense of warmth for you, Jack, that came from the guys was incredible."

I started my mini-documentary by standing on a spruce stump in the middle of a vast wasteland of clear-cut logging on Lyell Island. "I'm standing on a tree stump nearly twelve-feet across," I intoned. "It stood two hundred feet tall and if it hadn't been cut down, it would have fallen down. It was an old spruce. Don't kid yourself that when you cut down the one hundred hectares you see behind me that you can make it like Stanley Park tomorrow."

Then I went around and interviewed Frank Beban, union officials, the Indians, the school marm and the people who lived on the islands. I decided the workers, many of whom were Haida, deserved a job and I hollered on their behalf.

From my vantage point, logging on Lyell Island really only offended the well-heeled anthropological researchers on university grants who visited the remote islands on freebie junkets. The Haida would have logged the place too! But the professional tree-huggers and affluent academics were upset because they could hear the whistlepunks when they sailed near Lyell Island and—God forbid!—they could actually see clear-cut logging areas! Here they were living on fancy little yachts at $1,700 per head a week, and throwing up over the side because of this rape of nature. I was disgusted.

I make no excuses for the old "cut-and-get-out" policies of the companies large and small. But at least they acknowledge the error of their ways. Those days, I hope, are gone, and no small thanks to the more sensible environmentalists, too. Survival of the industry, the veritable base of B.C.'s economy, depends on the intelligent harvesting of the crops of trees. I get very angry when I see a former federal cabinet minister declaim after a flight over the coastal forests that the devastation reminds him of the "semi-arid deserts of Ethiopia."

The days of major clear-cuts have gone. Silviculture and replanting is catching up. Helicopter and high-lead logging will stop some of the devastation caused by road-building and erosion.

I was the first reporter to focus on the jobs being wiped out. Don't get me wrong: I, too, am in favour of preserving much of Moresby Island as irreplaceable primeval forest. But for God's sake, the people who were buying $26,000 advertisements in *The Globe and Mail* should realize that the forest industry is dependent on tree farm licences in the Charlottes and elsewhere.

British Columbia was in a disastrous state during the early

and mid 1980s. I tried to tell people that. The loss of forest industry jobs had crippled the provincial economy and the further loss of timber supply was jeopardizing too many other jobs.

There were few problems in booming central Canada, where most of the pressure to stop logging was based. In those days, they had eight percent unemployment, while ours stood at fourteen percent. I was not about to stand idly by and let Eastern bleeding hearts steal the very basis of our forest economy. Without the trees, B.C. is in real trouble.

I didn't have to conjure up that indignation, even though I was one of the most highly paid broadcasters in Canada. I can't forget my working class origins. I will always take the average worker's point of view.

No one wants to cut down a tree, but if we stop cutting down trees some of us will starve to death. It's all very well and good to have a service economy and have tourists, but if this blind, save-every-tree movement continues, the loss of an industry that pays well and provides good benefits will leave many of us sitting on the corner selling Lotto tickets or working at some hamburger joint earning minimum wage.

My diatribe convinced the Social Credit government to issue the cutting permits to Frank Beban logging. But not long after the loggers got back to work, the Haida Indians blockaded Lyell Island.

Dressed in their traditional costumes, they erected pickets on the logging road. The confrontation ended in a number of Haida and Svend Robinson, a federal member of the NDP trying to capitalize on the dispute, being charged with contempt. Everyone was acquitted but Robinson, who was fined $750 for his participation in an illegal picket line. The Indians christened him "White Swan," because of his help.

"White Swan," what nonsense! I'm sick and tired of the native rights issue. Canada's aboriginal peoples should be just like the rest of us: full citizens with no special privileges or rights.

Yes, they deserve to be compensated for the land and resources appropriated by white society. But that deal should have been struck years ago by the politicians. That successive federal and provincial governments have passed the buck and refused to solve the problem is ridiculous. Leaving the decision to the courts, which is what is happening, not only is increasing tremendously the final cost of settling land claims, but also is an abrogation of responsibility. It should be settled so natives, industry and everyone else affected are treated fairly and we can all get on with the job of building a stronger, more humane and more economically sound country.

But Jim Fulton, the NDP member for Skeena, and a resident of the Queen Charlottes, lambasted me in the House of Commons for daring to speak out for the loggers. He even presented a petition attacking my reporting. "The petitioners call upon this House to make sure that Mr. Webster's personal vendetta against native rights and environmental groups, his fomenting of trouble and creating an atmosphere of hostility, is brought to his attention," Fulton said.

"You're always blaming the press," Speaker Ray Hnatyshyn said, dismissing Fulton.

In the end, however, the federal government sided with the Indians and environmentalists. The southern Queen Charlottes was reserved for a national park. I took the defeat badly. I said to Munro at the time, "Maybe I made a mistake."

"Bullshit! You didn't have any egg on your face as far as the workers were concerned," he said. "The media very easily slide into all these environmental, slippery slope arguments that if we don't save every square foot of wilderness, the planet is doomed. There can be rational, sustainable harvesting of the forests. You were the only guy who the workers felt tried to help us. Maybe we waited too late to appeal to you."

I appreciated that. Frank Beban, who was a personable, burly logger, died of a heart attack shortly after the park reserve was announced. I believe it was because of the stress he suffered during all those years of fighting to keep his workers employed.

I left television not long after that program, on May 1, 1987, at 5 P.M. precisely! After eight years of doing "Webster!" from 9 A.M. to 10 A.M., the program had moved to its supper hour location the previous year. That turned out to be its most successful time slot. I drew an average of 170,000 viewers over the sixty minutes of the show.

My final program was a ninety-minute special that featured highlights of my nine years on the tube and endless congratulations from the famous and not-so famous. I think most of the politicians were happy just to see me go!

Prime Minister Brian Mulroney called:

"Jack, British Columbia is going to be a different place without your voice—the whole country for that matter. For one thing, it's going to be an awful lot quieter," he said, sounding as if he were reading the prepared farewell for the first time. "B.C. never had to worry about being heard on this side of the mountains as long as you were on the air. Your message was always loud and clear. Sometimes a little louder than we wanted maybe. I've still got a few souvenirs on my own hide from our times together on the Webster show. But I've got to admit that where you gave us a few licks, we probably deserved it. And you were always impartial. You were rough on everybody.

"And Jack, if all of this praise has been embarrassing for you, I do have one final complaint: Why couldn't you in all these years have learned to speak at least one of our official languages?"

I appreciated the sentiment.

Opposition Liberal leader John Turner, NDP leader Ed Broadbent and B.C. Premier Vander Zalm all called to wish me well.

Svend Robinson, White Swan himself, called. He had been

the subject of the interview over which I received the most criti-
cism. During our earlier verbal sparring, I asked Robinson
where the NDP stood on street prostitution. I bullied him, demanding he answer 'yes' or 'no' to the question, "would your
party wipe out the bawdy house section of the criminal code
and legalize brothels?"

When he continued to reasonably explain that the present
laws weren't working and needed to be changed, I turned my
back on him. As the camera showed him talking to the back of
my head, I loudly insisted: "Answer the question—yes or no!"

Robinson finally conceded that he believed his party would
reform the laws and decriminalize prostitution. So upset was
NDP leader Ed Broadbent with the controversy that Robinson's
statement ignited that he temporarily stripped him of his role as
the party's justice critic.

I felt badly about the episode and was surprised when Robinson appeared via a remote link-up on my last program to wish
me well. In a deadpan, he said he had heard that I was retiring
to run a bawdy house on my farm at Saltspring. "Goodbye," he
concluded, than slowly he spun around on his chair so his back
faced the camera.

Fair's fair!

Singers k. d. lang and Anne Murray both called and offered
me a job as a backup vocalist. Earlier, when they had appeared
on my program, I had sung impromptu duets with each. I was
entranced by the Canadian Snowbird, but lang literally overwhelmed me. With her glassless spectacles, holes in her shoes,
and the demeanour of an ingenue, she captivated me. I even
taught her a silly Webster song from Scotland!

From Los Angeles, actor Michael J. Fox telephoned and
promised "if things get a little tight in a couple of years, I'll be
glad to help you out." Bryan Adams called to wish me well, too.

Fox was a Burnaby boy who first appeared on my program

simply because his parents were huge fans of mine and he thought it would be a giggle. Adams came on after we had had a rip-roaring discussion about politics at a lunch arranged by his manager, Bruce Allen, at Umberto Menghi's Al Porto in Gastown. Allen and I went back to my days at CJOR and we've always got along. He's the only man I can think of who was louder than both Wasserman and me!

It was a toss-up between Fox and Adams for most popular Webster guest of all-time. B.C. Tel said the number of calls that were made to my program by viewers wanting to talk to the two B.C. superstars caused their switching system to seize up. It was at moments like that that I realized how out of touch I was from today's generation of kids. Imagine, tens of thousands of young people out there who will remember me only as that old guy with a Scotch accent who interviewed rock singers!

My pal Pat Carney sent her two-cents worth as well. "He was a grouch thirty years ago, and he's a grouch now. But underneath it all he's just a sweetie-pie."

People asked why I was getting out of daily broadcasting. I hated that question. "This is not a requiem for Webster. It was just time for a change," I assured everyone. But the bottom line was I was 68 years old and bushed!

I had won most major broadcasting awards in Canada, including thee Can-Pro Awards, an Actra Award, a Canadian Association of Broadcasters award and a special award for courageous conduct for my role in the prison riot in 1963. I have been inducted into the Canadian News Hall of Fame and I have received honourary law degrees from the University of British Columbia and Simon Fraser University.

There was even a Jack Webster Foundation, sparked by a Canadian Club tribute dinner in 1986, and a trust fund to reward excellence in reporting, print and electronic, with cash awards and an annual dinner held to maintain the funding.

I thought they only named those funds after dead people, but I'm certainly not dead yet.

But I do think I was burned out towards the end. I wanted to spend time with my grandchildren and I wanted to relax. I didn't really care anymore if something was happening and I wasn't there.

Shirley MacLaine, my second love, was one of the few people towards the end who could always rouse me from that ennui. When she called from Denver to wish me good luck on my final show, I was weak in the knees. Yet, I had to be coaxed into the first interview I did with her in December 1978.

Then, she sat in front of the camera, gorgeous, glamorous and totally uncommunicative. She had me talking for the first two minutes because all she would say was 'Yes,' or 'No.' Finally she said, "You remind me of a cross between Archie Bunker and my father."

There is a physical resemblance between me and Carroll O'Connor.

But suddenly MacLaine leaned forward with a kleenex, put her hand on my knee and wiped the sweat from my brow as she continued: "You bring out the most extraordinary maternal instincts in me. I really could just come right over there onto your lap and tell you all the things you want to make you happy."

"That's enough," I stammered, leaking profusely from the forehead.

She giggled seductively, "Enjoying it?"

I was the colour of beetroot.

Only a few months before Margaret's death, we met again. I pretended to chide her for her previous performance. "You went out of your way to embarrass me to death," I began.

MacLaine just started to giggle.

"She started in monosyllables," I reminded the audience in mock chagrin. "She called me a cross between Archie Bunker and her father and then she made advances to me that caused me to sweat profusely. I trust you're going to act your age to-day."

She looked at the camera and laughed.

"You haven't changed, you haven't grown, you haven't realized a thing," she said. "You're worse than Archie Bunker . . . I'm glad to hear you've given up drinking."

She smiled warmly.

"You do look beautiful today," I said.

"It's my spiritual guide shining through."

"What are you, nudging 52 now?"

"Yes."

"For 52, you look smashing," I said, eyes atwinkle. I looked and sounded like a small boy in love.

"Anything would look smashing to you," she quipped.

I forged ahead. "There was a guy in your autobiography [*Out on a Limb*] to whom I took an intense dislike," I told her.

"My lover Gerry," she said without batting an eye. "Of course, you would."

"Why would I?" I said taken aback.

"Because you want to be my lover so anyone who got there first you would have a disposition against."

What do you say to that? I surrendered. From then on, our relationship on camera exuded warmth. She was right. In another place or another time, who knows?

"Will you put a little cloud of light around me to keep me happy and content for the next year?" I asked her.

"How can life be cloudy, Jack?" she said. "There are no clouds if it's light. It's perfectly crystal clear—absolutely. I've been doing that since I met you, since I fell in love with you five years ago, since I spoke about you from the stage. You have been in my conscious mind. Now you are rattling about with me in my super-conscious mind and I am convinced that in one incarnation you were probably a Roman Emperor and had your way with me."

"Excuse me while I swoon," I managed.

"You're very sexy," she said.

How's that for a reference!

"Shirley, Shirley, Shirley," I sang on my farewell show upon hearing her voice.

"Don't slobber all over yourself," she admonished. "I understand your love life has got so exhausting that you're retiring to take a rest."

"To take it up full time, you mean, you fool," I retorted. "You had the opportunity and you rejected me."

"Can I have a second chance?" she asked.

"Only in a second life."

Ain't it the truth!

EPILOGUE

"There's two things bother me. Jack gets far too much money for talking on the wireless, and I'd like to know where the devil he got that accent."

WILLIAM 'WULLIE' WEBSTER

● I think my children are proud of their old man. I didn't want any of them to follow me into the media. And they didn't. Linda became a librarian with the provincial government. Jenny is a housewife in North Vancouver. Jack is a lawyer in Vancouver. Joan, a graduate pharmacist, lives in England with her family. I am proud of all of them.

I didn't want them to pursue journalism because there are easier ways to make more money than this one. I wouldn't put my best friend through it when I look back on it. Oh, it was good fun. And the more the trouble, the better the fun.

I think Talk Radio has been a terrific development. It's a therapy and rehabilitation, cathartic and informative. There's no such thing as a bad talk show. But some *are* better than others. All are relief valves for society.

Current events are infinitely easier to understand when considered translated through Talk Radio. The informal interview followed by an open-line question and answer session is a far superior format than structured news programs or lectures. Unquestionably, the format allows listeners and viewers to identify more with the newsmakers. The hemming and hawing, the quips and banter, humanizes public figures, and the telephone allows the audience to participate. It's the interactive use of the medium that holds its greatest democratic promise.

But the strength of the form is also its weakness. Give most people a soap box and their first instinct is to rail and complain. They talk about the doctor who's never available, the rude policeman who gave them a ticket, the welfare cheat who lives in the same apartment building, the judge who took away their children. Talk shows give people a chance to blame everyone else for their problems while avoiding their own responsibility.

Newspaper editorials don't reach the ordinary people. When it came to rent control, private automobile insurance companies or the scandals over the lack of care for retarded children, it was the open lines that changed the complexion of B.C.

I was a pioneer in information. No matter what government was in power, if there was a new policy or initiative, that was meat for me. Providing straightforward information was a necessary part of the program. I reviewed every piece of new legislation, translated it into language people could understand and then tested it to see whether it met the requirements of good, common sense.

Not all the interviews I did lanced the egos of puffed up politicians or exposed the shenanigans of professional shysters. Some were pure entertainment, and they always posed the biggest problems for me. I liked to be hard-nosed. Subtlety is a skill I never quite managed to master.

Once I established a little bit of a reputation, my great strength in radio and television was that the big shots and the politicians were always willing to return. I don't think I was ever turned down for a second appearance. Mainly, they came back because my program was invaluable for anybody with a particular message to spread because I didn't edit, mainly because ninety percent of my shows were live.

I worried from time to time about politicians talking over my head, trying to speak directly to the audience and avoid my questions. But I would jump on them and bring them back to sanity every now and then.

I knew the world was changing one day in the 1960s when I was daydreaming during an interview with a doctor. I was watching the clock, thinking that the doctor was getting reasonably good questions from intelligent younger women. Suddenly I hear the words "vaginal itch."

"What!" I thought, perking up instantly. But I let it go, and probably asked a question about it myself. I realized the world had become a different place. Nowadays, they talk about everything. But in those days. . . .

I have Malcolm Lowry's roll-top desk at the farm. I've had it for more than twenty years. Einar Nielsen, a friend of Lowry who lived on Bowen Island, phoned me one night and said it was in a beach shack in which Lowry used to drink and write. It was at the bottom of a cliff so a friend of mine climbed down, pulled the desk apart and hauled it up. I had it refinished and it's in good shape.

I fantasized for a long time that I would write my book on it. I joked about it in one of my last programs. Using the smoke-and-mirrors technology of television, viewers saw a normal Jack Webster behind his desk across from another Webster, this one wearing a cravat and a poofy jacket. He was my caricature of a writer. And I, as Webster the interrogator, gave myself a hard time for being the author of "Terror in the Name of Talk."

It was great fun, but I found shortly after I retired that I had no burning desire to leave words for posterity. There was still the old egomania up to a point. But it was a question of going through the flotsam and jetsam of a lifetime in media. Thousands and thousands of stories; heck, more than 800 separate clips from the "Webster!" television show alone were used on evening newscasts!

I've read a lot of books but I'm a skip reader, down the

middle of the page. Newspapers, magazines, that's what I love. I have not been taken with intellectual pursuits. Honest! But I could keep up a conversation with the world's greatest architect or have great fun with Marshall McLuhan.

When I was in the Sudan they called me 'Abu Killam Kitir', the father of much talking. Which was a delightful piece of prophecy, looking back on my career.

I think that was the problem after Margaret died: Talk is so god-damn ephemeral! It evaporates immediately, leaving no residue and rarely any identifiable effect. I wondered during that final year on television whether any of it was really worth anything. What did all those years of yelling and complaining accomplish? I'm still not really sure.

For the first part of my career I was active; for the latter part I basically sat in a studio. The news came to me. Occasionally I did a walk-about, interviewing everyday people at the scene of a newsworthy event, a picket line, or maybe a major construction site such as the Revelstoke Dam. My relationship with most of the guests, to whom people presumed I was close, was short and sweet. They came, were interviewed and left. Rarely did I socialize with them or develop friendships. There wasn't time.

My father was once asked on my open-line show what he thought of my career. "There's two things bother me," Dad replied. "Jack gets far too much money for talking on the wireless, and I'd like to know where the devil he got that accent."

I swear I did not annually return to Scotland to broaden it! I plead guilty on his first point. It was crazy, my father thought, that the prime minister earned less than a professional talker!

My political analysis was always straightforward. I have no time for those who speak like bureaucrats and worry about arcane legalisms. I am more interested in the hurly-burly of daily life, the give and take of the politics of the present. I am not much for shades of grey. I, too, see things in black and white.

Throughout my career, I tried to emphasize my belief in the

power of persuasion and the value of an honestly held opinion. I guess I believe in talk, talk, talk. It is in communicating with each other that we bridge our differences.

I believe that if I influenced events it was solely with the force of my opinion, not the size of my stick. If there is one thing my life has confirmed it's the power of opinion. Not the pen, not the microphone, but the simple, honest to God, heartfelt conviction that one person *can* bring about change. And with the perspective retirement has given me, I am proud of that. It is not a cure for cancer, or a solution to world hunger. But it is a message that should never be forgotten.

Talk Radio and Television Talk have restored a measure of practical democracy. They provide a forum for discussion and debate.

It was tackling issues on a day-to-day basis, hopefully contributing to public understanding of complex matters from the economy to complicated labour disputes, that I made my mark. Occasionally, the right question at the right time produced a minor miracle or broke a log jam.

Talk media release pressure no other institutional forum can vent. It is the best form of communication ever developed for ordinary people. Look at them all now. They sneered at me. Especially my colleagues. Now, what do you have on CBC Newsworld? What do you have on CNN? Talk radio with pictures. The whole thing has exploded and is here to stay.

I believe in the power of strongly held opinion, forcibly argued, to bring about change. If I was wrong, I admitted it. I hope that I was a slave to neither rhetoric nor ratings, that I was humble in victory and contrite in defeat. Although, I don't think I was any more successful than anyone else in achieving that ideal.

I could have gone back to daily radio or television at any time during the past few years, but I didn't want to. What was it that is said about an unexamined life not being worth living? I wanted time to consider what I had done and to judge whether the sacrifices had been worth it.

I think they were.

Still, I couldn't tell you how the bottom line on the balance sheet of my life reads. That will be for someone else to tally when I'm gone. Until then, there is time yet to tilt at new windmills, and I have found renewed vigour in retirement.

Since leaving the cut and thrust of the daily media, I have traded my unofficial ombudsman's hat and accepted an appointment as a lay bencher of the Law Society of British Columbia. I have always believed strongly that lawyers receive such status within our society, that those who do not live up to the highest standards should be punished severely.

During my career, I regularly crossed swords with law societies in Canada—which discipline the profession—over issues such as the public's right to know about crooked barristers and the punishments they received. I feel very strongly that where there is any defalcation or misuse of trust funds, that the offending lawyer be permanently excluded from the legal profession.

No one expects all lawyers to be perfect, but they enjoy incredible privilege as officers of the court and members of a self-governing and self-disciplining society. It would not be human if they did not have a subconscious conflict of interest in defence of their closed-shop 'trade union.' With the vast increase in numbers of lawyers and the fairly new conscientiousness in handling today's much more sophisticated complaints, I predict that independent tribunals will be appointed to handle punishment decisions.

Until then, I will continue to nip at the heels of B.C. lawyers from my position as a lay bencher.

When all is said and done, Margaret's illness became paradoxically the source of my sorrow and my strength. If it hadn't been for the brutal discipline her ordeal imposed on my life, I would not have made it. There were too many temptations along the road. With her I had to be home at six o'clock. I had to tell her my every movement.

I overheard her once talking to a reporter who had come to interview me for a profile. "You know," she said, "we go on the ferries and people rush up to him and ask him for his autograph and he says, 'I can't stand it any more, all these people!'

"But we'll get back to the car and he'll say, 'If people didn't recognize me, I'd die.'"

She thought for a moment, then continued, "You know, I should be the one interviewed. I've been married to him for forty-four years and I've shared him with the public for all these years. Do you know the only thing I want to know?"

The reporter shook his head. "Webster, where have you been all these years?" she said slowly.

Margaret, I was just making the rounds.

I still am. And I'm still searching for an answer to the question: What are people for?